A Practical Guide to North Indian Classical Vocal Music

This book is a step-by-step practical guide to North Indian music. With the help of this book, the reader can understand the basic aspects of North Indian music and learn to appreciate it better. It describes the ten basic *rā.gs* of North Indian classical music. It also gives instructions on how to sing and how to play the musical instruments. This book describes the tonal patterns and the tonal embellishments. By following the practical exercises given in this book, you can train your voice, sing notes correctly, develop your own ability to improvise, and make your own tonal patterns. This book is your giude to creating and singing your own *rā.g*.

Dr Indurama Srivastava did M.A. in Sanskrit from Allahabad University, obtained Master of Music from Banaras Hindu University, and PhD. in Musicology from the University of Utrecht, The Netherlands. Her earlier book was on *Dhrupad*. She lives in The Netherlands and is actively involved in Indian music.

A Practical Guide to North Indian Classical Vocal Music

The Ten Basic *rā.gs* with Compositions and Improvisations

Indurama Srivastava

Transcription in staff notation

Nelly van Ree Bernard

Munshiram Manoharlal Publishers Pvt. Ltd.

ISBN 978–81–215–1175–9
First published 2008

Published by
Munshiram Manoharlal Publishers Pvt. Ltd.
Post Box 5715, 54 Rani Jhansi Road, New Delhi 110 055, India
www.mrmlbooks.com

Anabhyāsaḥ kāṭhinyaḥ
(Difficulty is another name for lack of practice.)

Dedicated to my teachers
Sri Nawab Ali Khan
Sri Ramashraya Jha
Smt. Leelawati Carwal
Sri M.V. Thakar
Dr M.R. Gautam
Sri B. Bhatt
Dr Smt. Premlata Sharma

Contents

Figures

Preface

A Practical Guide to North Indian Classical Vocal Music is for those who want to learn the practical aspects of Indian Classical vocal music. Indian Classical vocal music consists of two main styles, viz., *dhru.pad* and *khyā.l.* This book deals only with the *khyā.l* style.

Many books have been written on Indian music. They generally deal only with the theory of Indian music. The books that cover the practical aspects are mostly written in Hindi. Besides that, in these books very little attention is paid to the needs of the uninitiated but well-interested person who desires to learn the basic essentials and practical aspects of Indian music. Some of the well-known Hindi books are: Pt. V.N. Bhatkhande's series *Hindustānī Saṅgīta Paddhati Kramika Pustaka Mālikā,* Pt. V.N. Patvardhan's series *Rāga Vijñāna,* Pt. Onkar Nath Thakur's series *Saṅgītāñjali,* Pt. N.L. Gune's series *Saṅgīta Pravīṇa Darśikā,* Pt. Ramashraya Jha's series *Abhinava Gītāñjali,* Pt. J.N. Pathak's series *Rāga Darpaṇa,* and Prof. Harishchandra Srivastava's series *Madhura Svara-lipi Saṅgrah.* They are excellent books. They give a detailed description of the *rā.gs* along with their compositions. Since they are in Hindi, people who do not have knowledge of Hindi cannot benefit from them. Moreover, these books give no guidance on practical aspects such as how to sit, how to play the instrument, and how to train the voice required for Indian music. All these subjects are dealt with in the present book. In addition, this book gives the delineation of the ten basic *rā.gs* also in staff notation

There are three chapters and an appendix in this book. Chapter one outlines the characteristic features of the two current systems of Indian music. It also mentions which system is popular in which province. The nomenclature of the notes of both North Indian and South Indian systems are given. A table of classification of the ten basic melodic scales (*thā.ṭs*) of the North Indian system along with their *rā.gs* is given and the tone material of a representative *rā.g* of each *thā.ṭ* is also provided. This table is useful for beginners and helps them see in one glance which particular *rā.g* belongs to which melodic family (*thā.ṭ*).

All the styles of North Indian vocal music have been explained with a short description. A description of the musical instruments used for vocal music has also been included along with the photographs.

Chapter two deals with the basic exercises. With the help of these exercises a learner can train his/her voice and sing the compositions of North Indian Classical music in the right way. How to play the harmonium and the *tān.pū.rā* have also been explained.

A set of exercises is given in this chapter to help students develop the ability to improvise.

In addition, practical exercises for learning the tonal embellishments are given so that a learner can understand these and train his/her voice accordingly.

The third chapter focuses on the rendering of a *rā.g* in *khyā.l* style of North Indian system. This is followed by the delineation of the ten basic *rā.gs*. There are three different compositions given for each *rā.g*. The first composition is complete with examples of improvisation in both slow and fast tempos. The other two compositions are provided only with Hindi texts along with their meanings. The name of the *tā.l* and the number of beats a *tā.l* contains, are mentioned with all the compositions.

The appendix gives the transcription of the above mentioned compositions and improvisations in staff notation. The transcription is done by Mrs Nelly van Ree Bernard. It is especially aimed at those who can only read notes in staff notation. These compositions are not only meant for singing but can also be played on musical instruments.

Most compositions that I have mentioned in this book are those that I learned from my first teacher Sri Nawab Ali Khan of Kheri. Some of these compositions are also mentioned in Pt. Bhatkhande's series but here and there they differ in melody and text.

In the index where a name of a *rā.g* is mentioned, a name of the *thā.ṭ* is also written in brackets.

INDURAMA SRIVASTAVA

Bennebroek, The Netherlands
November 2007

Acknowledgments

I am grateful to my teachers who taught me the art of singing and inspired me with their skill and profound knowledge. This book is a result of their investment in me. My heartfelt thanks to them.

I am thankful to F. Van Lamsweerde and Ms Mayon Zeeman for making useful suggestions. My student, Billy posed for the pictures and I am thankful to her.

Finally, I would like to express my thanks to my husband, Onkar and children, Apoorv and Nidhi for all the love, support, and constant encouragement throughout, without which this book would not have come into existence.

A Note on Transliteration and Pronunciation

This book is about modern North Indian Classical vocal music. Hence, the musical terms used here are given in Hindi (the language of the modern North Indian Classical music). The script of Hindi, like that of Sanskrit, is De.va Nā.ga.rī (in Hindi, it is often pronounced as De.v Nā.grī). In Sanskrit, the implicit vowel that every consonant carries, is pronounced. In modern Hindi, especially in the prose form, if the last consonant of the word carries the vowel short *a*, it is very often not pronounced. If the last vowel of the word is long as in *ka.ma.lā*, the middle implicit short *a* that a consonant carries, is not pronounced and *ka.ma.lā* is pronounced as *kam.lā.* In view of this practice, the musical terms, ending with the vowel short *a*, have been written in this book without the implicit vowel *a* just as they are pronounced in modern Hindi.

In the musical compositions, however, the consonants are pronounced with the implicit vowel *a* and, therefore, the musical text has been written with the implicit vowel *a.* The full names of the notes in Sanskrit are also mentioned with the implicit vowel *a.*

Syllable division has been denoted by dot (.) to facilitate the pronunciation of Hindi words.

Pronunciation

Vowels

- *a* as in b<u>u</u>t
- *i* as in s<u>i</u>t
- *u* as in p<u>u</u>t
- *ā* as in f<u>a</u>ther
- *ī* as in s<u>ea</u>t
- *ū* as in r<u>oo</u>m

ri Sanskrit vowel, pronounced as in bear with rolled r
e as in gate
ai as in pear
o as in boat
au as in not

Unaspirated consonants
k as in baker
g as in go
c as in church
j as in just
ṭ (*t* with point underneath) as in steam
ḍ as in deep
t as in tomato
d as in then
p as in put
b as in but
ṛ "retroflex flap. The tongue is retroflexed as for pronouncing *ḍ*, but the tip, instead of making firm contact with the roof of the mouth, is flapped quickly forward, touching the roof of the mouth only lightly or not at all, and finishes behind the lower teeth."*
(No similar sound occurs in English.)

Aspirated consonants
kh as in back hand
gh peg hole
ch much hope
jh bridge hand
ṭh out house
ḍh round hole
th theory
dh sound of th of father with aspiration
ph keep high
bh abhor
ṛh aspirated retroflex flap. (No similar sound in English.)

*R.S. McGregor, *Outline of Hindi Grammar* (Oxford: Oxford University Press, 1972), p. xviii.

Semi-vowels

- *y* as in yes
- *r* as in room
- *l* as in love
- *v* as in valley

Others

- *ṅg* as in king
- *ṇ* cerebral nasal as in Devanāgarī pronunciation *koṇa*
- *n* as in name
- *m* as in moon
- *ṅ* nasalization of a vowel as in no
- *ṣ* cerebral sibilant as in Devanāgarī pronunciation *dhanuṣa*
- *ś* palatal sibilant as in fish
- *s* as in seat
- *h* as in hand

CHAPTER 1

Introduction: The Background

North Indian music (known as Hindustani music) is one of two systems of Indian classical music. The other system is called South Indian music and is also known as Karnatak or Carnatic music. The North Indian system of music is popular in the northern states of India such as Assam, Bengal, Bihar, Gujarat, Haryana, Jammu and Kashmir, Madhya Pradesh, Maharashtra, Orissa, Punjab, Rajasthan, and Uttar Pradesh. South Indian music is popular in the southern states such as Andhra Pradesh, Kerala, Mysore, and Tamil Nadu. Both systems have the same roots and right up to the fourteenth century, both had the same literature on music. Both have the same basic components, i.e., *rā.g* and *tā.l* and both accept the same number of notes as well as octaves. The main difference, however, lies in the manner in which the notes are presented.

The nomenclature of the notes is also a little different among these two systems. The characteristic feature of North Indian music is that a note is held steady for a long time, while in South Indian music the notes are always ornamented by a trill or a shake. As a result, the notes in the South Indian music are constantly swinging between the preceding and the succeeding notes. Rao states, "the South Indian mind delights in the use of oscillating graces more than the North Indian. It is, therefore, our characteristic love of graces and not weakness of the tones that accounts for their peculiar negotiation."[1]

A general belief is that South Indian music has retained its pristine ancient Indian tradition while the North Indian music has lost it due to Islamic influence which mainly affected

[1]T.V. Subba Rao, *Studies in Indian Music* (Bombay: Asia Publishing House, 1962), 18.

the north of India. In fact, both north and south India faced many foreign invasions. Much ancient literature including that of music was destroyed by the invaders. As a result, it became difficult for Indian musicians and musicologists to rediscover and decipher this lost tradition. Nevertheless, attempts were made by musicologists to revive this heritage as best as they could. The music that came out of this revival took two directions that are now known as the Hindustani and the Karnatak systems of music. Both draw their ancestry from the same common roots (or what remained of these roots after the foreign invasions) and both were inevitably influenced by the cultural and political influences brought on by waves of invasions.

Harmony, in the sense of a simultaneous sounding of notes, plays a great role in western music. However, it does not play any role in Indian Classical music. On the other hand, improvisation plays a big role in Indian Classical music. Only a small part of the music is pre-composed while the larger part is improvised. The compositions and the melodies are usually composed beforehand, though generally not by the performer himself. A performer with poetic talent is, however, free to compose his/her own texts and melodies. The improvised and the composed parts are termed in Sanskrit books on music as *ani.bad.dha* and *bad.dha,*[2] respectively.

Notes and Beats

Notes (*Svar*)

In Indian music, a note or a tone is called *svar.* There are seven main notes. Their names in ascending order are: *ṣa.dja, ṛi.ṣa.bha, gān.dhā.ra, ma.dhya.ma, pañ.ca.ma, dhai.va.ta,* and *ni.ṣā.da.* The abbreviated and more commonly used names of these notes are *Sa, Re* (*Ri* in the Karnatak system), *Ga, Ma, Pa, Dha,* and *Ni.* These notes are collectively referred to as *Sar.gam* which is an acronym of the first four notes of the scale. *Sar.gam* is analogous to the tonic Sol-Fa system in the

[2]Śārṅgadeva, *Saṅgītaratnākara,* vol. II, ed. S. Sastri (Adyar: Adyar Library Series, 1959), 204.

western music. The corresponding names of these notes in tonic Sol-Fa are doh, ray, me, fah, soh, lah, and te or C, D, E, F, G, A, and B, respectively. When the note in Indian music are sung in ascending order such as *Sa, Re, Ga, Ma, Pa, Dha, Ni,* and *Ṡa,* it is called *ā.ro.h* (meaning ascent). When they are sung in the descending order such as *Ṡa, Ni, Dha, Pa, Ma, Ga, Re,* and *Sa,* it is called *ava.ro.h* (meaning descent). In Indian music, an interval of seven notes counting from *Sa* to *Ni* is called *sap.tak.* The term *sap.tak* is derived from *sap.ta* meaning seven and the term *sap.tak,* refers to an interval of seven notes. In practice, though, one *sap.tak* consists of eight notes, since it is customary to add the first note of the next higher *sap.tak* to the preceding seven notes. Pandit Onkar Nath Thakur[3] uses the term *aṣ.ṭak* instead of *sap.tak. Aṣ.ṭak* means an interval of eight notes. There are three *sap.tak*s or octaves in Indian vocal music: low, middle, and high. These are called *man.dr* (low), *ma.dhy* (middle), and *tā.r* (high) *sap.tak.* In writing, the notes of the low octave (*man.dr sap.tak*) are written with a dot below the notes, such as *Ṇi, Ḍha,* and *P̣a.* The notes of the high octave (*tā.r sap.tak*) are written with a dot above the notes such as *Ṡa, Ṙe, Ġa,* and *Ṁa.* The notes of the middle octave (*ma.dhy sap.tak*) are written without any dot.

A note in Indian music does not always carry the same fixed frequency. It is the interval between the notes that is fixed. Every musician is free to determine the pitch of *Sa* (the starting note of the scale) on the basis of the range of his or her voice. The pitch of the remaining higher or lower notes is automatically determined on the basis of the pitch of *Sa.* That is why the pitch of *Sa* is very crucial in Indian music.

In one *sap.tak,* in addition to the seven notes, there are also five half notes that are slightly modulated forms of *Re, Ga, Ma, Dha,* and *Ni.* Of these five notes, the notes *Re, Ga, Dha,* and *Ni* are modulated by lowering the pitch from the original position while the note *Ma* can only be modulated by raising the pitch from its original position. The original position of the note is called *śud.dh* meaning pure or unmodulated.

[3]Onkar Nath Thakur, *Saṅgītāñjali,* part 1 (Bombay: Onkar Nath Thakur Estate, 1977), 11.

In western music, they are called natural notes. The modulated positions are called *vi.kṛit* meaning altered or modified. The notes *Sa* and *Pa* are fixed. These two notes (*Sa* and *Pa*) are, therefore, called *a.cal-svar* or immovable notes while the rest are called *cal-svar* meaning movable notes. In its original position, a *cal-svar* is called *śud.dh* (natural) and in its lower position is called *ko.mal* (flat). The higher or raised position of a note is called *tī.vr* (sharp). As stated earlier, the only note that can be modified by raising its pitch is *Ma.* The lower positions of *Re, Ga, Dha,* and *Ni* are, respectively, called *ko.mal Re* (D flat), *ko.mal Ga* (E flat), *ko.mal Dha* (A flat), and *ko.mal Ni* (B flat). The raised position of *Ma* is called *tī.vr Ma* or F sharp. Naturally, there can be no such thing as *ko.mal Ma.* In the terminology of Indian music, the act of raising a note upwards is called as *svar-ca.rhā.nā* (literally raising a note) and the act of moving a note downwards is called as *svar-utā.rnā* (literally lowering a note).

The twelve half-notes (7 *śud.dh* + 4 *ko.mal* + 1 *tī.vr Ma*) in the Indian music (both in the North as well as in the South) are as follows:

North Indian Music	*South Indian Music*
1. *Sa*	*Sa*
2. *ko.mal Re*	*śud.dh Ri*
3. *śud.dh Re*	*ca.tuś.śru.ti Ri* or *śud.dh Ga*
4. *ko.mal Ga*	*ṣaṭ.śru.ti Ri* or *sā.dhā.raṇ Ga*
5. *śud.dh Ga*	*an.tar Ga*
6. *śud.dh Ma*	*śud.dh Ma*
7. *tīvr Ma*	*pra.ti Ma*
8. *Pa*	*Pa*
9. *ko.mal Dha*	*śud.dh Dha*
10. *śud.dh Dha*	*ca.tuś.śru.ti Dha* or *śud.dh Ni*
11. *ko.mal Ni*	*ṣaṭ.śru.ti Dha* or *kai.śik Ni*
12. *śud.dh Ni*	*kā.ka.lī Ni*

In the above nomenclature, the *śud.dh Re* and *śud.dh Dha* of the North Indian music can also be called *śud.dh Ga* and *śud.dh Ni* in the South Indian music. The note *Re* of the North Indian music can be sung as *Re* as well as *Ga* in the South

Indian music. In the same way, *Dha* can be sung as *Dha* as well as *Ni.* Thus, *śud.dh Re, ko.mal Ga, śud.dh Dha,* and *ko.mal Ni* of North Indian music have two names in South Indian music.

Beats: a time measure of a rhythmic cycle

In Indian music, a beat is called *mā.trā.* One beat is called *e.k-mā.trā,* half-a-beat is *ā.dhī-mā.trā,* one-fourth of a beat is *cau.thāī-mā.trā,* one-sixth of a beat is *e.k-ba.tā.chai-mā.trā,* and so on. The beats are indicated by the monosyllabic sounds called *bo.l.* These monosyllabic sounds or *bo.ls* are vocalized imitations of sounds produced by the *tab.lā* or *mṛi.daṅ.g* (percussion instruments). These *bo.ls* are *dhā, dhe, dhin, ga, ge, ka, ki, kī, na, ne, ra, ta, te, tī, tā, tin, tū,* and *tūṅ.* These monosyllabic sounds are used to delineate the structure of a rhythmic cycle. One monosyllabic sound, when used separately, stands for one beat except *ra* that always indicates one-fourth of a beat and is always combined with three other monosyllabic sounds. Half-a-beat is indicated by uttering two monosyllabic sounds in quick succession, i.e., within the time interval of one beat. When *dhā* and *ge* are uttered in quick succession, they sound *dhage.* One-fourth of a beat is indicated by uttering four monosyllabic sounds within the time span of one beat. The four *bo.ls* used to indicate one-fourth of a beat are *te* + *ṭe* + *ke* + *ṭe.* When these are uttered in quick succession, they sound as *ti.ṭa.ki.ṭa.* In common parlance, musicians often utter these *bols* as *tira.kiṭa* or *tiṭa.kiṭa* in preference to *teṭe.keṭa.* The *bo.l tira.kita* is, thus, only an altered form of *teṭe.keṭa* and more commonly used because it is easier to pronounce.

The three basic components of Indian music are: *Rā.g, Tā.l,* and *La.y.*

Rā.g

A *rā.g* is an organized group of notes (*svar*) that come in a fixed sequence and form a melody. A *rā.g* is governed by certain rules. These are as follows:

1. The notes of a *rā.g* are presented in a specified ascending and descending order (*ā.ro.h* and *a.va.ro.h*). A *rā.g* may or may not comprise all the notes of the octave; but the total number of notes may never be less than five. The

number of notes in ascent can differ from their number in descent.

2. The notes in a *rā.g* can be arranged in a straight or a zigzag sequence.
3. The character of a *rā.g* is determined by the notes it contains, the sequence in which these notes are arranged (straight or zigzag), the emphasis placed on certain notes, and the use of certain ornaments.
4. The note *Sa* is always present in every *rā.g.*
5. *Ma* and *Pa* are never absent simultaneously. Either one or the other is always present in a *rā.g.*
6. In every *rā.g,* any two notes must be given more importance than the others. Even among these two notes there is a hierarchy, where one is important than the other. The two important notes are called *vā.dī svar* and *sam.vā.dī svar.* The *vā.dī svar* is the more important of the two and is, therefore, called the king of the *rā.g.* It is emphasized either by its repetition or by holding it for a longer period. The *sam.vā.dī svar,* is less important than the *vā.dī svar,* and is, therefore, called the minister. The *vā.dī svar* and *sam.vā.dī svar* are delineated sometimes by emphasizing them but occasionally also by skilfully skipping them and, thus, making them conspicuous by their absence.
7. Every *rā.g* has a special mood and an appropriate time of the day or night when it is to be performed. Some *rā.gs* are typically morning *rā.gs*, some are evening *rā.gs*, some are night *rā.gs*, and some are sung at dawn or dusk. Musicians, however, do not always strictly adhere to this rule.

Tā.l

A *tā.l* is a cycle of beats (*mā.trā*). Its structure is defined by a fixed number of beats of different stresses and values with which many rhythmic patterns are formed. These patterns are called *tā.ls*. Every pattern has a name. These *tā.ls* are played on percussion instruments typically *tab.lā, mṛi.daṅ.g* or *pa.khā.vaj,* and *ḍho.lak.* The beats can also be demonstrated by hand movements either by clapping or by tapping the palm of one hand with the fingers of the other hand. A player is free to improvise but may not distort the framework or the basic structure of the rhythmic cycle. The first beat or the starting beat in a *tā.l* is very important and, thus, is shown by an emphasis. It is called *sa.m.* When a *tā.l* is played on a percussion instrument, the *sa.m* is indicated by a hard stroke. The other beats, less stressed than that of *sa.m* are indicated in either of two ways: (1) by a light stroke and (2) simply by a movement of the palm without making a sound. This is usually done on the left *tab.lā.*

When a *tā.l* is demonstrated by hand, the hard strokes are indicated by claps. These are called *tā.lī.* The light strokes are indicated by tapping of the fingers of one hand against the palm of the other hand or against the thigh. The silent stroke is either indicated by putting the back side of the right hand on the palm of the left hand or just by waving the palm. It is called *kh̲ā.lī* (meaning empty or silent beat). The stressed beats, other than the *sa.m,* that are indicated by harder strokes (but never harder than the *sa.m*) are called *dū.sa.rī tā.lī* (second stroke or clap), *tī.sa.rī tā.lī* (third stroke or clap), *cau.thī tā.lī* (fourth stroke or clap), and so on depending upon the ordinal number beginning from the *sa.m.* In writing, *sa.m* (the first stressed beat) is indicated by the sign V or sometimes the plus sign. The other stressed beats are indicated by the digits 2, 3, 4, and so on and the *kh̲ā.lī* is indicated by zero. A *tā.l* is demonstrated by monosyllabic sounds of the *tab.lā.* These vocalized beats of a *tā.l* are called *ṭhe.kā.*[4] Some other rules concerning the *tā.l* are:

1. Every *tā.l* is divided into different parts (*vi.bhā.g*) which are formed by stressed beats and determine the V rhythm of the *tā.l.*
2. The number of beats in a *tā.l* may never be less than six.

La.y

La.y means tempo. There are three main *la.y*s (tempi) in Indian music: *vi.lam.bit* or slow, *ma.dhy* or medium, and *dru.t*

[4]Ibid.

or fast. In modern times, a tempo even faster than the one used in *dru.t* is becoming popular and is called *ati-drut la.y* meaning an extremely fast tempo. The slowness or fastness of the tempo depends entirely upon the mood of the performer. Generally, *dru.t la.y* is two times faster than *ma.dhy la.y* and *ma.dhy la.y* is two times faster than *vi.lam.bit la.y. Ma.dhy la.y* (medium tempo) is also called *ṭhā.h* or *ba.rā.bar-kī-la.y.*

Thā.ṭ (also called *ṭhā.ṭh* or *me.l*)

The *thā.ṭs* can be seen as a parent scale. All the *rā.gs* in both Hindustani as well as Karnatak systems are arranged in a genealogy. A family that a *rā.g* belongs to is called a *thā.ṭ.* In the Karnatak music, a *thā.ṭ* is called *me.la.kar.tā* or *me.l. Thāṭ* or *me.l* is an abstract concept that is used only for indicating the genealogy. The *rā.g* and the *thā.ṭ* classification was first introduced in the fourteenth century in south India by Mādhavācārya (Vidyāraṇya). He was the Prime Minister of the kingdom of Vijayanagara under the reign of Krishnadevaraya. This classification was largely influenced by Persian music.[5] Later, in the seventeenth century, a renowned south Indian musicologist, Vyaṅkaṭamukhī wrote a book called *Caturdaṇḍi-prakāśikā* literally "the elucidator of the four signposts." In this book, he classified all the *rā.gs* in 72 *me.ls*. His classification was based entirely on a mathematical calculation of the permutations and combinations of the twelve semi-tones of the octave. The three basic rules, on which the grouping of *rā.gs* in South Indian music is based, are as follows:

1. A *me.l* has seven notes.
2. The notes of a *me.l* are always presented in ascending order.
3. *Me.l,* since it is an abstract concept used only for the grouping of *rā.gs*, need not have a pleasing quality that is a basic requirement of *rā.gs*.

The North Indian music has one extra rule, viz., that a *thā.ṭ* (*me.l*) may never have the two forms of the same note

[5]K.C. Brihaspati, *Bhārata kā Saṅgīt Siddhānt* (Prakashan Shakha Suchana Vibhag, U.P., 1959), 28.

(i.e., *śud.dh* and *vi.kṛi.t*) together. This criterion reduces the number of *me.ls* or *thā.ṭs* (which in South Indian music is seventy-two) to only thirty-two. However, Pt. Vishnu Narayan Bhatkhande (1906-33), a leading musicologist of the North Indian music, selected only ten *thā.ṭs* as being important and grouped all the prevalent *rā.gs* of that time in to these ten *thā.ṭs*. Some musicologists such as V.N. Patwardhan[6] do not support this restriction and, thus, accept thirty-two *thā.ṭs*. However, the most prevalent system of grouping of *rā.gs* in to *thā.ṭs* in the North Indian music is that of Pt. Bhatkhande. The names of these ten *thā.ṭs* in the North Indian music and their corresponding names in the South Indian music are as follows:

North Indian Music	*South Indian Music*
1. *Bi.lā.val*	*Dhī.ra.śaṅ.karā.bha.raṇ*
2. *Kal.yā.ṇ*	*Me.ca.kal.yā.ṇī*
3. *Kha.mā.j*	*Ha.ri.kām.bho.jī*
4. *Kā.fī*	*Kha.ra.ha.ra.pri.yā*
5. *Bhai.rav*	*Māyā.mā.la.va.gauṛ*
6. *Ā.sā.va.rī*	*Naṭ-Bhai.ra.vī*
7. *Bhai.ra.vī*	*Ha.num-To.ṛī*
8. *Mār.vā*	*Ga.man-Śri.yā*
9. *Pūr.vī*	*Kā.m-Var.dha.nī*
10. *To.ṛī*	*Śubh-pan.tu.va.rā.lī*

Each *thā.ṭ* represents one family comprising many *rā.gs*. The tone material of these *thā.ṭs*, and the list of the *rā.gs* belonging to these *thā.ṭs* are given in a tabular form below. Each *thā.ṭ* has one representative *rā.g* that has the same name. The only exception to this rule is *thā.ṭ Ka.lyā.ṇ* where the representative *rā.g* is called *Ya.man* instead of *Ka.lyā.ṇ*

THE CLASSIFICATION OF THE NORTH INDIAN *RĀ.GS*

The ten *thā.ṭs*, their tone material, popular *rā.gs*, and the tone material of their representative *rā.gs* are given below.

[6]V.N. Patwardhan, *Rāga Vijñan*, part 1 (Pune: Sangit Gaurav Granthmala, 1965), 10-13.

Thā.ṭ	*Tone material*	*Rā.gs comprising the Thā.ṭ*	*Tone material of representative rā.g*
1. *Bi.lā.val*	*S R G M P D N*	*Al.hai.yā-bi.lā.val,*	*Rā.g Bi.lā.val*
		Bhin.na-Ṣa.dj,	*S ^{G}R G P ^{N}D N Ṡ*
		Bi.hā.g, Bi.lā.val,	*Ṡ N D P, M G M R S*
		Chā.yā-ti.lak,	
		Deś.kā.r, De.va.gi.ri,	
		Gu.ṇa.ka.lī, Hans.dhva.nī,	
		Jal.dhar-ke.dār,	
		Ka.mal.rañ.ja.nī,	
		Ku.ku.bh, Lac.chā.sā.kh,	
		Ma.lu.hā-ke.dā.r,	
		Mā.ṅḍ, Me.vā.ṛ,	
		Naṭ.bi.lā.val, Pa.hā.ṛī,	
		Sa.ra.pa.rdā,	
		Śaṅ.ka.rā, Śukl-bi.lā.val,	
		Ya.ma.nī-bi.lā.val	
2. *Kal.yā.ṇ*	*S R G Ṁ P D N*	*Bhū.pā.lī,*	*Rā.g Ya.man*
		Can.dra.kā.nt,	*Ṇ^{G}R^{R}G, Ṁ P^{N}D Ṇ Ṡ*
		Chā.yā.naṭ,	*Ṡ Ṇ ^{N}D P ^{P}Ṁ G ^{S}R S*
		Gaur.sā.ra.ṅg,	
		Go.ra.kh-ka.lyā.ṇ,	
		Ha.mīr, Hin.dol,	
		Jait-ka.lyā.ṇ, Kā.mo.d,	
		Ke.dā.r, Māl.śrī,	
		Nan.d, Pū.ri.yā.kal.yā.ṇ,	
		Sā.va.nī-kal.yā.ṇ,	
		Śri-kal.yā.ṇ,	
		Śud.dh-kal.yā.ṇ,	
		Śyā.m.kal.yā.ṇ,	
		Ya.man, Ya.man-kal.yā.ṇ	
3. *Kha.mā.j*	*S R G M P D N̲*	*Baṛ.hans, De.ś, Dur.gā,*	*Rā.g Kha.mā.j*
		Ga.uṛī.mal.hār, Gā.rā,	*S, G M P D N Ṡ*
		Jai.jai.van.tī,	*Ṡ N̲ D P M G R S*
		Jhiṅ.jho.ṭī, Kalā.va.tī,	
		Kha.mā.j, Kham.bā.va.tī,	
		Naṭ-mal.hār, Nā.rā.ya.ṇī,	
		Rā.ge.śva.rī, So.ra.th,	
		Ti.lak-kāmo.d, Til.aṅg	

4. *Kā.fī*	$S\ R\ \underline{G}\ M\ P\ D\ \underline{N}$	*Ā.bho.gī, Ba.hā.r, Baṛ.hans-sā.ra.ṅg, Ba.ra.vā, Bā.ge.śva.rī Bhīm.pa.lā.sī, Brin.dā.va.nī-sā.ra.ṅg, De.va.sā.kh, Dha.nā.śrī, Dhā.nī, Ga.uṛ.mal.hār, Hans.kiṅ.ki.ṇī, Jo.g, Jo.g-kaun.s, Kau.śi.k, Kau.śī.kān.ha.ṛā, Kā.fī, Lan.kā-da.han, Ma.dhu-mā.dha.vī, Me.gh-mal.hār, Miṅ.yāṅ-mal.hār, Nā.rā.ya.ṇī-(kā.fī-a.ṅg), Nā.ya.kī-kān.ha.ṛā, Nī.lām.ba.rī, Paṭ.dī.p, Paṭ-mañ.ja.rī, Pī.lū, Pra.dī.pa.kī, Pu.lin.di.kā, Rām.dā.sī-mal.hār, Sain.dha.vī, Sā.man.t-sā.ra.ṅg, Sin.dhū.rā, Su.gh.rā.ī, Sū.hā, Sū.hā-sugh.rā.ī, Sur-mal.hār, Śa.hā.nā, Śiv-rañ.ja.nī, Śrī-rañ.ja.nī, Śud.dh-sā.ra.ṅg*	*Rā.g Kā.fī* $S\ R\ ^{M}\underline{G}\ ,\ M\ P,\ D\ ^{D}\underline{N}\ \dot{S}$ $\dot{S}\ \underline{N}\ D,\ P,\ M\ ^{M}\underline{G}\ R\ S$
5. *Bhai.rav*	$S\ \underline{R}\ G\ M\ P\ \underline{D}\ N$	*A.hī.r-bhai.rav, A.hīr-la.li.t, Ā.nan.d-bhai.rav, Baṅ.gāl-bhai.rav, Bhai.rav, Dev.rañ.ja.nī, Gau.rī (bhai.rav a.ṅg), Gu.ṇa.krī, Jaṅ.gū.lā, Jhī.laf, Jo.gi.yā, Kā.liṅ.ga.rā, La.li.t pañ.ca.m, Me.gh-mal.hār (bhai.rav aṅ.g), Pra.bhā.t, Pra.bhā.va.tī, Rām.ka.lī, Sau.rā.ṣṭ bhai.rav, Śiv-bhai.rav, Vai.rā.gī-bhai.rav, Vi.bhā.s*	*Rā.g Bhai.rav* $^{S}\underset{\cdot}{N}\ S\ ^{\underline{R}}G\ M\ ^{N}\underline{D},\ \underset{\cdot}{N}\ \dot{S}$ $\dot{S}\ N\ ^{N}\underline{D}\ P,\ M\ G\ ^{G}\underline{R},\ S$
6. *Ā.sā.va.rī*	$S\ R\ G\ M\ P\ \underline{D}\ N$	*A.bhī.rī, A.dā.nā, Ā.sā.va.rī, Dar.bā.rī, De.v.gān.dhā.rī, Gān.dhā.rī,*	*Rā.g Āsā.va.rī* $S,\ R\ M\ P,\ ^{\underline{N}}\underline{D}\ \dot{S}$ $\dot{S}\ \underline{N}\ \underline{D}\ P,\ M\ P\quad D\ M\quad P,$ $^{M}\underline{G}\ ^{M}\underline{G}\ R\ S$

		Go.pi.kā-ba.san.t, *Jaṅ.ga.lā, Ja.un.pu.rī,* *Jhī.laf (Āsā.varī a.ṅg),* *Kān.ha.ṛā,*18 kinds of *Kān.ha.ṛā, Kha.ṭ,* *Ko.mal.de.sī,* *Sin.dha-bhai.ra.vī*	
7. *Bhai.ra.vī*	$S\,\underline{R}\,\underline{G}\,M\,P\,\underline{D}\,\underline{N}$	*Bhai.ra.vī, Bho.pā.l,* *Bi.lās.khā.nī-to.ṛī,* *Can.dra.kauns,* *Dha.nā.śrī, Jaṅ.gol,* *Māl.kauns, Mo.ṭkī,* *Śud.dh-sā.man.t,* *U.tarī.guṇ.ka.lī,* *Va.san.t.mu.khā.rī*	*Rā.g Bhai.ra.vī* $S\,\underline{R}\,{}^{\underline{R}}\underline{G}\,M\,P,\ \underline{D}\,\underline{N}\,\dot{S}$ $\dot{S}\,\underline{N}\,\underline{D}\,P,\ M\,\underline{G}\,\underline{R}\,S$
8. *Mā.rvā*	$S\,\underline{R}\,G\,\dot{M}\,P\,\underline{D}\,N$	*Ba.rā.rī, Bhan.khār,* *Bha.ti.yār, Jait,* *La.li.t, La.li.t-gau.rī,* *Mā.lā-gau.rī, Mā.rvā,* *Pañ.cam, Pū.rbā,* *Pū.ri.yā, Pū.ri.yā-kal.yāṇ,* *Sāj.gi.ri, So.hi.nī,* *Vi.bhā.s (Mā.rvā a.ṅg)*	*Rā.g Mā.rvā* $\underset{\cdot}{N}\,\underline{R}\,G\,\dot{M}\,D\,N\,\dot{\underline{R}}$ $\dot{R}\,N\,D\,\dot{M}\,G\,{}^{\dot{M}}\underline{R}\,N\,\underline{R}\,S$
9. *Pū.rvī*	$S\,\underline{R}\,G\,\dot{M}\,P\,\underline{D}\,N$	*Cai.tī-gau.rī, Dī.pak,* *Hans-nā.rā.ya.ṇī,* *Jait-śrī, Mā.lvā, Pa.ra.j,* *Pū.ri.yā-dha.nā.śrī,* *Pū.rvī, Re.vā, Śrī,* *Śrī-ṭan.k, Tri.ve.nī,* *Va.san.t, Vi.bhā.s*	*Rā.g Pū.rvī* $N\,\underline{R}\,G\,\dot{M}\,\underline{D}\,N\,\dot{S}$ $\dot{S}\,N\,\underline{R}\,N\,\underline{D}\,P\,\dot{M}\,G\,M$ $G,\ \underline{R}\ S$
10. *To.ṛī*	$S\,\underline{R}\,\underline{G}\,\dot{M}\,P\,\underline{D}\,N$	*Ba.hā.durī-to.rī,* *Gur.ja.rī-to.ṛī,* *Lā.cā.rī-to.ṛī, Lak.ṣmī-* *to.ṛī, Mul.tā.nī,* *Mul.tā.nī-to.ṛī*	*Rā.g To.ṛī* $N\,\underline{R}\,\underline{G}\,\dot{M}\,\underline{D},\ N\,\dot{S}$ $\dot{S}\,N\,\underline{D}\,P,\ M\,\underline{D}\,\dot{M}\,\underline{G}\,\underline{R}$ $\underline{G}\,\underline{R}\,S$

Even though the list of the *rā.gs* as given above is comprehensive, it can never be exclusive, since a musician is always free to create his/her own new *rā.g.*

MUSICAL STYLES

Any composition can be rendered in a *rā.g.* The performance of a *rā.g* is begun with a rhythm-free part followed by a rhythmic part. In the rhythm-free, part an improvisation is done in slow tempo. However, in some styles where the rhythm-free part is long, it is begun in slow tempo but finished in medium or fast tempo. The tempo and the duration of rhythm-free improvisation phase depend on the particular musical style. The rhythm-free part is followed by the rhythmic part. The rhythmic part comprises two parts. One is the structured part delineating the composition and the other is the unstructured part that is the improvisation. The rhythmic part is accompanied by a percussion instrument. The player of the percussion instrument accompanies the performer till the end of the performance.

The musical styles can be divided into three categories depending on the strictness with which they follow the rules of a *rā.g* and a *tā.l*.

1. Classical category
2. Semi-classical category
3. Light-classical category

1. Classical Category

The two main musical styles *dhru.pad* and *k͟hyā.l* come under this category. The styles such as *dha.mā.r* and *sā.da.rā* are subsumed under *dhru.pad* while *lak.ṣa.ṇ.gī.t*, *ta.rā.nā*, *tri.va.ṭ*, *svar-mā.li.kā*, *ca.tu.ra.ṅg*, and *rā.g-mā.li.kā* are subsumed under *k͟hyā.l*. These can be sung in any *rā.g*.

Dhru.pad

The musical style *dhru.pad* is characterized by vigorous and forceful shakes (*ga.ma.k*), and long glidings (*mīṅ.ḍ*). These shakes and glidings demand a forceful voice to sing and for this reason the *dhru.pad* is called *mar.dā.nā-gā.yan* or the masculine style. The *dhru.pad* compositions (also called *dhru.pad*), have usually four sections, i.e., *sthā.yī*, *an.ta.rā*, *sañ.cā.rī*, and *ā.bhog*. However, some *dhru.pads* are exceptions to this rule and have only two sections, viz., *sthā.yī* and *an.ta.rā*. A *dhru.pad* style emphasizes the delineation of different tempi in the rhythm-free part as well as the rhythmic part. The *muk.tā.lā.p* or *ā.lā.p* (the slow rhythm-free improvisation) of *dhru.pad* is the longest among all the musical styles. The *tā.ls*, that are played with *dhru.pad* compositions, are *cau-tā.l, jhap-tā.l, sū.l-tā.l, tī.vra-tā.l, sur.fākh.tā-tā.l, ga.ja.jham.pā-tā.l, ru.dra-tā.l,* and *bra.hma-tā.l.* The popular *tā.ls* are *cau-tā.l* (12 beats), and *jhap-tā.l* (10 beats). The accompanying percussion instrument is *pa.khā.va.j* (also called *mṛi.da.ṅg*). It is a tubular drumstick shaped wooden instrument with drumhead made of hide stretched over a circular end on either side. It is placed on the floor and played by both hands on sides.

Dha.mā.r

Dha.mā.r is a variety of *dhru.pad.* It differs from the prototypical *dhru.pad* in the verbal content and the *tā.l.* The verbal content of *dha.mā.r* compositions deals with the Hindu festival Holī (the colour festival that falls in the month of Phalgun of the Hindu calendar, i.e., February/March). The *dha.mā.r* compositions describe the festivities related to Holī. In these compositions, Krishna along with Rādhā and his other male and female friends (*gwā.ls* and *go.pīs*), is described as playing with colours. The *tā.l* played in *dha.mā.r* has 14 beats in one cycle and is also called *dha.mā.r-tā.l.*

Sā.da.rā

Sā.da.rā is another variety of *dhru.pad.* Its compositions are sung in *jhap.tā.l* that has 10 beats in one cycle. The text of *sā.da.rā* compositions is usually related with war. It might be that, in earlier times, these were sung during times of war in order to encourage the warriors. Its tempo used to be a little faster than the tempo of *dhru.pad* but now *sā.da.rā* has lost its separate identity and has merged with *dhru.pad.*

Dhru.pad[7] was in its prime in the sixteenth and the seventeenth centuries. Gradually its popularity faded away and a new musical style evolved out of it called *khyā.l.* Attempts have been made nowadays by musicians to repopularize *dhru.pad.*

Khyā.l

A *khyā.l* style is characterized by its delicate tonal embellishments such as shake (*ga.ma.k*), gliding (*mīṅ.ḍ*), tonal push

[7]For more details see I. Srivastava, *Dhrupada,* A Study of its Origin, Historical Development, Structure, and Present State (Delhi: Motilal Banarsidass, 1980).

(*khaṭ.kā*), small quick *tā.ns* as well as shakes on descending tones (*mur.kī*), grace notes (*ka.n*), and trill (*ā.ndo.lan*). In *k͟hyā.l*, the focus is more on the melody than the text. As a result, the text of *k͟hyā.l* compositions is often unclear to such a degree that it is sometimes difficult to understand the meaning. The *k͟hyā.l* compositions are also called *ban.diś* or *cī.z*. The text and the *muk.tā.lā.p* (rhythm free slow improvisation) of *k͟hyā.l* is shorter than that of *dhru.pad*. The total embellishments are more delicate in *k͟hyā.l* than those used in *dhru.pad*. The *k͟hyā.l* compositions have only two sections viz., *sthā.yī* and *an.ta.rā* while *dhru.pad* has four.

There are different theories about the origin of the *k͟hyā.l* style. According to some, *k͟hyā.l* was invented by Amir Khusro in the thirteenth century. According to others, it was started by Sultan Husain Sharki of Jaunpur in the fifteenth century. Even if it might have originated in the fifteenth century or earlier, it came to flourish into its full glory only in the nineteenth century. The early *k͟hyā.l* compositions that we come across were composed by Niyamat Khan (Sadāraṅg) at the time of Muhammad Shah Rangile (1719-48). Because of the delicate ornamentations used in *k͟hyā.l*, it is called *za.nā.nā gā.yan* or the female style as opposed to the *dhru.pad* that is called the male style.

There are two kinds of *k͟hyā.l* compositions: slow and fast. A composition that is sung in slow tempo is called *vi.lam.bit-k͟hyā.l* or *ba.ṛā-k͟hyā.l* and the one that is sung in medium or fast tempo is called *drut-k͟hyā.l* or *cho.ṭā-k͟hyā.l*. A slow composition (*ba.ṛā-k͟hyā.l*) is never sung alone. It is always followed by a fast composition while the fast composition (*cho.ṭā-k͟hyā.l*) can be sung independently. When *cho.ṭā-k͟hyā.l* is sung without *ba.ṛā-k͟hyā.l*, its tempo is medium otherwise it is faster.

The percussion instrument that accompanies *k͟hyā.l* is *tab.lā*. It is a pair of small drums. The *tā.ls*, that are played with *ba.ṛā-k͟hyā.l* (slow composition) are *ek-tā.l*, *tī.n-tā.l*, *jhū.mrā-tā.l*, *jhap-tā.l*, and *ā.ṛā.cau.tā.l*. The *tā.ls*, that are played with *cho.ṭā-k͟hyā.l*, are played in fast or medium tempo. These are *drute-k-tā.l* and *jhap-tā.l*.

In the course of time, several *gha.rā.nās* (schools) emerged from the *k͟hyā.l* style. The popular *gha.rā.nās* are Gwālior *gha.rā.nā*, K͞irānā *gha.rā.nā*, Paṭiyālā *gha.rā.nā*, Āgrā *gha.rā.nā*, and Jaipur *gha.rā.nā.* The famous singers whose names are associated with Gwālior *gha.rā.nā,* are: Pandit Viṣṇu Digambar and Pandit Onkar Nath Thakur. The famous singer whose name is associated with Kirānā *gha.rā.nā* is Ustad Abdul Karim Khan. The name of Ustad Baḍe Ghulam Ali Khan is associated with Paṭiyālā *gha.rā.nā* and Ustad Alladiya Khan represents Jaipur *gha.rā.nā.*

The verbal content of *khyā.l* may be any subject ranging from religious devotion to erotic love.

The other styles that are subsumed under the *khyā.l* style are: *lak.ṣa.ṇ.gī.t, ta.rā.nā, tri.va.ṭ, svar-mā.li.kā, ca.tu.ra.ṅg,* and *rā.g-mā.li.kā* (also called *rā.g-mā.lā*). These are performed independently like *cho.ṭā-khyā.l.* The text of these styles is different from that of *khyā.l.* For this reason, they are seen as different styles even though in other respects they are similar to *khyā.l.* These have two sections viz., *sthā.yī* and *an.ta.rā.* However, *ca.tu.ra.ṅg* is the only exception that has four parts. The *tā.ls* that are played with these styles are also the same as of *cho.ṭā-khyā.l* and the tempo is either medium or fast.

Lak.ṣa.ṇ.gī.t

The text of *lak.ṣa.ṇ.gī.t* compositions describes all the characteristic features of a *rā.g* in which it is sung.

Ta.rā.nā

The text of *ta.rā.nā* compositions is formed by meaningless syllables, such as *ta, na, de, re, na, tom, dīm,* and *nom.* It requires good practice to pronounce these syllables in a very fast tempo during improvisation.

Tri.va.ṭ

The text of *tri.va.ṭ* compositions is formed by the syllables that are used by the drum players to denote the strokes on the drums, such as *ka, ta, ga, gha, dha,* and so forth. *Tri.va.ṭ* is not so popular now and most people look upon it as just another type of *ta.rā.nā.*

Svar-mā.li.kā or Sar.gam

The text of *svar-mā.li.kā* compositions is formed by the tonal syllables such as *sa, re, ga, ma, pa, dha,* and *ni.*

Ca.tu.ra.ṅg

The word *ca.tu.ra.ṅg* literally means four colours and refers to four types of texts used in this musical form. A *ca.tu.ra.ṅg* composition has four parts. The first part is formed by meaningful words. The second part is formed by abbreviations of the notes (*sa, re, ga, ma*). The third part is formed by euphonious syllables (*ta, na, dīm, tom*) that are the same as used in *ta.rā.nā*, and the fourth one is formed by the monosyllabic names of beats (*dha, dhin, tā, tin, tirakiṭ*) that are used by the drum-players.

Rā.g-mā.li.kā or Rā.g-mā.lā

The word *rā.g-mā.li.kā* means a garland of *rā.gs*. Here, the singer uses a number of *rā.gs* changing the *rā.g* from one line to the other. The text is formed by using the names of different *rā.gs*. A good performer blends the main notes of different *rā.gs* in such a way that when the name of the *rā.g* comes in the text he/she sings the notes that belong to that *rā.g*.

2. Semi-classical Category

The musical styles of this category do not follow the rules concerning *rā.g* and *tā.l* as rigidly as in the classical category. The text is usually short and romantic. The delineation of emotions described in the text, is more important than the purity of the *rā.g*. For this reason, they appeal more to the common people than to the puritans of Indian music. The main musical styles of this group are *ṭhum.rī*, *ṭap.pā*, and *dā.drā*. They are usually sung towards the end of a musical sitting of *khyā.l*.

Ṭhum.rī

The notes in *ṭhum.rī* are ornamented with delicate tonal glidings, swings, and shakes. The text is shorter than that of *khyā.l*. The *muk.tā.lā.p* (rhythm free slow improvisation) hardly lasts longer than a minute. The main feature of *ṭhum.rī* is its flexibility. It is not important in *ṭhum.rī* to stick to only one *rā.g*. If the text requires the usage of two or more *rā.gs*, so that the emotions of the composition can be better expressed, the singer does not hesitate to do that. At the same time, the singer should not lose touch of the original *rā.g.* The switching over from one *rā.g* to another is done very deftly otherwise the whole composition appears to be disjointed and the melody appears to be badly blended. This flexibility is not permitted in *khyā.l* or *dhru.pad.*

The compositions in *ṭhum.rī* have a romantic text. The text often describes the feelings of a lovelorn woman usually represented by Radha who is longing for Krishna. The cities that are famous for *ṭhum.rī* style are Varanasi (Banaras), Lucknow, Jaipur, Kolkata (Calcutta), and Paṭiyalā. In Banaras style, the same *ṭhum.rī* composition is sung in two tempi and in two different *tā.ls*. It is first sung in medium tempo and then the same text is sung in another *tā.l* in fast tempo usually in *ka.har.vā.* This kind of singing is called *lag.gī.* The *ṭhum.rī* compositions are generally sung in *rā.gs* such as *Bhai.ra.vī, Kha.mā.j, Ti.la.k-kā.mo.d, Pī.lū, Pa.hā.ḍī,* and *Kā.fī.* They are also sung in mixed *rā.gs* belonging to the *thā.ṭs, Kha.mā.j,* and *Kā.fī.* The *tā.ls* that are played in medium tempo are *dīp.can.dī, ja.t,* and *tī.n-tā.l.* The singer begins with medium tempo, then moves on to fast tempo, and then returns to the original tempo befor he/she concludes the performance.

Ṭap.pā

A *ṭap.pā* style has a short rhythm free *ā.lā.p* as well as a short composition much like a *ṭhum.rī.* It is characterized by very light and quick shakes. The notes are sung in a very fast tempo in ascent as well as descent. Each word of the composition is sung in the form of a small *tā.n.* It is called *mur.kī.* The *ṭap.pā* style requires special skill in order to sing *mur.kīs* that are sung in a very fast tempo.

Dā.drā

Dā.drā style is characterized by its tonal movement. Here, one beat is played hard and two succeeding ones are played light. The notes are embellished with glidings and swings. The text is short and romantic like that of *ṭhum.rī* and *ṭap.pā.*

3. Light Classical Category

Light classical musical styles are the folk songs that are making inroads into the established classical tradition. The rules concerning *rā.g* and *tā.l* that are typical of classical or semi-classical musical styles are not adhered to in these forms. The tonal ornaments that are used here are jerks, shakes, and glidings. The *ā.lā.p* is extremely short and sometimes it is skipped altogether. The compositions are long and the melodies are simple. The popular styles of this category are *ho.lī, cai.tī, sā.van, kaj.rī, bha.jan,* and *gha.zal.*

Ho.lī, cai.tī, sā.van, and *kaj.rī* are the seasonal folk songs. *Ho.lī* and *cai.tī* compositions are sung in the spring season and *sā.van* and *kaj.rī* compositions are sung in the monsoon season.

Ho.lī compositions describe the colourful festival of Holī. The songs have similar verbal content as those of *dha.mā.r* but *ho.lī* being a folk-song does not follow the rules concerning *rā.g* and *tā.l* as it is done in *dha.mār.* The *tā.ls* that are generally played with *ho.lī* songs are *rū.pak, dīp.can.dī,* and *ka.har.vā* or some akin forms of these. The *rā.gs* are mostly *Kā.fī, Pī.lū, Kha.mā.j,* and *Jhiṅ.jho.ṭī* that are sometimes mixed with other folk melodies.

Cai.tī[8] compositions are sung in the late spring season. Their text is romantic. The popular *tā.ls* of *cai.tī* compositions are *rū.pak, ja.t* and sometimes *ka.har.vā.* The *rā.gs* are mostly *Kha.mā.j, De.ś, Kham.bā.va.tī,* and *Ti.la.k-kā.mo.d* mixed with other folk melodies.

Sā.van and *kaj.rī* compositions are sung in the months of July and August. The text describes Krishna swinging with Rādhā and the *go.pīs.* It also describes things and events connected with the rainy season such as dark clouds, drizzling rain, lightning, the cuckoo bird, the croaking of frogs, and the dancing of the peacock. The popular *tā.ls* are *rū.pak* and *ka.har.vā.* The *rā.gs* are mainly *De.ś, Dur.gā,* and *Ti.la.k-kā.mo.d* mixed with other folk melodies. The text of these seasonal songs is long and the tempo is medium.

Bha.jan compositions have devotional texts. The tempo is medium. They are sung in *rā.gs* such as *Bhai.ravī, Dur.gā,*

[8]For detailed description see Shanti Jain, *Chaitee* (Lucknow, 1980).

De.ś, Jhiṅ.jho.ṭī, Ya.man, Ya.man-kal.yāṇ, Kha.mā.j, Pī.lū, and sometimes also in the not so common *rā.gs* such as *Ka.lā.va.tī* and *Śi.v-rañ.ja.nī.* The popular *tā.ls* are *ka.har.vā, tīn-tā.l, jhap-tā.l, dā.drā,* and *rū.pak.*

G͟ha.zal is a love song in the Urdu language. Its text is long and the tempo is medium. The popular *tā.ls* are *dā.drā, ka.ha.rvā, tīn-tā.l,* and *rū.pak. G͟ha.zals* are sung in *rā.gs* such as *ya.man, kha.mā.j, bi.hā.g, chā.yā.na.ṭ,* and *gauḍ-sā.ra.ng* mixed with other *rā.gs.*

Basic Musical Instruments

Harmonium

A harmonium is a reed organ with a keyboard. It is a wind instrument in which the wind acts on a set of metal reeds. The left hand pushes the bellows that generate wind and the fingers of the right hand press the keys to play the melody. It is a useful instrument for a beginner. By trying to sing at the same pitch as that being played on the harmonium, the beginner can learn to keep him/herself in tune. When a learner has acquired a good command of the notes, he/she can use *tān.pū.rā* or *tam.bū.rā* described on p. 22.

Fig. 1.1. Harmonium

Tab.lā

The *tab.lā* is the most popular percussion instrument of north India. It is a pair of drums that is used as an accompaniment as well as for solo performances. *Tab.lā* is played by the fingers. One of the drums is played by the left hand and is called *bāṅ.yāṅ* (meaning "left"). The other one is played by the right hand and is called *dāṅ.yāṅ* (meaning "right"). The left drum is made of either clay or metal and produces the bass sound. The right drum is made of a hollowed block of wood and produces high pitched sounds. The top of these drums is closed by hide that is kept tightened by leather braces. The middle of the hide is treated with a plaster that shows up as a black disc. This enables the player to produce special sounds. A large variety of sounds can be produced on the *tab.lā* by subtly altering the manner and force of percussion with the fingers.

Fig. 1.2. *Tab.lā*

Tān.pū.rā or Tam.bū.rā

The *tān.pū.rā* is a vitally important drone instrument in Indian music. It has a long wooden hollow neck connected to a big dried gourd (*tūm.bā*) at the end. This big dried gourd is covered with a thin sheet of wood and serves as a soundbox. The *tān.pū.rā* has usually four strings (but there are also *tān.pū.rās* with five to seven strings). These run down the entire length of the instrument. At one end, the strings are attached to tuning knobs (Hindi: *khūṅ.ṭī*) and at the other end, i.e., towards the base, they are fastened to an anchor fixed on the *tūm.bā*. On the other end, the strings pass over a curved bridge. The bridge is made of ivory or plastic. There are pieces of thread on the bridge under each string. Before playing the *tān.pū.rā* it has to be tuned. The four strings of *tān.pū.rā* (counting them from the left), are traditionally tuned as *pa, ṡa, ṡa, sa* (fifth, tonic, tonic and one octave below tonic). The first three strings counting from left are made of steel and the fourth one is made of brass. When *pa* is absent in a *rā.g*, the first string (i.e., the one to the extreme left) is tuned in *ma*. The tuning is done in two steps viz., the gross tuning and the fine tuning. The middle pair of steel strings are tuned first in high *Sa*, then the string on the right that is made of brass is tuned in *Sa* of middle octave and at the end the steel string on the left is tuned either in *pa* or *ma*. This constitutes the gross tuning. This is followed by fine tuning. It is done by pulling the beads (Hindi: *man.kā*) that each string has below the ivory bridge. The tonal accuracy in the tuning of *tān.pū.rā* is extremely important.

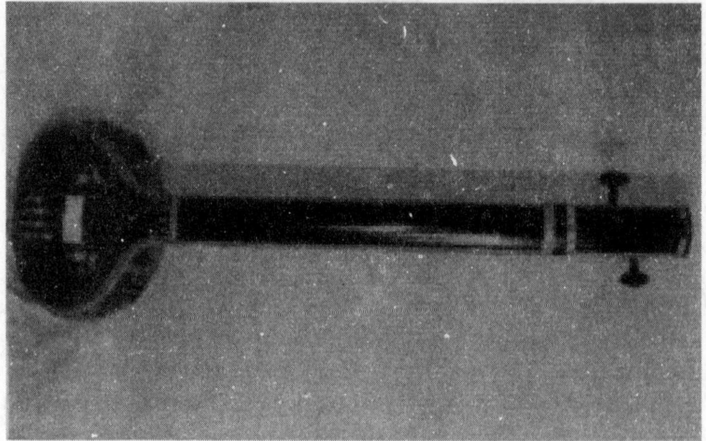

Fig. 1.3. *Tān.pū.rā*

The tuning is followed by optimization of resonance that is called *ja.vā.rī khol.nā*. It is done by striking the strings one by one with one hand while the other hand pulls the piece of thread very slowly from the upper end of the bridge to the lower end till the string creates the optimum resonance.

The thickness of the string determines the pitch that is produced by that string. Since the male voice is lower in pitch, the *tān.pū.rā* for males has generally thicker strings and a larger *tūm.bā* while that for females has generally thinner strings and a smaller *tūm.bā.*

CHAPTER 2

Preparation: Basic Requirements and Techniques

Vocal music demands a wide tonal range, an ear for tonal and rhythmic variations, and a long breath. Indian classical music, in particular, demands a resonant voice (voice full of microtones), a skill to sing a single note steadily and in tune in one breath, and an ability to sing several notes with their tonal ornamentations at a very fast tempo without compromising the clarity. These skills can be aquired by regular practice of special exercises that will be discussed in this chapter.

There are two traditional ways of singing notes[1] in Indian music. One is singing them in *sar.gam* (*Sa, Re, Ga, Ma, Pa, Dha,* and *Ni*) and the other one is singing them in *ā.kā.r* (an open *ā* sound as in father).

It is advisable to use the harmonium in the beginning in order to keep oneself in tune. Later, the harmonium can be replaced by *tān.pū.rā*.

THE TECHNIQUE OF PLAYING HARMONIUM

The keyboard of the harmonium contains two types of keys: the black keys and the white or light coloured keys. The black keys are short in length and fifteen in number. The white or light coloured keys are long and twenty-two in number. The total number of keys is thirty-seven (see fig. 1.1). The black keys are arranged in groups of twos and threes. Traditionally, the player sits on the floor with the harmonium in front of him or her. He/she can also sit on a chair with the harmonium on a table in front.

[1] *Nom tom* is another method but it is exclusively used in *dhru.pad* and *dha.mār* styles.

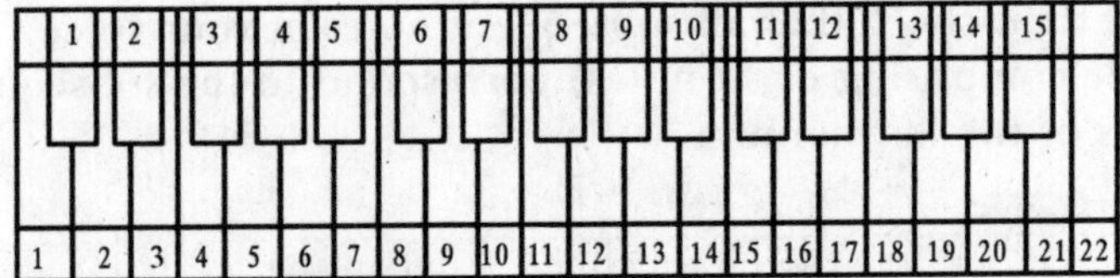

Fig. 2.1. Keyboard of Harmonium

- Going from the left to the right, the tones become steadily higher. Going from the right to the left, the tones become steadily lower.
- Each finger of the right hand starting from the thumb has been assigned an ordinal number. The thumb is 1, the index finger is 2, the middle finger is 3, the ring finger is 4, and the small finger is 5. The small finger is seldom used for playing harmonium.
- To play the harmonium, open the clip that keeps the harmonium closed. Now, place the fingers of the left hand at the backside of the flap and open the bellows of the harmonium. Place the thumb at the innerside of the harmonium so that you can control the volume of the harmonium at will. Pull the flap of the harmonium slowly till it touchs the harmonium frame. At the same time, play the keys of the harmonium with your right hand by pressing the keys. If you are left-handed, do it the other way round.

Selection of *Sa* on the Harmonium

Since every person has a different pitch of the voice and the tonal range, it is important that a learner finds out which key on the harmonium represents his or her, starting note, i.e., *Sa.* Once *Sa* as a starting note is selected properly, the whole octave corresponds exactly to the tonal range of one's own voice.

The starting note *Sa* for the female voice is generally the fourth black key of the harmonium counting from the left (see fig. 2.1), and for the male voice it is the second black key from the left (see fig. 2.1), not forgetting that this is a broad generalization and not every female or male has to confirm to this rule. The important point is that you find out on the harmonium the starting key that represents your *Sa*, and then check that all subsequent notes of your voice (in a scale comprising eight notes) correspond to the subsequent keys of the harmonium.

Sa Re GaMa Pa Dha NiSa

1 2 3 4 5 6 7 8 9 10 11 12 13 14 15

1 2 3 4 5 6 7 8 9 10 11 12 13 14 15 16 17 18 19 20 21 22

Fig. 2.2. Female voice with *Sa* on the fourth black key

Ordinal number of fingers to play notes of the middle octave when the *Sa* is the fourth black key. (See explanation *supra*, p. 25.)

Notes in ascending order:

key:	4th black	5th black	8th white	6th black	7th black	11th white	12th white	9th black
note:	*Sa*	*Re*	*Ga*	*Ma*	*Pa*	*Dha*	*Ni*	*Ṡa*
finger:	2	3	1	2	3	1	2	3

Notes in descending order:

key:	9th black	12th white	11th white	7th black	6th black	8th white	5th black	4th black
note:	*Ṡa*	*Ni*	*Dha*	*Pa*	*Ma*	*Ga*	*Re*	*Sa*
finger:	3	2	1	3	2	1	3	2

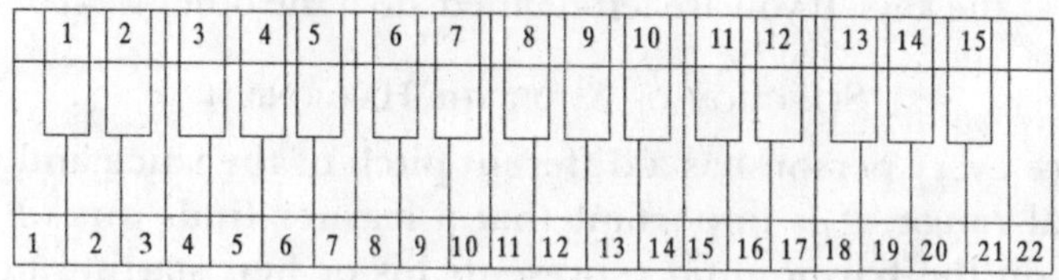

Fig. 2.3. Male voice with *Sa* on the second black key

Ordinal number of fingers to play notes of the middle octave when the *Sa* is the second black key. (See explanation *supra*, p. 25.)

Notes in ascending order:

key:	2nd black	4th white	5th white	4th black	5th black	8th white	9th white	7th black
note:	*Sa*	*Re*	*Ga*	*Ma*	*Pa*	*Dha*	*Ni*	*Ṡa*
finger:	2	1	2	3	4	1	2	3

Notes in descending order:

key:	7th black	9th white	8th white	5th black	4th black	5th white	4th white	2nd black
note:	*Sa*	*Ni*	*Dha*	*Pa*	*Ma*	*Ga*	*Re*	*Sa*
finger:	3	2	1	4	3	2	1	2

THE TECHNIQUE OF PLAYING *TĀN.PŪ.RĀ*

There are two ways of holding the *tān.pū.rā* while playing. It can be held either vertically or horizontally. Holding the *tān.pū.rā* vertically is more popular than holding it horizontally. There are no hard and fast rules as to when it should be played vertically and when horizontally. It all depends on the performer's conveniene. Still, playing it in a vertical position certainly povides a performer a better hearing and, thus, a quicker discovery of "off-tuning," i.e., its slightest shift from

Fig. 2.4. Playing *tān.pū.rā* vertically

tuning. The *tān.pū.rā* is played with the right hand while the left hand is used for supporting the instrument. The player also uses his/her left hand to correct the tension of the strings without any interruption in case it gets off-tuned during the performance. The left string, that is tuned as *pa,* is played by pushing the string lightly with the left side of the end of the middle finger of the right hand. Of the remaining three strings, the first two are tuned as high *Sa* and the third one is tuned as *Sa* of the middle octave. They are played by pushing the strings lightly with the end of the left side of the forefinger.

Some singers prefer to play *tān.pū.rā* horizontally. In that case the singer sits cross-legged and places the *tūm.bā* on his/her lap. The right elbow rests on the *tūm.bā.* The strings are played in the same manner as when playing it in a vertical position.

Fig. 2.5. Playing *tān.pū.rā* horizontally

The Technique of Voice Training

Remember three things before you start: (1) Be relaxed. (2) Listen attentively to the note you are playing. (3) Remember that practice makes a person perfect. Go on practising despite disappointments.

Four Sets of Exercises

There are four sets of exercises to help you train and cultivate your voice. Set no. 1 has four exercises that are meant to make your voice resonant and help you develop a long breath. Set no. 2 has three exercises that are meant to help you increase your tonal range. Set no. 3 has six exercises that are meant to teach you the basic tonal embellishments. Set no. 4 has three exercises that are meant to master the technique further.

Set no. 1: *Exercises for developing a long breath and making voice steady and resonant*

Exercise 1

Sit comfortably and play *Sa* on the harmonium. Listen to the pitch of *Sa* attentively for a few seconds. Take a long breath through your nose very gently without making any hissing sound or any unnatural physical movement while you breathe in. Now, close your lips lightly. Your upper and lower jaws should not touch each other. Make a humming sound. Ensure that your humming is in tune with the pitch of the harmonium. Sing it as long as your breath lasts. Try to feel a vibrating sensation in your lips. The more are the vibrations the more resonant is the voice. Play and sing all the notes of the middle octave one by one in ascending as well as descending order. Repeat each note at least three times.

Exercise 2

Take a long breath gently as in exercise 1. In this exercise, you are to utter two letters *ā* (as in father) and *ū* (as in room) one after another and then close your lips making a humming sound in one continuation. Make sure that your note remains the same. It is to be sung in one breath. The ratio of the duration of singing *ā, ū,* and humming is 2:4:1. The duration of *ā, ū,* and humming will naturally depend on the length of your breath. Play and sing all the notes of the middle octave one by one in ascending as well as descending order starting from *Sa.* Repeat this exercise at least three times.

Exercise 3

Take a long breath gently as in exercise 1. Play and sing all the notes of the middle octave one by one in *ā.kā.r* in ascending as well as in descending order. Each note should be sung in one breath. Repeat this exercise at least three times.

Exercise 4

Take a long breath gently as in exercise 1. Sing *Sa* by its name *Sa* and sing it as long as your breath lasts. Play and sing all the notes of the middle octave one by one in ascending as well as in descending order by their names, i.e., *sa re ga ma pa dha ni sā.* Repeat this exercise at least three times.

When you are sure that you know the correct pitch of all the notes of the middle octave, you can practice the following exercises. Now you need not play each note one after another while you sing, instead play three notes *Sa, Pa,* and high *Ṡa* simultaneously. This you can do by pressing the three keys *Sa, Pa,* and high *Ṡa* simultaneously. You can also do it by removing the wires, that are pressing the backside of these three keys and placing these wires on the adjacent keys. In this way, your one hand will be free and you can now use this for keeping the beat.

Set no. 2: *Exercises to increase tonal range*

Exercise 1

Play high *Ṡa* on harmonium. Listen to it attentively so that you are in tune with it. Take a long breath through your nose slowly and gently. Relax your facial muscles. Close your lips as in exercise 1 of set no. 1 and sing high *Ṡa* by its name. If you find the pitch of high *Ṡa* too high, sing it with your *head voice* (the upper part of the vocal chords). The change over from the throat to the head voice should be smooth so that it is unnoticeable. For that, you should decrease the volume of the last note that you were singing before you change to the head voice. For example, if you are going to sing high *Ṡa* in head voice, decrease the volume of *Ni* prior to changing over and increase the volume of high *Ṡa* that you are going to sing in head voice. When the volume of the last note is decreased and the volume of the following note is increased, the change over from throat voice to head voice is smooth. It is better to sing the notes of the higher octave in head voice. Singing in head voice will not strain the vocal chords and the voice will remain soft.

Sing high *Ṡa* as long as your breath lasts. Do it at least three times. After you have mastered this, sing high *Ṙe, Ġa, Ṁa,* and *Ṗa* one by one with your head voice. Sing each note for as long as your breath lasts.

After singing the notes of the higher octave, sing all the notes of the middle octave in descending order. Sing it five times.

Exercise 2

Now play the three notes *Sa, Pa,* and high *Ṡa* simultaneously. The tonal range of this exercise comprises three notes of the lower octave, the whole middle octave and five notes of the higher octave, i.e., *P̣a, Ḍha, Ṇi, Sa, Re, Ga, Ma, Pa, Dha, Ni, Ṡa, Ṙe, Ġa, Ṁa,* and *Ṗa.* Sing the notes in ascending as well as descending order from low *Pa* to high *Ṗa* and from high *Ṗa* to low *Pa* in *sar.gam.* Take a short breath through your mouth after every four notes. Repeat this exercise five times in *sar.gam* and then in *ā.kā.r.*

Exercise 3

Here the tonal range is the same as in exercise 2 but the tempo is increased. Take a short breath through your mouth after every eight notes. Sing in *sar.gam* and then in *ā.kā.r* five times.

Set no. 3: *Exercises to learn tonal embellishments*

There are six main tonal embellishments: *mī.ṅḍ* (tonal gliding), *kan* (something like grace note), *svar-ghu.mā.v* (tonal swinging), *khaṭ.kā* or *ga.ma.k* (kind of shake), *ā.ndo.lan* (kind of shake), and *mur.kī* (singing four or five notes in extremely quick succession with a light push (*khaṭ.kā*) in order to show their separation.

(*a*) Mīṅ.ḍ: *Mīṅ.ḍ* or tonal gliding is a gliding from one note to the other while subtly touching the notes in-between. It can be done in descending as well as ascending order.

Exercise 1

Mīṅ.ḍ between *Sa,* low *Pa,* and *Sa.*

Start singing *Sa* steadily and increase your volume slowly. Increasing the volume is shown in the example below by the sign <. While increasing the volume, glide over the notes *Ṇi, Ḍha* of the lower octave and decrease the volume slowly as you sing low *Pa.* The notes *Ni* and *Dha* are purposely not written in the example since you are to glide over them. Decreasing the volume is shown in the examples below by the sign >. After singing low *Pa* steadily for a short while, increase your volume a little and glide over *Dha, Ni* and then decrease your volume when you sing *Sa.* Sing the whole middle octave in this way.

Example:

ascent *Sa...* < < > *P̣a...* < < > *Sa...*
Re... < < > *Ḍha...* < < > *Re...*
Ga... < < > *Ṇi...* < < > *Ga...*
Ma... < < > *Sa...* < < > *Ma...*
Pa... < < > *Re...* < < > *Pa...*
Dha... < < > *Ga...* < < > *Dha...*
Ni... < < > *Ma...* < < > *Ni...*

descent *Ṡa...* < < > *Pa...* < < > *Ṡa...*
Ni... < < > *Ma...* < < > *Ni...*
Dha... < < > *Ga...* < < > *Dha...*
Pa... < < > *Re...* < < > *Pa...*
Ma... < < > *Sa...* < < > *Ma...*
Ga... < < > *Ṇi...* < < > *Ga...*
Re... < < > *Ḍha...* < < > *Re...*
Sa... < < > *P̣a...* < < > *Sa...*

Sing the above exercise two times in *sar.gam* as well as in *ā.kā.r.*

(*b*) Kaṇ: *Kaṇ* is a grace note. It is added as an ornament and is sung shortly before singing the main note.

Exercise 2

Sing *Sa* with a touch of low *Ṇi, Pa* with a touch of *Ma* and high *Ṡa* with a touch of *Ni* in *ā.kā.r.* The *kaṇ* notes are written in the example below on the left upper side of the main notes.

Example:

[Ṇi]*Sa* [Ma]*Pa* [Ni]*Ṡa*

Sing the above exercise three times.

(*c*) Svar-ghu.mā.v: *Svar-ghu.mā.v* or tonal swinging is a repetitional gliding from a higher note to a lower note by controlling the volume of the voice. Basically, it is a kind of *mīṅ.ḍ* with the exception that here the gliding movement is to be repeated at least once. The two notes in *svar-ghu.mā.v* can either be next to each other or there can be one or two notes between them.

Exercise 3a

Sing *Sa* steadily, increase your volume on *Sa* while gliding towards low *Ni*. Decrease the volume when you sing low *Ṇi*. Hold low *Ṇi* for a while. Now, again increase the volume of low *Ṇi* and glide towards *Sa*. Decrease the volume when you sing *Sa* and hold *Sa* for a while.

Example 3a:

Sa.<.<.>Ṇi..<.<.>Sa..<.<.>Ṇi.<.<.>Sa....

Exercise 3b

Sing *Sa* steadily, increase your volume on *Sa* while gliding towards low *Dha*. Decrease the volume when you sing low *Dha*. Hold low *Dha* for a while then increase your volume of low *Dha* and glide towards *Sa*. Decrease your volume when you sing *Sa*.

Example 3b:

Sa...<.>Ḍha.<Sa...<.>Ḍha.<Sa....

Sing the above exercises three times and sing in *ā.kā.r* only.

(*d*) Khaṭ.kā or ga.ma.k: *Khaṭ.kā* is the art of nimbly touching a lower note before singing the higher note which is the main note. After touching the lower note, the singer sings the higher note with more volume. This tonal manoeuvre or the shake sounds like a tonal push. The lower note can be just one note lower or can be more than one note lower. When it is just one note lower, the shake is light and it creates a light *khaṭ.kā*. When the lower note is lower by more than one note, the shake is stronger and thus creates a forceful *khaṭ.kā*. This effect is generated by the push and the volume. If you want to sing notes in fast tempo, you should create light *khaṭ.kā*s. When the distance between the lower and the higher notes is less, it is easier to sing in fast tempo and naturally the *khaṭ.kā*s will also be less forceful. The *khaṭ.kā*s are also referred to as *ga.ma.k*s which is a Sanskrit name for *khaṭ.kā*.

Exercise 4a

Sing all the notes of the middle octave in ascending as well as descending order with *khaṭ.kā* and sing them in *ā.kā.r* since it is easier. However, you can also sing them in *sar.gam*. If you sing the notes in *sar.gam*, do not utter the names of *khaṭ.kā* notes but utter only the names of main notes even though you start your exercise from the *khaṭ.kā* note. Start saying *Sa* while your pitch is actually low *Ni*. In the examples below, the *khaṭ.kā* note [the lower note] is indicated by the sign * and it is written in small letters. This is followed by the name of the main note. After singing the *khaṭ.kā* note quickly, sing the main note and hold it for a little while. Keep the beat on every *khaṭ.kā* note. Use your free hand for the beat.

Example 4a:

ascent **ṇi Sa...*, **sa Re..*, **re Ga..*, **ga Ma..*, short breath
**ma Pa..*, **pa Dha..*, **dha Ni..*, **ni Ṡa...* long breath
descent **ni Ṡa...*, **dha Ni..*, **pa Dha..*, **ma Pa..*, short breath
**ga Ma..*, **re Ga..*, **sa Re..*, **ṇi Ṡa...*, long breath

Sing it five times first in *ā.kā.r* then in *sar.gam*.

Exercise 4b

Sing the same note twice with light *khaṭ.kā* and after that take a short breath. Sing the whole scale in ascending as well as descending order only in *ā.kā.r*. Start it with *Sa*.

Example 4b:

ascent	**ṇi Sa..*	**ṇi Sa..* short breath
	**sa Re..*	**sa Re..* short breath
	**re Ga..*	**re Ga..* short breath
	**ga Ma..*	**ga Ma..* short breath
	**ma Pa..*	**ma Pa..* short breath
	**pa Dha..*	**pa Dha..* short breath
	**dha Ni..*	**dha Ni..* short breath
	**ni Ṡa..*	**ni Ṡa..* short breath
descent	**ni Ṡa..*	**ni Ṡa..* short breath
	**dha Ni..*	**dha Ni..* short breath
	**pa Dha..*	**pa Dha..* short breath
	**ma Pa..*	**ma Pa..* short breath
	**ga Ma..*	**ga Ma..* short breath
	**re Ga..*	**re Ga..* short breath
	**sa Re..*	**sa Re..* short breath
	**ṇi Sa..*	**ṇi Sa..* short breath

Sing it five times in *ā-kā.r.*

Exercise 4c

Sing the same note twice but this time with strong *khaṭ.kā*s. Follow the instructions of exercise 4b.

Example 4c:

ascent	**p̣a Sa..*	**p̣a Sa..* short breath
	**ḍha Re..*	**ḍha Re..* short breath
	**ṇi Ga..*	**ṇi Ga..* short breath
	**sa Ma..*	**sa Ma..* short breath
	**re Pa..*	**re Pa..* short breath
	**ga Dha..*	**ga Dha..* short breath
	**ma Ni..*	**ma Ni..* short breath
	**pa Ṡa..*	**pa Ṡa..* short breath
descent	**pa Ṡa..*	**pa Ṡa..* short breath
	**ma Ni..*	**ma Ni..* short breath
	**ga Dha..*	**ga Dha..* short breath
	**re Pa..*	**re Pa..* short breath
	**sa Ma..*	**sa Ma..* short breath

**ṇi Ga..* **ṇi Ga..* short breath
**ḍha Re..* **ḍha Re..* short breath
**ṗa Sa..* **ṗa Sa..* short breath

Sing it five times in *ā.kā.r.*

You can also practice with three or more same notes with light as well as strong *khaṭ.kā*s as you did in exercise 4a, 4b, and 4c.

(*e*) Ān.do.lan: *Ān.do.lan* or *ān.do.lit svar* is a tonal oscillation. Here, one higher note is sung before singing the main note, after that one lower note is sung and then again the main note is sung. All this is sung very quickly.

Exercise 5

Ān.do.lan on *Sa,*
Example: *re sa ṇi sa*
Ān.do.lan on *Re*
Example: *ga re sa re*
Ān.do.lan on *Ga*
Example: *ma ga re ga*
Ān.do.lan on *Ma*
Example: *pa ma ga ma*
Ān.do.lan on *Pa*
Example: *dha pa ma pa*
Ān.do.lan on *Dha*
Example: *ni dha pa dha*
Ān.do.lan on *Ni*
Example: *ṡa ni dha ni*

Sing it five times only in *ā.kā.r.*

(*f*) Mur.kī: *Mur.kī* is a kind of short *tā.n* of three or four notes. It is sung in an extremely fast tempo. The notes in *mur.kī* are sung in a sequence. The difference between *mur.kī* and *tā.n* is that *mur.kī* is shorter with no repetitive pattern while *tā.n* can be repetitive. Also, *mur.kī* is sung faster than *tā.n.* There are two types of *mur.kī*s. One is a short quick *tā.n* while the other is a kind of tonal shake.

Exercise 6—Mur.kī type 1

Here, a singer sings three or four notes in a sequence in an extremely fast tempo with light *khaṭ.kā*s. The notes can be sung in an ascent as well as in descent.

Example 6—*Mur.kī* type 1:

saregama or *magarema*
repamaga or *pamagare*
gamapadha or *dhapamaga*
manidhapa or *nidhapama*
padhaniṡa or *ṡanidhapa*

Exercise 6—Mur.kī type 2

The second type of *mur.kī* can be called tonal turn. The word *mur.kī* is from Hindi word *moṛ* meaning "turn." Here, a singer sings very quickly one note higher from the base note then skips the base note and sings the lower note with trill and holds it steady for a while.

Example 6—*Mur.kī* type 2:

If the base note is *Pa,* hold *Pa* steadily then touch *Dha* [one higher note] very briefly, skip *Pa* and sing *Ma* with trill and hold it for a while. You can also skip two notes when you descend. Sing it three times in *ā.kā.r.*

Before singing *mur.kī,* try to sing simple *tā.ns* in fast tempo.

Set no. 4: *Exercises to master the technique further*

Exercise 1

Now you should sing in one breath the whole middle octave in ascent as well as in descent in *ā.kā.r* with *khaṭ.kā.* Take short, quick, and gentle breath through your mouth after every fourth note and also keep a beat after every fourth note, starting from *Sa* (the first note).

Example 1:

ascent **ṇiSa. *saRe. *reGa. *gaMa., *maPa. *paDha. *dhaNi. *niṠa*

descent **niṠa. *dhaNi. *paDha. *maPa. *gaMa. *reGa. *saRe. *ṇiSa.*

Sing the above exercise ten times, first in *sar.gam* then in *ā.kā.r.*

Exercise 2

Sing all the eight notes of the middle octave with *khaṭ.kā* in ascending order in one breath. Take short quick breath through your mouth and then sing all the eight notes with *khaṭ.kā* in descending order. Keep the beat after every eighth note starting from *Sa*.

Example 2:

ascent *ṇiSa. *saRe. *reGa. *gaMa., *maPa. *paDha. *dhaNi. *niṠa

descent *niṠa. *dhaNi. *paDha. *maPa. *gaMa. *reGa. *saRe. *ṇiSa.

Sing the above exercise 20 times in *sar.gam* then in *ā.kā.r.*

Exercise 3

Sing the whole middle octave with *khaṭ.kā* in ascent as well as descent in one breath. Take short quick breath through your mouth after completing one cycle of ascent and descent. When you repeat this exercise, do not sing the last *Sa* of descent. In this way, you will get some more time to take your breath without loosing track of your beat.

Example 3:

ascent *ṇiSa. *saRe. *reGa. *gaMa. *maPa. *paDha. *dhaNi. *niṠa

descent *niṠa. *dhaNi. *paDha, *maPa. *gaMa. *reGa. *saRe

Sing the above exercise, twenty times in *sar.gam* then in *ā.kā.r.*

After this exercise, try to sing the whole middle octave two times in one breath. Once you have mastered this, you can try to sing the whole middle octave three times and after that four times and five times in one breath. This will help you to sing *tā.ns* in fast tempo.

Basic Tonal Patterns *Pal.ṭe*

The tonal patterns are called *pal.ṭe.* The word *pal.ṭe* is a plural form of *pal.ṭa* meaning turn or rotation. It is also called *a.laṅ.kār.* There are three basic tonal patterns. These are given below. Other tonal patterns are formed by a combination of these three basic tonal patterns.

Pattern no. 1: *Singing the same note*

Here, the patterns are formed by repeating the same note that can be sung two, three, or four times.

Exercise 1

Sing the same note two times. Take a short breath through your mouth when needed. The notes are to be sung with *khaṭ.kā*. In the exercises below, *khaṭ.kā* note (the push from one lower note) has been shown by an "*" such as **Sa*Sa* and that means *nisa nisa.*

Example:

ascent *Sa*Sa, *Re*Re, *Ga*Ga, *Ma*Ma, *Pa*Pa, *Dha*Dha, *Ni*Ni, *Ṡa*Ṡa

descent *Ṡa*Ṡa, *Ni*Ni, *Dha*Dha, *Pa*Pa, *Ma*Ma, *Ga *Ga, *Re*Re, *Sa*Sa

Exercise 2

Sing the same note three times.

Example:

ascent *Sa*Sa*Sa, *Re*Re*Re, *Ga*Ga*Ga, *Ma*Ma*Ma, *Pa*Pa*Pa, *Dha*Dha*Dha, *Ni*Ni*Ni, *Ṡa*Ṡa*Ṡa.

descent *Ṡa*Ṡa*Ṡa. *Ni*Ni*Ni, *Dha*Dha*Dha, *Pa*Pa*Pa, *Ma*Ma*Ma, *Ga*Ga*Ga, *Re*Re*Re, *Sa*Sa*Sa

Exercise 3

Sing the same the note four times.

Example:

ascent *Sa*Sa*Sa*Sa, *Re*Re*Re*Re, *Ga*Ga*Ga*Ga, *Ma*Ma*Ma*Ma, *Pa*Pa*Pa*Pa, *Dha*Dha*Dha*Dha, *Ni*Ni*Ni*Ni, *Ṡa*Ṡa*Ṡa*Ṡa

descent *Ṡa*Ṡa*Ṡa*Ṡa, *Ni*Ni*Ni*Ni, *Dha*Dha*Dha*Dha, *Pa*Pa*Pa*Pa, *Ma*Ma*Ma*Ma, *Ga*Ga*Ga*Ga, *Re*Re*Re*Re, *Sa*Sa*Sa*Sa

Pattern no. 2: *Singing the notes in a sequence*

Here, the patterns are formed by singing the notes in a sequence.

Exercise 1

Sing the first three notes in a sequence in ascent starting from *Sa* then descend one note and after that sing three notes again in ascent starting from the note you descended to. Such a pattern can also be sung with four or five notes instead of three. Sing it with *khaṭ.kā*.

Example:
ascent **Sa*Re*Ga, *Re*Ga*Ma, *Ga*Ma*Pa, *Ma*Pa*Dha, *Pa*Dha*Ni, *Dha*Ni*Ṡa*
descent **Dha*Ni*Ṡa., *Pa*Dha*Ni, *Ma*Pa*Dha, *Ga*Ma*Pa, *Re*Ga*Ma, *Sa*Re*Ga*
descent can also be sung as:
**Ṡa*Ni*Dha, *Ni*Dha*Pa, *Dha*Pa*Ma, *Pa*Ma*Ga, *Ma*Ga*Re, *Ga*Re*Sa*

Exercise 2

Sing four notes in a sequence in ascent starting from *Sa* then descend three notes and after that sing four notes again in ascent starting from the note you descended to.

Example:
ascent **Sa*Re*Ga*Ma, *Re*Ga*Ma*Pa, *Ga*Ma*Pa*Dha, *Ma*Pa*Dha*Ni, *Pa*Dha*Ni*Ṡa.*
descent **Pa*Dha*Ni*Ṡa, *Ma*Pa*Dha*Ni, *Ga*Ma*Pa*Dha, *Re*Ga*Ma*Pa, *Sa*Re*Ga*Ma*
descent can also be sung as:
**Ṡa*Ni*Dha*Pa, *Ni*Dha*Pa*Ma, *Dha*Pa*Ma*Ga, *Pa*Ma*Ga*Re, *Ma*Ga*Re*Sa*

Exercise 3

Sing five notes in a sequence in an ascent sarting from *Sa* then descend four notes and after that sing five notes again in ascent starting from the note you descended to.

Example:
ascent **Sa*Re*Ga*Ma*Pa, *Re*Ga*Ma*Pa*Dha, *Ga*Ma*Pa*Dha*Ni, *Ma*Pa*Dha*Ni*Ṡa,*
descent **Ma*Pa*Dha*Ni*Ṡa, *Ga*Ma*Pa*Dha*Ni, *Re*Ga*Ma*Pa*Dha, *Sa*Re*Ga*Ma*Pa*
descent can also be sung as:
**Ṡa*Ni*Dha*Pa*Ma, *Ni*Dha*Pa*Ma*Ga, *Dha*Pa*Ma*Ga*Re, *Pa*Ma*Ga*Re*Sa*

Pattern no. 3: *Skipping the notes*

Here, a tonal pattern is formed by skipping one or more notes between two notes. This is done in ascent as well as in descent.

Exercise 1: Skipping one note

Sing *Sa*, followed by *Ga* skipping *Re*. After this, descend to *Re*, skip the next note *Ga* and sing *Ma*.

Example:

ascent *Sa* Ga, *Re* Ma, *Ga* Pa, *Ma* Dha, *Pa* Ni, *Dha* Ṡa

descent *Dha* Ṡa, *Pa* Ṅi, *Ma* Dha, *Ga* Pa, *Re* Ma, *Sa* Ga

descent can also be sung as:

Ṡa Dha, *Ni* Pa, *Dha* Ma, *Pa* Ga, *Ma* Re, *Ga* Sa

Exercise 2: Skipping two notes

Example:

ascent *Sa* Ma, *Re* Pa, *Ga* Dha, *Ma* Ni, *Dha* Ṡa.

descent *Dha* Ṡa, *Pa* Ni, *Ma* Dha, *Ga* Pa, *Re* Ma, *Sa* Ga

descent can also be sung as:

Ṡa Dha, *Ni* Pa, *Dha* Ma, *Pa* Ga, *Ma* Re, *Ga* Sa

Exercise 3: Skipping three notes

Example:

ascent *Sa* Pa, *Re* Dha, *Ga* Ni, *Ma* Ṡa

descent *Ma* Ṡa, *Ga* Ni, *Re* Dha, *Sa* Pa

descent can also be sung as:

Ṡa Ma, *Ni* Ga, *Dha* Re, *Pa* Sa

Patterns formed by the combination of the above three basic patterns

Patterns formed with three notes

Example 1:

ascent *Sa* Re* Sa, *Re* Ga* Re, *Ga* Ma* Ga, *Ma* Pa* Ma, *Pa* Dha* Pa, *Dha* Ni* Dha, *Ni* Ṡa* Ni, *Ṡa* Ṙe* Ṡa

descent *Ṡa* Ṙe* Ṡa, *Ni* Ṡa* Ni, *Dha* Ni* Dha, *Pa* Dha* Pa, *Ma* Pa* Ma, *Ga* Ma* Ga, *Re* Ga* Re, *Sa* Re* Sa

Example 2:

ascent *Re* Re* Sa, * Ga* Ga* Re, * Ma* Ma* Ga, * Pa* Pa* Ma,
Dha Dha* Pa, * Ni* Ni* Dha, * Ṡa* Ṡa* Ni, * Ṙe* Ṙe* Ṡa

descent * Ṡa* Ṙe* Ṙe, * Ni* Ṡa* Ṡa, * Dha* Ni* Ni, * Pa* Dha* Dha,
* Ma* Pa* Pa, * Ga* Ma* Ma, * Re* Ga* Ga, * Sa* Re* Re

Example 3:

ascent * Sa* Ga* Sa, * Re* Ma* Re, * Ga* Pa* Ga, * Ma* Dha* Ma,
* Pa* Ni* Pa, * Dha* Ṡa* Dha, * Ni* Ṡa* Ni, * Ṡa* Ṙe* Ṡa

descent * Ṡa* Ṙe* Ṡa, * Ni* Ṡa* Ni, * Dha* Ni* Dha, * Pa* Dha* Pa,
* Ma* Pa* Ma, * Ga* Ma* Ga, * Re* Ga* Re, * Sa* Re* Sa

Patterns formed with four notes

Example 1:

ascent * Sa* Re* Re* Ga, * Re* Ga* Ga* Ma, * Ga* Ma* Ma* Pa,
* Ma* Pa* Pa* Dha, * Pa* Dha* Dha* Ni, * Dha* Ni* Ni* Ṡa.

descent * Dha* Ni* Ni* Ṡa, * Pa* Dha* Dha* Ni, * Ma* Pa* Pa* Dha,
* Ga* Ma* Ma* Pa, * Re* Ga* Ga* Ma, * Sa* Re* Re* Ga

Example 2:

ascent * Sa* Ga* Re* Sa, * Re* Ma* Ga* Re, * Ga* Pa* Ma* Ga,
* Ma* Dha* Pa* Ma, * Pa* Ni* Dha* Pa, * Dha* Ṡa* Ni* Dha,
* Ni* Ṙe* Ṡa* Ni, * Ṡa* Ġa* Ṙe* Ṡa

descent * Ṡa* Ġa* Ṙe* Ṡa, * Ni* Ṙe* Ṡa* Ni, * Dha* Ṡa* Ni* Dha,
* Pa* Ni* Dha* Pa, * Ma* Dha* Pa* Ma, * Ga* Pa* Ma* Ga,
* Re* Ma* Ga* Re, * Sa* Ga* Re* Sa

Example 3:

ascent * Sa* Re* Ma* Ga, * Re* Ga* Pa* Ma, * Ga* Ma* Dha* Pa,
* Ma* Pa* Ni* Dha, * Pa* Dha* Ṡa* Ni, * Dha* Ni* Ṙe* Ṡa

descent * Dha* Ni* Ṙe* Ṡa, * Pa* Dha* Ṡa* Ni, * Ma* Pa* Ni* Dha,
* Ga* Ma* Dha* Pa, * Re* Ga* Pa* Ma, * Sa* Re* Ma* Ga

Patterns formed with eight notes

Example:

ascent * Sa * Ga * Re * Ma * Re * Ga * Re * Sa,
* Re * Ma * Ga * Pa * Ga * Ma * Ga * Re,
* Ga * Pa * Ma * Dha * Ma * Pa * Ma * Ga,
* Ma * Dha * Pa * Ni * Pa * Dha * Pa * Ma,

*Pa *Ni *Dha *Ṡa *Dha *Ni *Dha *Pa,
*Dha *Ṡa *Ni *Ṙe *Ni *Ṡa *Ni *Dha,
*Ni *Ṙe *Ṡa *Ġa *Ṡa *Ṙe *Ṡa *Ni,
*Ṡa *Ġa *Ṙe *Ṁa *Ṙe *Ġa *Ṙe *Ṡa

descent *Ṡa *Ġa *Ṙe *Ṁa *Ṙe *Ġa *Ṙe *Ṡa
*Ni *Ṙe *Ṡa *Ġa *Ṡa *Ṙe *Ṡa *Ni
*Dha *Ṡa *Ni *Ṙe *Ni *Ṡa *Ni *Dha
*Pa *Ni *Dha *Ṡa *Dha *Ni *Dha *Pa
*Ma *Dha *Pa *Ni *Pa *Dha *Pa *Ma
*Ga *Pa *Ma *Dha *Ma *Pa *Ma *Ga
*Re *Ma *Ga *Pa *Ga *Ma *Ga *Re
*Sa *Ga *Re *Ma *Re *Ga *Re *Sa

These are some examples of tonal patterns. You can make many more of your own.

CHAPTER 3

The Performance

The ten basic *rā.gs* are outlined here in the *khyā.l* style together with examples of improvisations and compositions belonging to the *rā.gs*. One of the compositions in each *rā.g* is provided with *ā.lā.p* and *tā.n*. The other compositions are given without any improvisation. They are meant to give the learner an idea of the basic character of the *rā.g* and to help the learner improvise on his/her own. The compositions that are given are in medium tempo. A composition in *khyā.l* style has two parts, viz., *sthā.yī* (the first part) and *an.ta.rā* (the second part).

The rendering of a *rā.g* in *khyā.l* style: The four stages:

Stage 1: *Muk.t ā.lā.p,* also called just *ā.lā.p,* is a rhythm-free improvisation in slow tempo.

Stage 2: *Ban.diś* or *cī.z* or *khyā.l* is a composition sung with the accompaniment of *tab.lā* (a pair of drums).

Stage 3: *Tā.l-bad.dha ā.lā.p* also referred to *ā.lā.p* is a rhythmic improvisation in slow tempo and is sung with the accompaniment of *tab.lā.*

Stage 4: *Tā.n* is a rhythmic improvisation in fast tempo and is sung with the accompaniment of *tab.lā.*

Stage 1—*muk.tā.lā.p, rhythm-free improvisation in slow tempo*

A *muk.t ā.lā.p* or *ā.lā.p* is based on a tone material of a particular *rā.g.* The starting note of this part is usually *Sa.* However, in *rā.g Ya.man* it is low *Ṇi.* The starting note, that is mostly *Sa,* is sung for as long as one's breath lasts. After singing *Sa,* the chief combinations of notes of the *rā.g* are sung in the lower and middle octaves in order to create a total effect of the *rā.g.* The duration of *ā.lā.p* in *khyā.l* is short. It lasts for a couple of minutes and is followed by the composition.

Stage 2—*ban.diś or cī.z,* (*composition*)

At this point, it is important for a singer to remember three points concerning the rhythmic cycle (the *tā.l*) that is going to be played.

1. The total number of the beats in one rhythmic cycle.
2. The basic rhythmic structure with monosyllabic names (*ṭhe.kā*).
3. The ordinal number of the beat of the *tā.l* from which the composition starts.

The name and the tempo of the *tā.l* have been mentioned with every composition. The singer, usually starts the composition first and the *tab.lā* player follows her/him later. If the composition is made for *tīn.tāl* that has 16 beats in one cycle, the text is started in most compositions from the ninth beat of the *tā.l* that is called *k͟hā.lī* or silent beat. However, there are also compositions that start from other beats of the *tā.l.*

The text of *sthā.yī* (the first part of the composition) can have one, two, or three rhythmic cycles. The first rhythmic cycle is called the first line of the *sthā.yī.* The singer sings the first line of *sthā.yī* twice and the rest of the text of *sthā.yī* just once. After singing the whole text of *sthā.yī,* the singer sings the first line of *sthā.yī* once again. Hereafter, he/she sings the first line of the *an.ta.rā* (the second part of the composition) twice and the rest of the text of *an.ta.rā* just once. After singing *an.ta.rā,* the first line of *sthā.yī* is sung one more time before singing *ā.lāp* (the third stage).

Stage 3—*tā.l-bad.dh ā.lā.p* (*rhythmic improvisation in slow tempo*)

The third stage comprises singing the text of the composition together with rhythmic improvisation in slow tempo (*tā.l-bad.dh ā.lā.p*). The starting text of the composition, i.e., from the beginning till the first beat of *tā.l,* viz., *sam* is called *mukh.ṛā* (meaning face) the opening phrase. In most cases, the position of *mukh.rā* lies between the *k͟hā.lī* (silent beat) and the *sa.m.* It is common to start *ā.lā.p* from the *sa.m.* The *ā.lā.p* in *sthā.yī* (the first part) is begun with *Sa* and the notes of the lower and the middle octaves are introduced gradually.

The *ā.lā.p* is done in pieces and the pieces are formed with one, two, or more notes. When there is only one note in a piece, the singer sings that note for a long period. The starting piece of *ā.lā.p* has usually one or two notes. The last piece of *ā.lā.p* has more notes. Gradual addition of the higher notes in *ā.lā.p* is called *ba.ṛha.t.* The pieces of *ā.lā.p* mostly begin with *Sa* and end with *Sa.* The *ā.lā.p* can be sung in *ā.kā.r,* in *sar.gam,* or with the words of the composition. That all depends on the mood of the singer. When the words of the composition are used to sing the notes of *ā.lā.p,* it is called *bol-ā.lā.p.*

After singing the *ā.lā.p* in *sthā.yī* (the first part), the singer sings the first line of *an.ta.rā* (the second part) once, and he/she then sings the pieces of *ā.lā.p* in *an.ta.rā* the same way as in *sthā.yī.* The pieces of *ā.lā.p* in *an.ta.rā* usually start with high *Ṡa* and end with high *Ṡa.*

In the following examples of *ā.lā.p,* the text is shown as ===== and the improvisation or *tā.l-bad.dha ā.lā.p* is shown as /////.

Example 1:

The composition is set in *tīn.tā.l* (16 beats).

The text begins from the ninth beat and the *ā.lā.p* begins from *sam.*

beats:	1	2	3	4	5	6	7	8	9	10	11	12	13	14	15	16
tā.l:	X				2				0				3			
Text:									====	====	====	====	====	====	====	====
ā.lā.p:	////	////	////	////	////	////	////	////	====	====	====	====	====	====	====	====

If the *ā.lā.p* is long and requires more beats, the text is shortened. The total number of the beats of the *tā.l* cycle remains the same.

Example 2:

The *ā.lā.p* begins from *sa.m* and the text begins from the thirteenth beat.

beats:	1	2	3	4	5	6	7	8	9	10	11	12	13	14	15	16
tā.l:	X				2				0				3			
ā.lā.p:	////	////	////	////	////	////	////	////	////	////	////	////	====	====	====	====
Text:	====	====	====	====	====	====	====	====	====	====	====	====	====	====	====	====

The *ā.lā.p* can also be done in one and a half cycles of the *tā.l.* It all depends of the creativity of the singer.

After improvising in slow tempo in *sthā.yī* and *an.ta.rā*, the singer sings the whole text of *an.ta.rā* just once and, thereafter, sings the first line of *sthā.yī* once again. At this point, the tempo of the composition is increased a little while singing the first line of *sthā.yī* before singing the *tā.n* (the fourth stage).

Stage 4— *tā.n* (*a rhythmic improvisation in fast tempo*)

The fourth stage comprises singing the text of the composition together with rhythmic improvisation in fast tempo. The *tā.ns* can be sung in *ā.kā.r, sar.gam,* or with the text of the composition that is called *bol-tā.n.* Like *ā.lā.p,* the *tā.ns* are sung first in *sthā.yī* (the first part) and then in *an.ta.rā* (the second part). Many different tonal patterns are used in *tā.ns* to create a good variety.

However, there are some common *tā.n* patterns that are given below. In the following examples of *tā.ns*, the full names of the notes are not used and only the first letter of the notes is used such as for *Sa, Re, Ga, Ma,* the first letters *S, R, G, M* are used.

The *tā.ns* are sung in fast tempo and in the beginning generally two or four notes are sung in one beat. Later, a singer can sing eight or more notes in one beat. It all depends how fast he/she can sing. Following letters *SRGMPD* and *N* represent the notes *Sa, Re, Ga, Ma, Pa, Dha,* and *Ni,* respectively.

1. *Sa.ra.l-tā.n:*

In this *tā.n*, the notes are sung in a sequence.

Example 1:

SR GM PM GR or *SR GM PD NṠ, ṠN DP MG RS*

2. *Kū.ṭ-tā.n*

In this *tā.n*, the notes are not sung straight.

Example 2:

SGR RMG GPM ṠDN PD MP GM RG SS

3. *Phi.ra.t-kī-tā.n*

In this *tā.n*, a new higher note is added in every piece. The starting and the end note in every piece can also be different.

Example 3:

SRGR, SRGMGR, SRGMPMGR, SRGMPDPMGR, SRGMPDNDPMGR, SRGMPDNṠNDPMGRS

4. *A.laṅ.kā.rik-tā.n*

This is the *tā.n* of the conventional tonal patterns (*pal.ṭe*).

Example 4:

SRG, RGM, GMP, MPD, PDN, DNṠ, ṠND, NDP, DPM, PMG, MGR, GRS

5. *Ga.ma.k-kī-tā.n*

This *tā.n* is sung with light and strong *khaṭ.kās*.

Example 5:

*S*S* R*R* G*G* M*M* P*P* D*D* N*N* Ṡ*Ṡ*, Ṡ*Ṡ*, N*N* D*D* P*P* M*M* G*G* R*R* S*S**

6. *Chū.ṭ-kī-tā.n*

In this *tā.n*, some notes are skipped.

Example 6:

SG SP MG RR, GP GN DP MM, DṠ DĠ ṘṠ NN, GP GN DP MM, SG SP MG RS

7. *Ā.ro.hī-tā.n*

The notes here are sung in an ascending order. According to some musicians, *ā.ro.hī* and *a.va.ro.hī tā.ns* are in fact just like *phi.rat-kī-tā.n* and need to be mentioned separately.

Example 7:

SR GM PD NN, RG MP DN ṠṠ, DN ṠṘ ṠṠ, SR GM PD NN, PP DD NN ṠṠ

8. *A.va.ro.hī-tā.n*

The notes here are sung in descending order.

Example 8:

DD PM GR, NN DP MG RR, ṠN DP MG RS

9. *Bol-tā.n*

Any *tā.n* that is sung with the words of the composition and not in *ā.kā.r* or *sar.gam,* is called *bol-tā.n.*

Example 9:

Notes of *tā.n* are sung with the text of the composition.

10. *Mi.śr-tā.n*

It is an amalgam of above-mentioned *tā.ns.*

Example 10:

SR GG RG PP MG MR, GM PP MP NN DP DM, PD NN DN ṘṘ ND PM GR SS

Delineation of the Ten Basic *Rā.gs*

Rā.g Bi.lā.val

Melodic pattern

ā.ro.h (ascent)	–	*S* ^{G}*R G P* ^{N}*D N Ṡ*
a.va.ro.h (descent)	–	*Ṡ N D P, M G M R S*
vā.dī (prominent note)	–	*D*
sam.vā.dī (consonant of *vā.dī*)	–	*G*
sa.ma.y (time)	–	forenoon

mu.khy svar sañ.ga.ti (chief combinations of notes)—*GRGP, MGMR, GMP MGMR*

Stage 1

muk.t ā.lā.p

1. *S ... NS,* ^{N}*D -* ^{N}*D - P ... MP,* ^{N}*D ... N - S ...*
2. *S -* ^{G}*R -* ^{R}*G ..., G - M G ..., M G - M R - S ...*
3. ^{N}*D NS* ^{G}*R* ^{R}*G RGP..., DG - MR - GP ..., MG - MR - S ...*
4. *RRSNS ...,* ^{N}*D -* ^{N}*D - N S ..., G - RG P ... MP, GR GG P ..., MG -M R - S ...*

Stage 2

COMPOSITION 1

Text[1]:

sthā.yī *tu hī a.dhā.ra sa.ka.la tri.bhu.va.na ko, pā.la.ka sa.ca.rā.ca.ra bhū.ta.na ko.*

an.ta.rā *tū hī vi.snu tū nā.rā.ya.na kā.ra.na tū pa.ra.brah.ma ja.ga.ta ko.*

Meaning: O *Parabrahma* (Eternal Supreme Spirit)! You are the Supporter of all the three worlds (the earth, the sky and the middle space between them), (You are) the Supporter of all animate and inanimate. You are Viṣṇu (Omnipresent), and you are Nārāyaṇa (the one whose abode is also in water), and you are the *raison d'être* of this cosmos.

[1] V.N. Bhatkhande, *Hindustānī Saṅgīt Paddhati Kramik Pustak Mālikā*, vol. I (Hathras: Sangeet Karyalaya, 1971), p. 30.

COMPOSITION 1: *Notation*

Rā.g Bi.lā.val, tī.n-tāl—medium tempo

ṭhe.kā-tī.n-tā.l

1	2	3	4	5	6	7	8	9	10	11	12	13	14	15	16
dha	*dhin*	*dhin*	*dha*	*dha*	*dhin*	*dhin*	*dha*	*dha*	*tin*	*tin*	*ta*	*ta*	*dhin*	*dhin*	*dha*
x				2				0				3			
								sthā.yī							
												^{P}G	*P*	*ND*	*N*
												tū	–	*hī*	*a*
x				2				0				3			
Ṡ	–	*Ṡ*	*Ṡ*	$^{N}\dot{S}$	*Ṙ*	*Ṡ*	*N*	*D*	*P*	*MG*	*MR*	^{M}G	*M*	*P*	*MG*
dhā	–	*ra*	*sa*	*ka*	*la*	*tri*	*bhu*	*va*	*na*	*ko-*	––	*pā*	–	*la*	*ka-*
x				2				0					3		
M	*R*	*S*	–	^{N}D	*N*	*Ṡ*	*N*	*D*	*P*	*MG*	*MR*				
sa	*ca*	*rā*	–	*ca*	*ra*	*bhū*	–	*ta*	*na*	*ko-*	––				
x				2				0							
								an.ta.rā							
												P	–	^{P}N	^{D}N
												tū	–	*hī*	–
												3			
Ṡ	–	*Ṡ*	–	$^{N}\dot{S}$	*Ġ*	$^{R}\dot{G}$	*Ṁ*	*Ġ*	*Ṙ*	*Ṡ*	*Ṡ*	$^{N}\dot{S}$	–	*Ġ*	*Ṙ*
vi	–	*ṣṇu*	–	*tū*	–	*nā*	–	*rā*	–	*ya*	*ṇa*	*kā*	–	*ra*	*ṇa*
x				2				0				3			
Ṡ	–	^{N}D	*P*	*D*	*N*	*Ṡ*	*ṠN*	*D*	*P*	*MG*	*MR*				
tū	–	*pa*	*ra*	*bra*	–	*hma*	*ja-*	*ga*	*ta*	*ko-*	––				
x				2				0							

Stage 3

ā.lā.p-sthā.yī													^{P}G	*P*	*ND*	*N*
													tū	–	*hī-*	*a*
	x			2				0				3				
1.	*Ṡ*	–	*Ṡ*	*Ṡ*	*Ṡ*	*Ṙ*	*Ṡ*	*N*	*D*	*P*	*MG*	*MR*	*S*	–	–	–
	dhā	–	*ra*	*sa*	*ka*	*la*	*tri*	*bhu*	*va*	*na*	*ko-*	—	*ā*	–	–	–
	x				2				0				3			
	^{N}D	–	^{N}D	–	*N*	–	–	–	*S*	–	–	–	^{P}G	*P*	*ND*	*N*
	–	–	–	–	–	–	–	–	–	–	–	–	*tū*	–	*hī-*	*a*
	x				2				0				3			
2.	^{N}D	–	*N*	*D*	*NS*	^{G}R	*G*	–	*M*	*R*	*S*	–	^{P}G	*P*	*ND*	*N*
	ā	–	–	–	—	—	–	–	–	–	–	–	*tū*	–	*hī-*	*a*
	x				2				0				3			
3.	*Ṡ*	–	*Ṡ*	*Ṡ*	*Ṡ*	*Ṙ*	*Ṡ*	*N*	*D*	*P*	*MG*	*MR*	*SR*	*G*	–	*RG*
	dhā	–	*ra*	*sa*	*ka*	*la*	*tri*	*bhu*	*va*	*na*	*ko-*	—	*ā-*	–	–	—
	x				2				0				3			
	P	–	–	–	*M*	*G*	–	–	*M*	*R*	*S*	–	^{P}G	*P*	*ND*	*N*
	–	–	–	–	–	–	–	–	–	–	–	–	*tū*	–	*hī-*	*a*
	x				2				0				3			
4.	*GGRS*	^{G}RG	*P*	–	*D*	*G*	–	*M*	*R*	–	*S*	–	^{P}G	*P*	*ND*	*N*
	ā--	—	–	–	–	–	–	–	–	–	–	–	*tū*	–	*hī*	*a*
	x				2				0				3			
5.	*PP*	^{N}D	–	–	^{N}D	*N*	*Ṡ*	–	*Ṡ*	*N*	^{N}D	–	*P*	–	–	–
	ā	–	–	–	–	–	–	–	–	–	–	–	–	–	–	–
	x				2				0				3			
	M	*G*	–	–	*M*	*R*	–	–	*S*	–	*GP*	*NN*	*GP*	*NN*	*GP*	*NN*
	–	–	–	–	–	–	–	–	–	–	*tū-*	*hīa*	*tū-*	*hīa*	*tū-*	*hīa*
	x				2				0				3	sing the whole line		

ā.lāp-an.ta.rā

Sing the first line of *an.ta.rā* once before starting the improvisation.

													P	–	N	–
													tū	–	*hī-*	–
	x				2				0				3			
1.	Ṡ	–	Ṡ	–	Ṡ	–	–	–	–	–	–	–	P	–	N	–
	ā	–	–	–	–	–	–	–	–	–	–	–	*tū*	–	*hī*	–
	x				2				0				3			
2.	ṠṘṠN	^{N}D	^{N}D	P	–	–	GP	^{N}D	–	N	Ṡ	–	P	–	N	–
	ā	–	–	–	–	–	––	––	–	–	–	–	*tū*	–	*hī*	–
	x				2				0				3			
3.	Ṡ	–	Ṡ	–	P	–	–	N	–	D	N	–	Ṡ	–	–	–
	vi	–	*ṣṇu*	–	*ā*	–	–	–	–	–	–	–	–	–	–	–
	x				2				0				3			
	S	Ṙ	–	-Ġ	Ṁ	Ṙ	–	^{Ṡ}Ṙ	Ṡ	–	–	–	P	–	N	–
	–	–	–	–	–	–	–	–	–	–	–	–	*tū*	–	*hī*	–
	x				2				0				3			
4.	Ṡ	–	Ṡ	–	Ṡ	–	–	–	ṠṘ	ṠN	D	–	P	–	MG	M
	vi	–	*ṣṇu*	–	*ā*	–	–	–	––	––	–	–	–	–	––	–
	x				2				0				3			
	R	^{P}G	R	^{P}G	–	P	–	D	–	N	Ṡ	–	P	–	N	–
	–	–	–	–	–	–	–	–	–	–	–	–	*tū*	–	*hī*	–
	x				2				0				3			
5.	Ṡ	–	Ṡ	–	Ṡ	–	Ġ	–	Ṁ	Ṙ	Ṡ	–	Ṡ	NṘ	Ṡ	N
	vi	–	*ṣṇu*	–	*ā*	–	–	–	–	–	–	–	–	––	–	–
	x				2				0				3			
	D-	P	–	G	–	P	–	D	N	Ṡ	–	–	P	–	N	–
	–	–	–	–	–	–	–	–	–	–	–	–	sing the whole *an.ta.rā*			

Stage 4 (increase your tempo a little)

tā.n-sthā.yī																
												G	*P*	*N*	*N*	
													tū	–	*hī*	*a*
	x				2				0				3			
1.	*Ṡ*	–	*Ṡ*	*Ṡ*	*GR*	*GP*	*DN*	*DP*	*MG*	*MR*	*SNR*	*SS*	*G*	*P*	*N*	*N*
	dhā	–	*ra*	*sa*	*ā*	––	––	––	––	––	––	––	*tū*	–	*hī*	*a*
	x				2				0				3			
2.	*SR*	*GR*	*GP*	*DN*	*DN*	*ṠṘ*	*ṠN*	*DP*	*MG*	*MR*	*SR*	*SS*	*G*	*P*	*N*	*N*
	ā	––	––	––	––	––	––	––	––	––	––	––	*tū*	–	*hī*	*a*
	x				2				0				3			
3.	*PP*	*GP*	*PG*	*PP*	*MG*	*NN*	*DN*	*ND*	*NN*	*DP*	*MG*	*MR*	*G*	*P*	*N*	*N*
	ā	––	––	––	––	––	––	––	––	––	––	––	*tū*	–	*hī*	*a*
	x				2				0				3			
4.	*SR*	*GP*	*MG*	*MR*	*NN*	*DP*	*MG*	*MR*	*SN*	*DP*	*MG*	*MR*	*ṘṘ*	*ṠN*	*DP*	*MG*
	––	––	––	––	––	––	––	––	––	––	––	––	––	––	––	––
	x				2				0				3			
	MR	*ṀṘ*	*ṠN*	*DP*	*MG*	*MR*	*SR*	*ṠṠ*	*GP*	*NN*	*ṠṠ*	*GP*	*NN*	*ṠṠ*	*GP*	*NN*
	––	––	––	––	––	––	––	––	*tū*	*hīa*	*dhār*	*tū-*	*hīa*	*dhāe*	*tū-*	*hīa*
	x				2				0				3			
	Ṡ	–	*Ṡ*	*Ṡ*	*Ṡ*	*Ṙ*	*Ṡ*	*N*	*D*	*P*	*MG*	*MR*				
	dhā	–	*ra*	*sa*	*ka*	*la*	*tri*	*bhu*	*va*	*na*	*ko-*	––				
	x				2				0				3			

tā.n-an.ta.rā

													P	–	*N*	–
													tū	–	*hī*	–
	x				2				0				3			
1.	*Ṡ*	–	*Ṡ*	–	*ṠN*	*DP*	*MG*	*MR*	*GP*	*ND*	*NN*	*ṠṠ*	*P*	–	*N*	–
	vi	–	*ṣṇu*	–	*ā*	——	——	——	——	——	——	——	*tū*	–	*hī*	–
	x				2				0				3			
2.	*Ṡ*	–	*Ṡ*	–	*GP*	*DN*	*ṠṘ*	*ṠN*	*DP*	*GP*	*DN*	*ṠṠ*	*P*	–	*N*	–
	vi	–	*ṣṇu*	–	*ā*	——	——	——	——	——	——	——	*tū*	–	*hī*	–
	x				2				0				3			
3.	*Ṡ*	–	*Ṡ*	–	*NṠ*	*GṀ*	*ṘṘ*	*ṠN*	*DP*	*GP*	*DN*	*ṠṠ*	*P*	–	*N*	–
	vi	–	*ṣṇu*	–	*ā*	——	——	——	——	——	——	——	*tū*	–	*hī*	–
	x				2				0				3			
4.	*ĠṀ*	*ṘṠ*	*ṠṘ*	*ṠṠ*	*DP*	*MG*	*MR*	*SS*	*GP*	*DN*	*ṠṘ*	*ṠṠ*	*P*	–	*N*	–
	ā	——	——	——	——	——	——	——	——	——	——	——	*tū*	–	*hī*	–
	x				2				0				3			
	Ṡ	–	*Ṡ*	–	*Ṡ*	*Ġ*	*Ġ*	*Ṁ*	*G*	*R*	*Ṡ*	*Ṡ*	*Ṡ*	–	*G*	*R*
	vi	–	*ṣṇu*	–	*tū*	–	*nā*	–	*rā*	–	*ya*	*na*	*kā*	–	*ra*	*na*
	x				2				0				3			
	Ṡ	*N*	^{N}D	*P*	^{N}D	*N*	*Ṡ*	*ṠN*	*D*	*P*	*MG*	*MR*	^{P}G	*P*	*N*	*N*
	tū	–	*pa*	*ra*	*bra*	–	*hma*	*ja-*	*ga*	*ta*	*ko-*	——	*tū*	–	*hī*	*a*
	x				2				0				3			
	Ṡ	–	–	*Ṡ*	*G*	*P*	*N*	*N*	*Ṡ*	–	–	*Ṡ*	*G*	*P*	*N*	*N*
	dhā	–	–	*ra*	*tū*	–	*hī*	*a*	*dhā*	–	–	*ra*	*tū*	–	*hī*	*a*
	x				2				0				3			
	Ṡ	–	–	*Ṡ*												
	dhā	–	–	*ra*												

Composition 2

Rā.g Bi.lā.val lak.ṣaṇ-gī.t, tī.n-tā.l—medium tempo

Text[2]:

sthā.yī *ta.ba ka.ha.ta bi.lā.va.la bhe.da ca.tu.ra, ja.ba me.la mi.lā.va.ta śud.dha su.ra.na ko, prā.ta sa.ma.ya ni.ta pra.tha.ma pra.ha.ra*

an.ta.rā *dhai.va.ta vā.dī ga sa.ma.vā.dī, aṣ.ṭa bhe.da sa.ba gā.ya ma.dhu.ra*

Meaning: When all the natural notes are used in the melody, the virtuosi call it *Bi.lā.va.l. Bi.lā.va.l* is sung in the first quarter of the day. The note *dha* is *vā.dī* and *ga* is *sam.vā.dī* in this *rā.g.* There are eight types of *Bi.lā.va.l* and all of them are sweet.

[2]V.N. Bhatkhande, op. cit. (Hathras: Sangeet Karyalaya, 1954), vol. II, p. 76.

Notation

								sthā.yī							
						Ṡ	*Ṡ*	*D*	*P*	*M*	*G*	*P*	–	*ND*	*N*
						ta	*ba*	*ka*	*ha*	*ta*	*bi*	*lā*	–	*va-*	*la*
x				2				0				3			
Ṡ	–	*Ṡ*	*Ṡ*	*ND*	*N*	*P*	*P*	*DN*	*ṠṘ*	*Ṡ*	*ṠN*	*D*	*P*	*M*	*G*
bhe	–	*da*	*ca*	*tu-*	*ra*	*ja*	*ba*	*me-*	*--*	*la*	*mi-*	*lā*	–	*va*	*ta*
x				2				0				3			
G	*R*	*G*	*M*	*GR*	*G*	*S*	–	*S*	*M*	*G*	*P*	*P*	*P*	*N*	*N*
śu	–	*ddha*	*su*	*ra-*	*na*	*ko*	–	*prā*	–	*ta*	*sa*	*ma*	*ya*	*ni*	*ta*
x				2				0				3			
Ṡ	*Ġ*	*Ṡ*	*Ṡ*	*ND*	*N*										
pra	*tha*	*ma*	*pra*	*ha-*	*ra*										
x				2				*an.ta.rā*							
								P	–	*ND*	*N*	*Ṡ*	–	*Ṡ*	–
								dhai	–	*va-*	*ta*	*va*	–	*di*	–
x				2				0				3			
Ṡ	*Ġ*	*Ġ*	*Ṁ*	*ĠṘ*	*ĠṘ*	*Ṡ*	–	*Ṡ*	*Ġ*	*Ġ*	*Ġ*	*Ṁ*	*Ṙ*	*Ṡ*	*Ṡ*
ga	–	*sa*	*ma*	*vā-*	*--*	*dī*	–	*a*	–	*ṣṭa*	*bhe*	–	*da*	*sa*	*ba*
x				2				0				3			
DN	*ṠṘ*	*Ṡ*	*ṠN*	*D*	*N*										
gā-	*--*	*ya*	*ma-*	*dhu*	*ra*										
x				2											

Composition 3

Rā.g Bi.lā.val, tī.n-tā.l—medium tempo

Text[3]:

sthā.yī *gu.ru mo.he gā.na dā.na gu.ṇa dī.je, gu.ṇa ke sā.ra bi.na gu.ṇa na.hīṅ ā.ve*

an.ta.rā *gu.ru kri.pā soṅ gu.ṇa mo.he ā.ve, ka.da.na ka.ha.ta ai.so gu.ni.ya.na soṅ*

Meaning: *Guru*, please teach me the art of singing. Without knowing the essence of this art, I cannot master it. This art can only be mastered with the blessing of the teacher. The poet Kadana tells this to all the virtuosi.

[3]This is composed by the father of Jamaluddin Bharatiya, a musician and an instrumentalist in Amsterdam.

Notation

								sthā.yī							
												G	*P*	*D*	*N*
												gu	*ru*	*mo*	*he*
x				2				0				3			
Ṡ	*N*	*D*	*P*	*M*	*G*	*P*	*M*	*G*	*R*	*S*	–	*S*	*R*	*G*	*R*
gā	–	*na*	*dā*	–	*na*	*gu*	*na*	*dī*	–	*je*	–	*gu*	*ṇa*	*ke*	*sā*
x				2				0				4			
G	*P*	*D*	*N*	*Ṡ*	*Ṙ*	*Ġ*	*Ṙ*	*ṠN*	*DP*	*MG*	*RS*				
–	*ra*	*bi*	*na*	*gu*	*na*	*na*	*hīṅ*	*ā-*	--	--	*ve-*				
x				2				0							
								an.ta.rā							
												P	*P*	*ND*	*N*
												gu	*ru*	*kī*	*kri*
												3			
Ṡ	–	*Ṡ*	–	*Ġ*	*ĠṘ*	*Ġ*	*Ṁ*	*Ġ*	*Ṙ*	*Ṡ*	–	*Ṡ*	*Ṡ*	*Ġ*	*Ṁ*
pā	–	*soṅ*	–	*gu*	*ṇa-*	*mo*	*he*	*ā*	–	*ve*	–	*ka*	*da*	*na*	*ka*
x				2				0				3			
Ġ	*Ṙ*	*Ṡ*	*Ṡ*	*D*	*N*	*Ṡ*	*Ṙ*	*ṠN*	*DP*	*MG*	*RS*				
ha	*ta*	*ai*	*so*	*gu*	*ni*	*ya*	*na*	*soṅ-*	--	--	--				
x				2				0				3			

Rā.g Ya.ma.n

Melodic pattern

ā.ro.h (ascent)	– *N* ^{G}*R* ^{R}*G Ṁ P* ^{N}*D N Ṡ*
ā.va.ro.h (descent)	– *Ṡ N* ^{N}*D P Ṁ G* ^{S}*R S*
vā.dī (prominent note)	– *G*
sam.vā.dī (consonant of *vā.dī*)	– *N*
sa.ma.y (time)	– early night
mu.khya svar saṅ.ga.ti (chief combinations of notes)	– *N*^{G}*RS, N*^{G}*RG, ṀR*^{R}*G, ṀDN, NRS*

Stage 1

muk.t-ā.lā.p

1. *Ṇ... Ḍ,* $^{\underset{\cdot}{N}}$*ḌṆ... Ḍ,* ^{D}*Ṃ.*$^{\underset{\cdot}{N}}$*Ḍ.Ṇ...Ḍ,* ^{S}*Ṇ.*^{S}*Ṇ.,* $^{\underset{\cdot}{N}}$*S...*
2. *Ṇ.R., S..., Ṇ* ^{G}*R* ^{G}*R* ^{R}*G...R,* ^{R}*G.R., Ṇ.R.S...*
3. ^{R}*Ṇ* ^{G}*R* $^{\dot{M}}$*G* ^{G}*Ṁ..., R.G.., G R Ṇ R S...*
4. *ṆRGṀ P..., P.Ṁ.*^{G}*R.*^{G}*R.G...,* ^{G}*G.R.Ṇ.Ḍ.Ṇ.R., S...*

Stage 2

COMPOSITION 1

Text[4]:

sthā.yī *gu.ru bi.na kai.se gu.ṇa gā.ve, gu.ru na mā.ne to gu.ṇa.na.hiṅ ā.ve,*
gu.ni.ya.na meṅ be.gu.ni ka.hā.ve

an.ta.rā *mā.ne to ri.jhā.ve sa.ba.ko, ca.ra.na ga.he sā.de.pa.na se ja.ba, ā.ve a.ca.pa.la tā.la su.ra*

Meaning: Without a teacher or a guide how can one learn the true art of singing. If one does not take a teacher, one cannot learn the fineries of singing. The learner then remains artless among the virtuosi. If, on the other hand, the learner takes a teacher, he can learn the art of enchanting everyone with his/her singing. If the pupil touches the feet of the *guru* in reverence with a simple heart, he/she learns the skills of rhythm and melody in no time.

[4]V.N. Bhatkhande, op.cit., vol. I (Hathras Sangeet Karyalaya, 1971), p. 27.

COMPOSITION 1: *Notation*

Rā.g Ya.man, tī.n-tā.l—medium tempo

								sthā.yī							
								$^{\dot{M}}P$	P	N	D	$^{\dot{M}}P\dot{M}$	D	P	–
								gu	ru	bi	na	kai	–	se	–
								0				3			
Ṁ	R	Ṁ	Ṁ	P	–	–	–	$^{\dot{M}}P$	N	D	$^{\dot{M}}P$	–	Ṁ	G	R
gu	na	gā	–	ve	–	–	–	gu	ru	na	mā	–	ne	to	–
x				2				0				3			
gu	R	GṀP	R	G	–	S	–	^{N}S	S	R	R	$^{\dot{M}}G$	Ṁ	$^{G}\dot{M}$	–
gu	ṇa	na-	hīṅ	ā	–	ve	–	gu	ni	ya	na	meṅ	–	be	–
x				2				0				3			
P	P	–	N	$^{N}\dot{M}$	D	P	–								
gu	ni	–	ka	hā	–	ve	–								
x				2											
								an.ta.rā							
								$^{\dot{M}}P$	–	G	Ṁ	P	–	Ṡ	D
								mā	–	ne	–	to	–	ri	–
								0				3			
Ṡ	–	Ṡ	–	N	Ṙ	Ṡ	–	Ṡ	Ṡ	Ġ	Ṙ	ṠN	Ṙ	Ṡ	Ṡ
jhā	–	ve	–	sa	ba	ko	–	ca	ra	na	ga	he-	–	sā	–
x				2				0				3			
N	D	Ṡ	Ṡ	N	D	Ṁ	P	^{M}P	G	^{G}P	(P)	G	R	NR	S
de	–	pa	na	se	–	ja	ba	ā	–	ve	–	a	ca	pa-	la
x				2				0							
ṆR	GM	PD	NṠ	ND	PṀ	GR	SS								
tā-	--	--	--	--	--	la-	sura								
x				2											

Stage 3

ā.lā.p-sthā.yī									$^{\dot{M}}P$	*P*	*N*	*D*	$^{\dot{M}}P\dot{M}$	*D*	*P*	–
									gu	*ru*	*bi*	*na*	*kai*	–	*se*	–
	x				2				0				3			
1.	*S*	–	–	–	–	–	–	–	$^{\dot{M}}P$	*P*	*N*	*D*	$^{\dot{M}}P\dot{M}$	*D*	*P*	–
	ā	–	–	–	–	–	–	–	*gu*	*ru*	*bi*	*na*	*kai*	–	*se*	–
	x				2				0				3			
2.	*Ṇ*	–	*R*	–	*S*	–	–	–	$^{\dot{M}}P$	*P*	*N*	*D*	$^{\dot{M}}P\dot{M}$	*D*	*P*	–
	ā	–	–	–	–	–	–	–	*gu*	*ru*	*bi*	*na*	*kai*	–	*se*	–
	x				2				0				3			
3.	*Ṇ*	–	^{G}R	–	^{R}G	–	–	–	*Ṁ*	–	–	–	*G*	–	*R*	–
	ā	–	–	–	–	–	–	–	–	–	–	–	–	–	–	–
	x				2				0				3			
	Ṇ	–	*R*	–	*S*	–	–	–	$^{\dot{M}}P$	*P*	*N*	*D*	$^{\dot{M}}P\dot{M}$	*D*	*P*	–
	–	–	–	–	–	–	–	–	*gu*	*ru*	*bi*	*na*	*kai*	–	*se*	–
	x				2				0				3			
4.	*ṆR*	*GṀ*	*P*	–	–	–	*M*	–	*D*	–	*P*	–	–	–	*M*	–
	ā-	––	–	–	–	–	–	–	–	–	–	–	–	–	–	–
	x				2				0				3			
	D	–	*N*	–	–	–	*M*	–	*D*	–	*P*	–	–	–	*R*	–
	–	–	–	–	–	–	–	–	–	–	–	–	–	–	–	–
	x				2				0				3			
	G	–	*R*	–	*S*	–	–	–	$^{\dot{M}}P$	*P*	*N*	*D*	$^{\dot{M}}P\dot{M}$	*D*	*P*	–
	–	–	–	–	–	–	–	–	*gu*	*ru*	*bi*	*na*	*kai*	–	*se*	–
	x				2				0				3			
	Ṁ	*R*	*Ṁ*	*Ṁ*	*P*	–	–	–								
	gu	*ṇa*	*gā*	–	*ve*	–	–	–								

ā.lā.p-an.ta.rā									$^{\dot{M}}P$	–	*P*	*G*	*Ṡ*	–	*Ṡ*	*D*
									mā	–	*ne*	–	*to*	–	*ri*	–
	x				2				0				3			
1.	*P*	–	–	–	$^{P}\dot{M}$	–	*G*	–	*Ṁ*	–	*D*	–	^{D}N	–	–	–
	ā	–	–	–	–	–	–	–	–	–	–	–	–	–	–	–
	x				2				0				3			
	N	–	*Ṙ*	–	*Ṡ*	–	–	–	$^{\dot{M}}P$	–	*P*	*G*	*P*	–	*Ṡ*	*D*
	–	–	–	–	–	–	–	–	*mā*	–	*ne*	–	*to*	–	*ri*	–
	x				2				0				3			
2.	*Ṡ*	–	–	–	*N*	–	*Ṙ*	–	*Ġ*	–	–	–	*N*	–	*Ṙ*	*N*
	ā	–	–	–	–	–	–	–	–	–	–	–	–	–	–	–
	x				2				0				3			
	Ġ	–	–	–	*Ṙ*	–	*Ṡ*	–	$^{\dot{M}}P$	–	*P*	*G*	*P*	–	*Ṡ*	*D*
	–	–	–	–	–	–	–	–	*mā*	–	*ne*	–	*to*	–	*ri*	–
	x				2				0				3			
3.	*Ṡ*	–	*Ṡ*	–	*N*	*Ṙ*	*Ṡ*	–	*NṘ*	*ĠṀ*	–	–	–	–	*R*	–
	jhā	–	*ve*	–	*sa*	*ba*	*ko*	–	*ā*	–	–	–	–	–	–	–
	x				2				0				3			
	Ġ	–	–	–	*Ṙ*	–	*N*	*D*	*Ṁ*	–	*D*	–	*N*	–	–	–
	–	–	–	–	–	–	–	–	–	–	–	–	–	–	–	–
	x				2				0				3			
	N	–	*R*	–	*Ṡ*	–	–	–	$^{\dot{M}}P$	–	*P*	*G*	*P*	–	*Ṡ*	*D*
	–	–	–	–	–	–	–	–	*mā*	–	*ne*	–	*to*	–	*ri*	–
	x				2				0				3			
	Ṡ	*Ṡ*	*Ġ*	*Ṙ*	*N*	*Ṙ*	*Ṡ*	*Ṡ*	*Ṡ*	*Ṡ*	*Ġ*	*R̲*	*ṠN*	*R̲*	*Ṡ*	–
	jhā	–	*ve*	–	*sa*	*ba*	*ko*	–	sing the whole *an.ta.rā* and first line of *sthā.yī*							
	x				2				0				3			

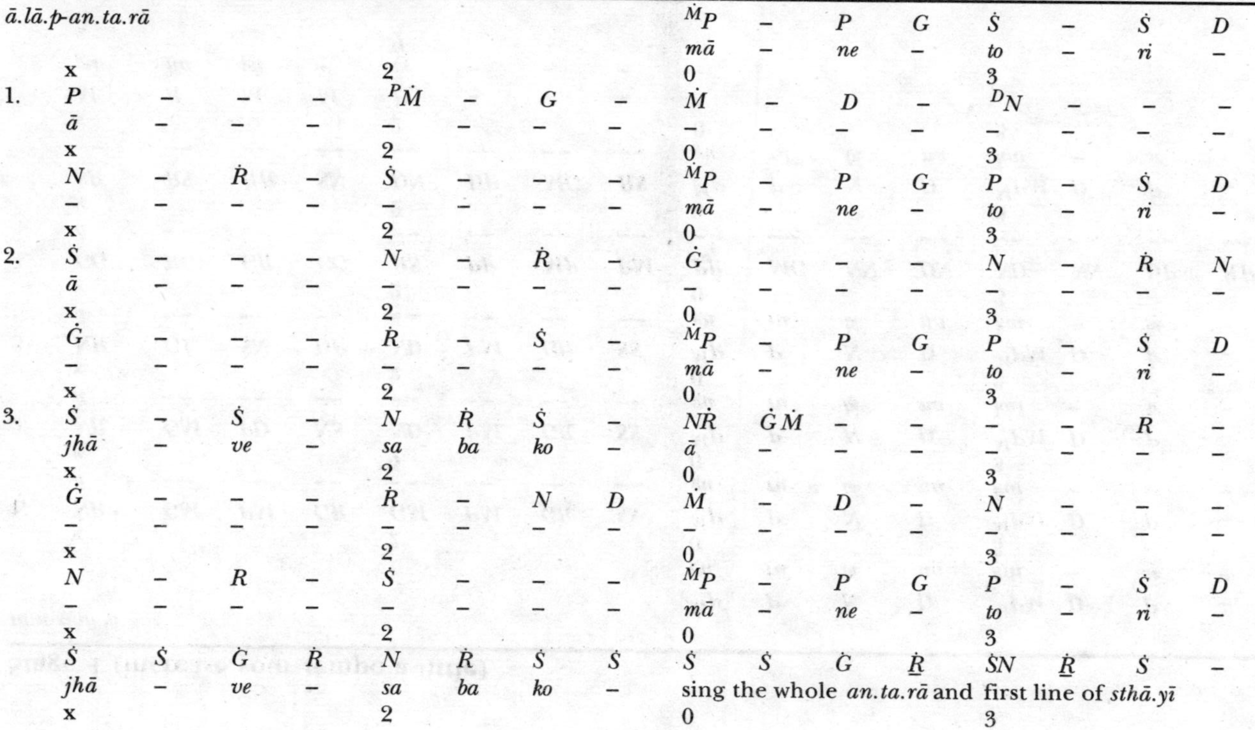

Stage 4 (increase your tempo a little)

tā.n-sthā.yī

									ṀP	*P*	*N*	*D*	*ṀPṀ*	*D*	*P*	–
									gu	*ru*	*bi*	*na*	*kai*	–	*se*	–
	x				2				0				3			
1.	*NR*	*GṀ*	*PṀ*	*GR*	*GṀ*	*PṀ*	*GR*	*SS*	*ṀP*	*P*	*N*	*D*	*ṀPṀ*	*D*	*P*	–
	ā	--	--	--	--	--	—	--	*gu*	*ru*	*bi*	*na*	*kai*	–	*se*	–
	x				2				0				3			
2.	*NR*	*GṀ*	*PD*	*NṠ*	*ND*	*PṀ*	*GR*	*SS*	*ṀP*	*P*	*N*	*D*	*ṀPṀ*	*D*	*P*	–
	ā	--	--	--	--	--	--	--	*gu*	*ru*	*bi*	*na*	*kai*	–	*se*	–
	x				2				0				3			
3.	*NṘ*	*ĠṘ*	*ṠN*	*DP*	*ND*	*PṀ*	*GR*	*SS*	*ṀP*	*P*	*N*	*D*	*ṀPṀ*	*D*	*P*	–
	ā	--	--	--	--	--	--	--	*gu*	*ru*	*bi*	*na*	*kai*	–	*se*	–
	x				2				0				3			
4.	*GG*	*RG*	*GR*	*GG*	*RS*	*PP*	*ṀP*	*PṀ*	*PP*	*ṀG*	*NN*	*DN*	*ND*	*NN*	*DP*	*ṘṘ*
	ā	--	--	--	--	--	--	--	--	--	--	--	--	--	--	--
	x				2				0				3			
	ṠṘ	*ṘṠ*	*ṘṘ*	*ṠN*	*DN*	*DP*	*ṀG*	*RS*	*ṀP*	*P*	*N*	*D*	*ṀPṀ*	*D*	*P*	–
	--	--	--	--	--	--	--	--	*gu*	*ru*	*bi*	*na*	*kai*	–	*se*	–
	x				2				0				3			
	M	*R*	*Ṁ*	*Ṁ*	*P*	–	–	–								
	gu	*ṇa*	*gā*	–	*ve*	–	–	–								
	x				2											

tā.n-an.ta.rā									*ṀP*	–	*P*	*M*	*P*	–	*Ṡ*	*D*
									mā	–	*ne*	–	*to*	–	*ri*	–
	x				2				0				3			
1	*PṀ*	*GṀ*	*PN*	*DP*	*ṀG*	*ṀP*	*DN*	*ṠṠ*	*ṀP*	–	*P*	*Ṁ*	*P*	–	*Ṡ*	*D*
	ā	--	--	--	--	--	--	--	*mā*	–	*ne*	–	*to*	–	*ri*	–
	x				2				0				3			
2	*PD*	*PṠ*	*ṘṠ*	*ND*	*PṀ*	*GṀ*	*DN*	*ṠṠ*	*ṀP*	–	*P*	*Ṁ*	*P*	–	*Ṡ*	*D*
	ā	--	--	--	--	--	--	--	*mā*	–	*ne*	–	*to*	–	*ri*	–
	x				2				0				3			
3	*ĠĠ*	*ṘṠ*	*ND*	*PṀ*	*GṀ*	*DN*	*DN*	*ṠṠ*	*ṀP*	–	*P*	*Ṁ*	*P*	–	*Ṡ*	*D*
	ā	--	--	--	--	--	--	--	*mā*	–	*ne*	–	*to*	–	*ri*	–
	x				2				0				3			
4	*ĠR*	*ṠR*	*ṠN*	*ṠN*	*DN*	*DP*	*DP*	*ṀP*	*ṀG*	*MG*	*ṘṠ*	*NR*	*GṀ*	*PṀ*	*GṀ*	*PD*
	ā	--	--	--	--	--	--	--	--	--	--	--	--	--	--	--
	x				2				0				3			
	NN	*DP*	*MD*	*PM*	*GṀ*	*DN*	*ṘṘ*	*ṠṠ*	*ṀP*	–	*P*	*Ṁ*	*P*	–	*Ṡ*	*D*
	--	--	--	--	--	--	--	--	*mā*	–	*ne*	–	*to*	–	*ri*	–
	x				2				0				3			
	Ṡ	–	*Ṡ*	–	*N*	*Ṙ*	*Ṡ*	–	sing the whole *an.ta.rā* +							
	jhā	–	*ve*	–	*sa*	*ba*	*ko*	–	frist line of *sthā.yī* and				conclude with following *ti.hā.ī*			
	x				2				0				3			
									ṀP	*P*	*N*	*D*	*ṀPṀ*	*D*	*P*	–
									gu	*ru*	*bi*	*na*	*kai*	–	*se*	–
									0				3			
	ṀP	*P*	*N*	*D*	*ṀPṀ*	*D*	*P*	–	*ṀP*	*P*	*N*	*D*	*ṀPṀ*	*D*	*P*	–
	gu	*ru*	*bi*	*na*	*kai*	–	*se*	–	*gu*	*ru*	*bi*	*na*	*kai*	–	*se*	–
	x				2				0				3			
	Ṁ	–	*R*	–	*Ṁ*	–	*Ṁ*	–	*P*	–	–	–				
	gu	–	*na*	–	*gā*	–	–	–	*ve*	–	–	–				

COMPOSITION 2

Rā.g Ya.ma.n, lak.ṣa.ṇ-gī.t, e.k-tā.l—medium tempo

Text[5]:

sthā.yī *sa.ba gu.ni.ja.na ya.ma.na gā.ta, tī.va.ra su.ra ka.ra.ta sā.dha*
sasa rere gaga mama papa dhadha nini rere gare sare sani dhapa

an.ta.rā *su.ra vā.dī gan.dhā.ra sā.dha sa.ma.vā.dī ka.ra ni.śā.da*
rā.ta sa.ma.ya pra.tha.ma pra.ha.ra ca.tu.ra su.ja.na ma.na ri.jhā.t.

Meaning: All artful singers sing *ya.ma.n.* They practice to hold sharp *ma* correctly and sing *sasa rere gaga mama papa dhadha nini rere gare sare sani dhapa.* They sing *ga* as *vā.dī* note and *ni* as *sam.vā.dī.* The virtuosi win the hearts of listeners by singing it at the first quarter of the night.

ṭhe.kā e.k-tā.l —12 beats

1	2	3	4	5	6	7	8	9	10	11	12
dhiṅ	*dhiṅ*	*dhage*	*tirakit*	*tū*	*nā*	*ka*	*tā*	*dhage*	*tirakit*	*dhī*	*nā*
x		0		2		0		3		4	

[5]V.N. Bhatkhande, *Hindustānī Saṅgīta Paddhati Kramik Pustak Mālikā* (Hathras: Sangeet Karyalaya, 1954), vol. II, p. 21.

Composition 2: Notation

						sthā.yī					
Ṡ	*Ṡ*	*N*	*ND*	*Ṁ*	*P*	*P*	*P*	*P*	*G*	–	*G*
sa	*ba*	*gu*	*ni-*	*ja*	*na*	*ya*	*ma*	*na*	*gā*	–	*ta*
x		0		2		0		3		4	
G	–	*G*	*R*	*G*	*P*	*R*	*G*	*R*	*SN*	*R*	*S*
tī	–	*va*	*ra*	*su*	*ra*	*ka*	*ra*	*ta*	*sā-*	–	*dha*
x		0		2		0		3		4	
S	*S*	*R*	*R*	*G*	*G*	*Ṁ*	*Ṁ*	*P*	*P*	*D*	*P*
sa	*sa*	*re*	*re*	*ga*	*ga*	*ma*	*ma*	*pa*	*pa*	*dha*	*pa*
x		0		2		0		3		4	
N	*N*	*Ṙ*	*Ṙ*	*Ġ*	*Ṙ*	*Ṡ*	*Ṙ*	*Ṡ*	*N*	*D*	*P*
ni	*ni*	*re*	*re*	*ga*	*re*	*sa*	*re*	*sa*	*ni*	*dha*	*pa*
x		0		2		0		3		4	
						an.ta.rā					
$^{\dot{M}}$*P*	*G*	*P*	–	*D*	*P*	*Ṡ*	–	*Ṡ*	*Ṡ*	–	*Ṡ*
su	*ra*	*vā*	–	*dī*	*gan*	*dhā*	–	*ra*	*sā*	–	*dha*
x		0		2		0		3		4	
^{N}*Ṡ*	*Ṡ*	*Ṙ*	–	*Ġ*	*Ṙ*	*Ṡ*	*Ṡ*	*N*	^{D}*N*	*D*	*P*
sa	*ma*	*vā*	–	*dī*	–	*ka*	*ra*	*ni*	*śā*	–	*da*
x		0		2		0		3		4	
P	–	*G*	*P*	*P*	*P*	*N*	*Ṡ*	*N*	*P*	*D*	*P*
rā	–	*ta*	*sa*	*ma*	*ya*	*pra*	*tha*	*ma*	*pra*	*ha*	*ra*
x		0		2		0		3		4	
Ṡ	*Ṡ*	*N*	*ND*	*Ṁ*	*P*	*P*	*G*	*P*	^{G}*R*	–	*S*
ca	*tu*	*ra*	*su-*	*ja*	*na*	*ma*	*na*	*ri*	*jhā*	–	*ta*

COMPOSITION 3

Rā.g Ya.man, tī.n-tā.l—medium tempo

Text[6]:

sthā.yī *e.rī ā.li pi.yā bi.na sa.khi ka.la na pa.ra.ta mo.he gha.ri pa.la chi.na di.na*

an.ta.rā *ja.ba te pi.yā pa.ra.de.sa ga.va.na kī.no, ra.ti.yāṅ ka.ṭa.ta mo.rī tā.re gi.na gi.na*

Meaning: O my friend, I do not get any rest, even for a moment, without my beloved husband. Since the moment he has left for a distant land, I have been spending my nights by counting the stars.

[6]V.N. Bhatkhande, op.cit. (Hathras: Sangeet Karyalaya, 1954), vol. II, p. 35.

Composition 3: *Notation*

								sthā.yī							
								N	–	*P*	–	–	*R*	–	*S*
								e	–	*rī*	–	–	*ā*	–	*li*
x				2				0				3			
G	*R*	*G*	*G*	–	–	*PṀ*	*GṀ*	*PN*	*DN*	*P*	–	–	*R*	–	*S*
pi	*yā*	*bi*	*na*	–	–	*a-*	*rī-*	*e-*	--	*rī*	–	–	*ā*	–	*li*
x				2				0				3			
G	*R*	*P*	^{P}G	–	–	*P*	*P*	*G*	*Ṁ*	*G*	*P*	*Ṁ*	*D*	*P*	*P*
pi	*yā*	*bi*	*na-*	–	–	*sa*	*khi*	*ka*	*la*	*na*	*pa*	*ra*	*ta*	*mo*	*he*
x				2				0				3			
N	*D*	*P*	*P*	^{G}R	*R*	*S*	*S*								
gha	*ri*	*pa*	*la*	*chi*	*na*	*di*	*na*								
x				2											
								an.ta.rā							
								$^{\dot{M}}P$	*P*	*Ṡ*	*Ṡ*	*Ṡ*	–	*Ṡ*	*Ṡ*
								ja	*ba*	*te*	*pi*	*yā*	–	*pa*	*ra*
								0				3			
$^{P}\dot{S}$	*N*	*N*	*D*	*N*	*D*	*P*	*P*	$^{\dot{M}}P$	$^{P}\dot{G}$	*Ṙ*	*Ṡ*	*N*	*D*	*P*	*P*
de	–	*sa*	*ga*	*va*	*na*	*kī*	*no*	*ra*	*ti*	*yāṅ*	*ka*	*ṭa*	*ta*	*mo*	*rī*
x				2				0				3			
ṀP	*DP*	*ṀP*	*P*	*R*	*R*	*S*	*S*								
tā-	--	--	*re*	*gi*	*na*	*gi*	*na*								

Rā.g Kha.mā.j

Melodic pattern

ā.ro.h (ascent) – *S, G M P D N Ṡ*
a.va.ro.h (descent) – *Ṡ N̲ D P M G R S*
vā.dī (prominent of note) – *D*
sam.vā.dī (consonant of *vā.dī*) – *G*
sa.ma.y (time) – late evening
mu.khy svar saṅ.ga.ti (chief combinations of notes) – *MPD, GMG, N̲DMPD, MG, MGRS*

Statge 1

muk.t-ā.lā.p

1. *S..., N̲.D.S..., S G.^{M}G M G... M G R S...*
2. *S G M P.^{P}G.M G..., SG MD P..., D G P M G..., N̲^{N}D.M P D M G..., P M G R S...*
3. *NS GM PG..., MD.P, Ṡ.N̲.D.P., G M G P M N̲.D.P., GMP(Ṡ)N̲ D P D P G M G..., M G.RN S...*

Stage 2

COMPOSITION 1

Text[7]:

sthā.yī *nū.pu.ra kī jha.na.kā.r ma.dhu.ra mri.du ma.na ha.ra.nī ma.ta.vā.rī pyā.rī*

an.ta.rā *saṅ.ga meṅ sa.khi.yāṅ bī.ca kan.hai.yā bhū.le dhu.na su.na sa.ba na.ra nā.rī*

Meaning: The jingling of the anklets is soft and sweet. It is captivating, lovely, and making the people intoxicated. Krishna is in the centre of the damsels of Brij. On hearing the melody on Krishna's flute, all the men and women loose control of themselves.

[7]J.S. Kulashreshtha, *Sangeet Kishore* (Hathras: Sangeet Karyalaya, 1988), p. 23.

Composition 1, *Notation*

Rā.g Kha.mā.j, tīn-tā.l—medium tempo

								sthā.yī							
								ṠN	*Ṡ*	*N̲*	*N̲*	*DP*	*D*	*M*	*G*
								nū-	–	*pu*	*ra*	*kī*	–	*jha*	*na*
								0				3			
G	*M*	*P*	*D*	*Ṡ*	*N*	*Ṡ*	*Ṡ*	*Ṡ*	*Ṡ*	*Ġ*	*Ṁ*	*Ġ*	*Ṙ*	*Ṡ*	*Ṡ*
kā	–	*ra*	*ma*	*dhu*	*ra*	*mri*	*du*	*ma*	*na*	*ha*	*ra*	*nī*	–	*ma*	*ta*
x				2				0				3			
N	–	*Ṡ*	–	*ṠN*	*Ṡ*	*N̲*	*D*								
vā	–	*rī*	–	*pyā-*	–	*rī*	–								
x				2											
								an.ta.rā							
								G	*M*	*D*	*N*	*Ṡ*	*N*	*Ṡ*	–
								saṅ	*ga*	*men*	–	*sa*	*khi*	*yāṅ*	–
								0				3			
N	–	*N*	*Ṡ*	*ṠN*	*Ṡ*	*N̲*	*D*	*Ġ*	–	*Ġ*	*Ṁ*	*Ġ*	*ĠṘ*	*N*	*Ṡ*
bī	–	*ca*	*ka*	*nhai*	–	*yā*	–	*bhū*	–	*le*	–	*dhu*	*na-*	*su*	*na*
x				2				0				3			
N	*N*	*Ṡ*	*Ṡ*	*ṠN*	*Ṡ*	*N̲*	*D*								
sa	*ba*	*na*	*ra*	*nā-*	–	*rī*	–								
x				2											

Stage 3

ā.lā.p-sthā.yī									*ṠN*	*Ṡ*	*N̲*	*N̲*	*DP*	*D*	*M*	*G*
									nū-	–	*pu*	*ra*	*kī-*	–	*jha*	*na*
									0				3			
	x				2											
1.	*NS*	*G*	–	*PM*	*G*	–	–	*RS*	*ṠN*	*Ṡ*	*N̲*	*N̲*	*DP*	*D*	*M*	*G*
	ā	–	–	––	–	–	–	––	*nū-*	–	*pu*	*ra*	*kī-*	–	*jha*	*na*
	x				2				0				3			
2.	*G*	*M*	*P*	*D*	*Ṡ*	*N*	*Ṡ*	*Ṡ*	*S*	–	*G*	–	–	*M*	*ᴰN̲N̲*	*D*
	kā	–	*ra*	*ma*	*dhu*	*ra*	*mri*	*du*	*ā*	–	–	–	–	–	––	–
	x				2				0				3			
	P	–	*M*	*P*	*D*	*M*	*G*	–	*ṠN*	*Ṡ*	*N̲*	*N̲*	*DP*	*D*	*M*	*G*
	–	–	–	–	–	–	–	–	*nū-*	–	*pu*	*ra*	*kī-*	–	*jha*	*na*
	x				2				0				3			
3.	*N*	*S*	–	*G*	*M*	–	*N̲*	–	–	*D*	*P*	–	*(Ṡ)*	*N̲*	–	*D*
	ā	–	–	–	–	–	–	–	–	–	–	–	–	–	–	–
	x				2				0				3			
	P	*M*	*G*	–	*R*	*S*	–	–	*ṠN*	*Ṡ*	*N̲*	*N̲*	*DP*	*D*	*M*	*G*
	–	–	–	–	–	–	–	–	*nū-*	–	*pu*	*ra*	*kī-*	–	*jha*	*na*
	x				2				0				3			
4.	*GM*	*DN*	*Ṡ*	–	*NṠ*	*Ġ*	–	*Ṁ*	*Ġ*	*Ṙ*	*Ṡ*	–	*Ṡ*	*N̲*	*D*	*P*
	ā-	––	–	–	––	–	–	–	–	–	–	–	–	–	–	–
	x				2				0				3			
	–	*M*	*P*	*ᴾD*	*M*	*G*	*R*	*S*	*ṠN*	*S*	*N̲*	*N̲*	*DP*	*D*	*M*	*G*
	–	–	–	–	–	–	–	–	*nū-*	–	*pu*	*ra*	*kī-*	–	*jha*	*na*
	x				2				0				3			
5.	*S*	–	–	–	*GM*	*PD*	*NṠ*	–	*PN*	*ṠṘ*	*Ṡ*	*N̲*	*D*	*P*	*G*	–
	ā	–	–	–	––	––	––	–	––	––	–	–	–	–	–	–
	x				2				0				3			
	M	*D*	*P*	*M*	*G*	*R*	*S*	–	*ṠN*	*Ṡ*	*N̲*	*N̲*	*DP*	*D*	*M*	*G*
	–	–	–	–	–	–	–	–	*nū-*	–	*pu*	*ra*	*kī*	–	*jha*	*na*
	x				2				0				3			

sing the whole line.

ā.lā.p-an.ta.rā									*G*	*M*	*D*	*N*	*Ṡ*	*N*	*Ṡ*	–
									saṅ	*ga*	*meṅ*	–	*sa*	*khi*	*yāṅ*	–
	x				2				0				3			
1.	*Ṡ*	–	*N̲*	*D*	–	*Ṡ*	–	–	*G*	*M*	*D*	*N*	*Ṡ*	*N*	*Ṡ*	–
	ā	–	–	–	–	–	–	–	*saṅ*	*ga*	*meṅ*	–	*sa*	*khi*	*yāṅ*	–
	x				2				0				3			
2.	*N*	–	–	*Ṡ*	–	*Ṙ*	*Ṡ*	*N̲*	*D*	*P*	–	*M*	*G*	–	*M*	*P*
	ā	–	–	–	–	–	–	–	–	–	–	–	–	–	–	–
	x				2				0				3			
	G	*M*	*D*	*N*	–	*Ṡ*	–	–	*G*	*M*	*D*	*N*	*Ṡ*	*N*	*Ṡ*	–
	–	–	–	–	–	–	–	–	*saṅ*	*ga*	*meṅ*	–	*sa*	*khi*	*yāṅ*	–
	x				2				0				3			
3.	*Ṡ*	–	–	*Ġ*	–	*Ṁ*	*Ġ*	–	*Ṙ*	*Ṡ*	*N̲*	–	*D*	*P*	–	*M*
	ā	–	–	–	–	–	–	–	–	–	–	–	–	–	–	–
					2				0				3			
	G	*M*	*D*	*N*	–	*Ṡ*	–	–	*G*	*M*	*D*	*N*	*Ṡ*	*N*	*Ṡ*	–
	–	–	–	–	–	–	–	–	*saṅ*	*ga*	*meṅ*	–	*sa*	*khi*	*yāṅ*	–
	x				2				0				3			
4.	*N*	–	*N*	*Ṡ*	*ṠN*	*Ṡ*	*N̲*	*D*	*GG*	*RS*	*G*	*M*	*P*	–	–	*GM*
	bī	–	*ca*	*ka*	*nhai-*	–	*yā*	–	*ā-*	––	–	–	–	–	–	––
	x				2				0				3			
	N̲	*D*	*N*	*Ṡ*	–	*N*	*Ṡ*	–	*G*	*M*	*D*	*N*	*Ṡ*	*N*	*Ṡ*	–
	–	–	–	–	–	–	–	–	*saṅ*	*ga*	*meṅ*	–	*sa*	*khi*	*yāṅ*	–
	x				2				0				3			
5.	*GM*	*PD*	*NṠ*	–	–	*NṠ*	*Ṙ*	*N̲*	*D*	*P*	–	*M*	*P*	*D*	*M*	*G*
	ā-	––	––	–	–	––	–	–	–	–	–	–	–	–	–	–
	x				2				0				3			
	G	*M*	*P*	*D*	*N*	–	*Ṡ*	–	*G*	*M*	*D*	*N*	*Ṡ*	*N*	*Ṡ*	–
	–	–	–	–	–	–	–	–	*saṅ*	*ga*	*meṅ*	–	*sa*	*khi*	*yāṅ*	–
	x				2				0				3 sing the whole *an.ta.rā.*			

Stage 4 (increase your tempo a little)

tā.n-sthā.yī									*ṠN*	*Ṡ*	*N̲*	*N̲*	*DP*	*D*	*M*	*G*
									nū	–	*pu*	*ra*	*kī-*	–	*jha*	*na*
	x				2				0				3			
1.	*NS*	*GM*	*PG*	*MN̲*	*DP*	*MG*	*RS*	*NS*	*ṠN*	*Ṡ*	*N̲*	*N̲*	*DP*	*D*	*M*	*G*
	ā-	––	––	––	––	––	––	––	*nū-*	–	*pu*	*ra*	*kī-*	–	*jha*	*na*
	x				2				0				3			
2.	*SS*	*GM*	*PD*	*NṠ*	*N̲N̲*	*DP*	*MG*	*RS*	*ṠN*	*Ṡ*	*N̲*	*N̲*	*DP*	*D*	*M*	*G*
	ā-	––	––	––	––	––	––	––	*nū-*	–	*pu*	*ra*	*kī-*	–	*jha*	*na*
	x				2				0				3			
3.	*G*	*M*	*P*	*D*	*ṠN*	*Ṡ*	*Ṡ*	*Ṡ*	*GM*	*PD*	*ṠN*	*DP*	*GM*	*PD*	*NṠ*	*ṘṠ*
	kā	–	*ra*	*ma*	*dha*	*ra*	*mri*	*du*	*ā-*	––	––	––	––	––	––	––
	x				2				0				3			
	N̲D	*PM*	*GM*	*PD*	*ṠN*	*DP*	*MG*	*RS*	*ṠN*	*Ṡ*	*N̲*	*N̲*	*DP*	*D*	*M*	*G*
	––	––	––	––	––	––	––	––	*nū-*	–	*pu*	*ra*	*kī-*	–	*jha*	*na*
	x				2				0				3			
4.	*G*	*M*	*P*	*D*	*Ṡ*	*N*	*Ṡ*	*Ṡ*	*N̲N̲*	*DP*	*MG*	*NS*	*GM*	*PD*	*GM*	*PD*
	kā	–	*ra*	*ma*	*dhu*	*ra*	*mri*	*du*	*ā-*	––	––	––	––	––	––	––
	x				2				0				3			
	NṠ	*PD*	*NṠ*	*ĠṀ*	*ĠṘ*	*ṠN*	*DP*	*MG*	*ṠN*	*Ṡ*	*N̲*	*N̲*	*DP̲*	*D*	*M*	*G*
	––	––	––	––	––	––	––	––	*nū-*	–	*pu*	*ra*	*kī-*	–	*jha*	*na*
	x				2				0				3			
5.	*GG*	*SG*	*MP*	*GM*	*N̲N̲*	*DP*	*MP*	*GM*	*ṠN̲*	*DP*	*ṘṠ*	*N̲D*	*ṠN̲*	*DP*	*MP*	*GM*
	ā-	––	––	––	––	––	––	––	––	––	––	––	––	––	––	––
	x				2				0				3			
	PM	*GR*	*SN*	*SS*	*ṠNṠ*	*N̲N̲*	*DPD*	*MG*	*ṠNṠ*	*N̲N̲*	*DPD*	*MG*	*ṠNṠ*	*N̲N̲*	*DPD*	*MG*
	––	––	––	––	*nū--*	*pura*	*kī--*	*jhana*	*nū--*	*pura*	*kī--*	*jhana*	*nū--*	*pura*	*kī--*	*jhana*
	x				2				0				3			
	G	*M*	*P*	*D*	*Ṡ*	*N*	*Ṡ*	*Ṡ*								
	kā	–	*ra*	*ma*	*dhu*	*ra*	*mri*	*du*								
	x				2											

tā.n-an.ta.rā									*G*	*M*	*D*	*N*	*Ṡ*	*N*	*Ṡ*	–
									saṅ	*ga*	*meṅ*	–	*sa*	*khi*	*yān*	–
	x				2				0				3			
1.	*ṠN*	*ṠṘ*	*ṠṈ*	*DP*	*MG*	*MP*	*DN*	*ṠṠ*	*G*	*M*	*D*	*N*	*Ṡ*	*N*	*Ṡ*	–
	ā-	––	––	––	––	––	––	––	*saṅ*	*ga*	*meṅ*	–	*sa*	*khi*	*yān*	–
	x				2				0				3			
2.	*ṠN*	*DP*	*MG*	*RS*	*NS*	*GM*	*DN*	*ṠṠ*	*G*	*M*	*D*	*N*	*Ṡ*	*N*	*Ṡ*	–
	ā-	––	––	––	––	––	––	––	*saṅ*	*ga*	*meṅ*	–	*sa*	*khi*	*yān*	–
	x				2				0				3			
3.	*N*	–	*N*	*Ṡ*	*ṠN*	*Ṡ*	*Ṉ*	*D*	*ṠṈ*	*DṈ*	*DP*	*MG*	*RS*	*GM*	*DM*	*DN*
	bī	–	*ca*	*ka*	*nhai-*	–	*yā*	–	*ā*	––	––	––	––	––	––	––
	x				2				0				3			
	ṠṠ	*ĠṀ*	*ĠṘ*	*ṠṈ*	*DP*	*MP*	*DN*	*ṠṠ*	*G*	*M*	*D*	*N*	*Ṡ*	*N*	*Ṡ*	–
	––	––	––	––	––	––	––	––	*saṅ*	*ga*	*meṅ*	–	*sa*	*khi*	*yān*	–
	x				2				0				3			
4.	*NN*	*ṠṘ*	*ṠN*	*DṈ*	*DP*	*MP*	*GM*	*ṈṈ*	*DP*	*MG*	*RS*	*NS*	*GM*	*SG*	*MP*	*GM*
	ā-	––	––	––	––	––	––	––	––	––	––	––	––	––	––	––
	x				2				0				3			
	ṈD	*PM*	*GM*	*DN*	*ṠṠ*	*ĠṀ*	*ĠṘ*	*ṠṠ*	*G*	*M*	*D*	*N*	*Ṡ*	*N*	*Ṡ*	–
	––	––	––	––	––	––	––	––	*saṅ*	*ga*	*meṅ*	–	*sa*	*khi*	*yān*	–
	x				2				0				3			
	N	–	*N*	*Ṡ*	*ṠN*	*Ṡ*	*Ṉ*	*D*	*G*	–	*G*	*M*	*Ġ*	*ĠṘ*	*N*	*Ṡ*
	bī	–	*ca*	*ka*	*nhai-*	–	*yā*	–	sing the whole *an.ta.rā* + the 1st line of *sthā.yī* and conclude it with							
	x				2				0				3			
	following *ti.hā.ī.*								*ṠN*	*Ṡ*	*Ṉ*	*Ṉ*	*DP*	*D*	*M*	*G*
									nū-	–	*pu*	*ra*	*kī-*	–	*jha*	*na*
	x				2				0				3			
	ṠN	*Ṡ*	*Ṉ*	*Ṉ*	*DP*	*D*	*M*	*G*	*ṠN*	*Ṡ*	*Ṉ*	*Ṉ*	*DP*	*D*	*M*	*G*
	nū-	–	*pu*	*ra*	*kī-*	–	*jha*	*na*	*nū-*	–	*pu*	*ra*	*kī-*	–	*jha*	*na*
	x	sing this line in original tempo					and end the *khyā.l.*									

COMPOSITION 2

Rā.g Kha.mā.j lak.ṣaṇ-gī.t-tīn-tā.l—medium tempo

Text[8]:

sthā.yī *ri.sa.bha ta.ja.ta ā.ro.ha ba.nā.va.ta, sa.mpū.ra.na a.va.ro.ha di.khā.va.ta*

an.ta.rā *gani vā.dī sam.vā.dī su.hā.va.ta, rā.ga kha.mā.ja ma.dhya ni.śi gā.va.ta*

Meaning: In *rā.g Kha.mā.j*, the ascent is formed by excluding the note *ri.sa.bha* (*Re*) but in descent all the seven notes are used. The *vā.dī* of this *rā.g* is *Ga* and *sam.vā.dī* is *Ni. Rā.g Kha.mā.j* is sung at midnight.

[8]V.N. Bhatt, *Bal Sangeet Śhiksha* (Hathras: Sangeet Karyalaya, 1983), vol. III, p. 37.

Notation

								sthā.yī							
								S	*G*	*M*	*P*	*G*	*M*	*N̲*	*DP*
x				2				*ri*	*sa*	*bha*	*ta*	*ja*	*ta*	*ā*	--
								0				3			
PD	*NṠ*	*N̲*	*DP*	*MD*	*PD*	*M*	*G*	*N*	–	*N*	–	*N*	*Ṡ*	*N̲*	*D*
ro-	--	*ha*	*ba-*	*nā-*	--	*va*	*ta*	*sam*	–	*pū*	–	*ra*	*na*	*a*	*va*
x				2				0				3			
PD	*NṠ*	*N̲*	*DP*	*M*	*PD*	*M*	*G*								
ro-	--	*ha*	*di-*	*ṭhā*	--	*va*	*ta*								
x				2											
								an.ta.rā							
								G	*M*	*D*	*N*	*Ṡ*	–	*Ṡ*	*Ṡ*
								ga	*ni*	*vā*	–	*dī*	–	*sa*	*ma*
x				2				0				3			
N	–	*Ṡ*	*Ṡ*	*NṠ*	*ṘṠ*	*N̲*	*D*	*Ṡ*	*Ġ*	*Ṁ*	*ĠṘ*	*N*	*Ṡ*	*Ṡ*	*Ṡ*
vā	–	*dī*	*su*	*hā-*	--	*va*	*ta*	*rā*	–	*ga*	*kha-*	*mā*	–	*ja*	*ma*
x				2				0				3			
P	*N*	*Ṡ*	*R*	*N̲*	*N̲*	*DN̲*	*DP*								
–	*dhya*	*ni*	*śi*	*gā*	–	*va-*	*ta-*								

COMPOSITION 3

Rā.g Kha.mā.j-Dā.drā (6 beats)—medium tempo

Text[9]:

sthā.yī *ā.ja śyā.ma mo.ha li.yo bāṅ.su.rī ba.jā.ya ke, bāṅ.su.rī ba.jā.ya kā.nhā. mu.ra.lī su.nā.ya ke*

an.ta.rā *ha.ri ha.ri sa.ba ka.ha.ta jā.ta, gā.ga.ra si.ra dha.ra.ta jā.ta, nī.ra nā.ra bha.ra.na ca.lī, su.dha na ra.hī śa.rī.ra kī*

Meaning: Today, we were enchanted by the flute of Krishna. Kānhā (Krishna) played for us his bamboo flute. All the damsels of Brija. were so fascinated that they started repeating the name Hari while they were carrying the earthen pots to fetch water. They were so engrossed in Hari, they forgot even the existence of themselves.

ṭhe.kā-Dā.drā

1	2	3	4	5	6
dhā	dhī	nā	dhā	tī	nā
x			0		

Notation			*sthā.yī*		
G	S	S	G	–	M
ā	–	ja	śyā	–	ma
x			0		
P	–	P	D	P	D
mo	–	ha	li	–	yo
x			0		
Ṡ	–	N̲	D	PM	M
bāṅ	–	su	rī	--	ba
x			0		
PM	P	M	G	–	–
jā-	–	ya	ke	–	–
x			0		
N	–	N	Ṡ	–	R
bāṅ	–	su	rī	–	ba
x			0		
ṠN	Ṡ	N̲	D	P	D
jā-	–	ya	kā	nhā	–
x			0		

[9]Learnt this composition from Sri Chhannulal Mishra (Varanasi: 1975).

1	2	3	4	5	6
Ṡ-	N̲	D	PM	M	
mu	–	ra	lā	–	su
x			0		
PM	P	M	G	–	–
nā-	–	ya	ke	–	–
			an.ta.rā		
G	M	G	M	P	D
ha	ri	ha	ri	sa	ba
x			0		
N	Ṡ	N	Ṡ	–	Ṡ
ka	ha	ta	jā	–	ta
x			0		
N	–	N	N	Ṡ	Ṡ
gā	–	ga	ra	si	ra
x			0		
D	Ṡ	N̲	D	P	D
dha	ra	ta	jā	–	ta
x			0		
G	–	M	P	–	D
nī	–	ra	nā	–	ra
x			0		
N	Ṡ	N	Ṡ	Ṡ	–
bha	ra	na	ca	lā	–
x			0		
ṠN	ṘṠ	N̲	N̲	DP	M
su-	dha-	na	ra	hī-	śa
x			0		
MP	P	M	G	–	–
rī-	–	ra	kī	–	–
x			0		

Rā.g Kā.fī

Melodic pattern		
ā.ro.h (ascent)	–	*A R* $^{M}\underline{G}$, *M, P, D* $^{D}\underline{N}$ *Ṡ*
a.va.ro.h (descent)	–	*Ṡ* $\underline{N}$ *D, P, M* $^{M}\underline{G}$*R S*
Note: In practices often *N* is natural in ascent	–	
vā.dī (prominent note)	–	*P*
sam.vā.dī (consonant of *vā.dī*)	–	*S*
sa.ma.y (time)	–	forenoon
mu.khy svar saṅ.ga.ti (chief combinations of notes)	–	*SR*$\underline{G}$*SRP*, *SSRR*$\underline{GG}$*MMP*, *SP*, *PMDP*, *M*$\underline{G}$*RS*, *P*$\underline{GG}$*RS*

Stage 1

muk.t ā.lā.p

1. *S..., S* $\underline{N}$*D P ..., N-S...*
2. *S R-*$^{M}\underline{G}$ $^{M}\underline{G}$ *M-P..., M M P-*$^{M}\underline{G}$*-*$^{M}\underline{G}$*-R-S...,*
3. *S R* $\underline{G}$*S R-P...,* ^{P}M ^{P}M *P..., D M P.,* $^{M}\underline{G}^{M}\underline{G}$*R.,* ^{N}S ^{N}S ^{S}R ^{S}R $^{M}\underline{G}^{M}\underline{G}$*M M P...,* $^{M}\underline{G}$*-* $^{M}\underline{G}$*- R- S...*
4. *SR*$\underline{G}$*M P..., D-*$\underline{N}$*-D-P..., DPMP* $^{M}\underline{G}$*-*$^{M}\underline{G}$*-R...S...*

Stage 2

Composition 1

Text[10]:

sthā.yī *ma.na re su.na pu.rā.ṇa kī ka.thā*

an.ta.rā *su.ta va.ni.tā ban.dhu ke kā.ra.na pa.ci pa.ci ja.na.ma bi.tī.tā*

Meaning: O my heart, listen to the Purāṇas. You have been spending your life in tolling for your son, wife, and near and dear ones, now is the time to pay attention and realize the ultimate truth.

[10]V.N. Bhatkhande, op. cit. (Hathras: Sangeet Karyalaya, 1971), vol. I, p. 47.

Composition 1: *Notation*

Rā.g Kā.fī, tī.n-tā.l—medium tempo

								sthā.yī							
				P	*D*	*Ṉ*	–	*D*	*D*	*DP*	*G̱*	–	*G̱*	*RG̱*	*SR*
				ma	*na*	*re*	–	*su*	*na*	*pu-*	*rā*	–	*na*	*kī*	--
x				2				0				3			
P	*P*	–	–	*N*	*Ṡ*	*NṠṘ*	*Ṉ*	^{N}D	^{N}D	*D*	*G̱*	–	*G*	*RG̱*	*SR*
ka	*thā*	–	–	*ma*	*na*	*re-*	–	*su*	*na*	*pu-*	*rā*	–	*na-*	*kī*	--
x				2				0				3			
P	*P*	–	–	–	–	–	–								
ka	*thā*	–	–	–	–	–	–								
x				2											
								an.ta.rā							
								M	*M*	*P*	*D*	*N*	–	*Ṡ*	–
								su	*ta*	*va*	*ni*	*tā*	–	*ban*	–
								0				3			
NṠ	*ṘĠ̱*	*Ṙ*	*Ṡ*	*Ṙ*	*N*	*Ṡ*	*Ṡ*	*N*	*N*	*Ṡ*	*Ṡ*	*N*	*N*	*Ṡ*	*Ṡ*
dhu-	--	*ke*	–	*kā*	–	*ra*	*na*	*pa*	*ci*	*pa*	*ci*	*ja*	*na*	*ma*	*bi*
x				2				0				3			
NṠ	*RṈ*	*D*	*P*												
tī-	--	*tā*	–												
x				2											

Stage 3

ā.lā.p-sthā.yī					*P*	*D*	*Ṉ*	–	*D*	*D*	*DP*	*G̱*	–	*G̱*	*RG̱*	*SR*
					ma	*na*	*re*	–	*su*	*na*	*pu-*	*rā*	–	*na*	*kī-*	––
	x				2				0				3			
1.	*S*	–	–	–	*R*	*G̱*	*R*	*S*	*D*	*D*	*DP*	*G̱*	–	*G̱*	*RG̱*	*SR*
	ā	–	–	–	–	–	–	–	*su*	*na*	*pu-*	*rā*	–	*na-*	*kī-*	––
	x				2				0				3			
2.	*P*	*P*	–	–	*S*	–	–	–	*R*	*P*	–	–	^{M}*G̱*	–	^{M}*G̱*	–
	ka	*thā*	–	–	*ā*	–	–	–	–	–	–	–	––	–	––	–
	x				2				0				3			
	R	–	*S*	–	*P*	*D*	*Ṉ*	–	*D*	*D*	*DP*	*G̱*	–	*G̱*	*RG̱*	*SR*
	–	–	–	–	*ma*	*na*	*re*	–	*su*	*na*	*pu-*	*rā*	–	*na*	*kī-*	––
	x				2				0				3			
3.	*P*	*P*	–	–	*RG̱*	*RS*	*R*	*R*	^{M}*G̱*	^{M}*G̱*	*M*	*M*	*P*	–	–	–
	ka	*thā*	–	–	*ā*	–	–	–	–	–	–	–	–	–	–	–
	x				2				0				3			
	^{M}*G̱*	–	*R*	*S*	*P*	*D*	*Ṉ*	–	*D*	*D*	*DP*	*G̱*	–	*G̱*	*RG̱*	*SR*
	–	–	–	–	*ma*	*na*	*re*	–	*su*	*na*	*pu-*	*rā*	–	*na*	*kī-*	––
	x				2				0				3			
4.	*S*	–	–	–	*R*	*G̱*	*R*	*S*	*R*	–	*P*	–	*G̱*	–	*G̱*	–
	ā	–	–	–	–	–	–	–	–	–	–	–	–	–	–	–
	x				2				0				3			
	R	–	*S*	–	*P*	*D*	*Ṉ*	–	*D*	*D*	*DP*	*G̱*	–	*G̱*	*RG̱*	*SR*
	–	–	–	–	*ma*	*na*	*re*	–	*su*	*na*	*pu-*	*rā*	–	*na*	*kī-*	––
	x				2				0				3			
5.	*S*	*R*	*P*	–	*MP*	*D*	*M*	*P*	*Ṉ*	–	*D*	*P*	^{M}*G̱*	–	^{M}*G̱*	–
	ā	–	–	–	––	–	–	–	–	–	–	–	–	–	–	–
	x				2				0				3			
	R	–	*S*	–	*P*	*D*	*Ṉ*	–	*D*	*D*	*DP*	*G̱*	–	*G̱*	*RG̱*	*SR*
	–	–	–	–	*ma*	*na*	*re*	–	*su*	*na*	*pu-*	*rā-*	–	*na*	*kī-*	––

ā.lāp-an.ta.rā									*M*	*M*	*P*	*D*	*N*	–	*Ṡ*	–
									su	*ta*	*va*	*ni*	*tā*	–	*ban*	–
	x				2				0				3			
1.	*Ṡ*	–	–	–	*(Ṙ)N*	–	*Ṡ*	–	*M*	*M*	*P*	*D*	*N*	–	*Ṡ*	–
	ā	–	–	–	–	–	–	–	*su*	*ta*	*va*	*ni*	*tā*	–	*ban*	–
	x				2				0				3			
2.	*N̲Ṡ*	*R*	*(Ṁ)Ġ̲*	*(Ṁ)Ġ̲*	*(Ṡ)Ṙ*	–	*Ṡ*	–	*M*	*M*	*P*	*D*	*N*	–	*Ṡ*	–
	ā	–	–	–	–	–	–	–	*su*	*ta*	*va*	*ni*	*tā*	–	*ban*	–
	x				2				0				3			
3.	*NṠ*	*ṘĠ̲*	*Ṙ*	*Ṡ*	*Ṙ*	*N*	*Ṡ*	*Ṡ*	*Ṡ*	–	*Ṙ*	–	*N̲*	*D*	*P*	–
	dhu-	—	*ke*	–	*kā*	–	*ra*	*na*	*ā*	–	–	–	–	–	–	–
	x				2				0				3			
	G̲	–	*R*	*S*	*RG̲*	*MP*	*DN*	*Ṡ*	*M*	*M*	*P*	*D*	*N*	–	*Ṡ*	–
	–	–	–	–	—	—	—	–	*su*	*ta*	*va*	*ni*	*tā*	–	*ban*	–
	x				2				0				3			
4.	*MP*	*NṠ*	*Ṙ*	*(Ṁ)Ġ̲*	*(Ṁ)Ġ̲*	*(Ṁ)Ġ̲*	*Ṙ*	–	*Ṡ*	–	*N̲*	*D*	*P*	–	*G̲*	–
	ā	–	–	–	–	–	–	–	–	–	–	–	–	–	–	–
	x				2				0				3			
	R	–	*M*	*P*	*N*	–	*Ṡ*	–	*M*	*M*	*P*	*D*	*N*	–	*Ṡ*	–
	–	–	–	–	–	–	–	–	*su*	*ta*	*va*	*ni*	*tā*	–	*ban*	–
	x				2				0				3			
	NṠ	*ṘĠ*	*Ṙ*	*Ṡ*	*R*	*N*	*Ṡ*	*Ṡ*	*N*	*N*	*Ṡ*	*Ṡ*	*N*	*N*	*Ṡ*	*Ṡ*
	dhu-	—	*ke*	–	*kā*	–	*ra*	*na*	*pa*	*ci*	*pa*	*ci*	*ja*	*na*	*ma*	*bi*
	x				2				0				3			
	NṠ	*ṘN̲*	*D*	*P*	*P*	*D*	*PD*	*N̲*	*D*	*D*	*DP*	*G̲*	–	*G̲*	*RG̲*	*ṠR*
	tī-	—	*tā*	–	*ma*	*na*	*re-*	–	*su*	*na*	*pu-*	*rā*	–	*na*	*kī-*	—
	x				2				0				3			
	P	*P*	–	–												
	ka	*thā*	–	–												

Stage 4 (increase your tempo a little)

tā.n-sthā.yī

1.					*P*	*D*	*Ṇ*	–	*D*	*D*	*DP*	*G̱*	*SR*	*G̱S*	*RR*	*PP*
					ma	*na*	*re*	–	*su*	*na*	*pu-*	*rā*	*ā-*	—	—	—
	x				2				0				3			
2.	*MP*	*DP*	*MG̱*	*RS*	*P*	*D*	*Ṇ*	–	*D*	*D*	*DP*	*G̱*	*NS*	*RS*	*RG̱*	*RG̱*
	—	—	—	—	*ma*	*na*	*re*	–	*su*	*na*	*pu-*	*rā*	*ā-*	—	—	—
	x				2				0				3			
	MG̱	*MP*	*MP*	*DP*	*DṆ*	*DP*	*MG̱*	*RS*	*D*	*D*	*DP*	*G̱*	–	*G̱*	*RG̱*	*SR*
	—	—	—	—	—	—	—	—	*su*	*na*	*pu-*	*rā*	–	*na*	*kī*	—
	x				2				0				3			
3.	*P*	*P*	–	–	*P*	*D*	*Ṇ*	–	*D*	*D*	*DP*	*G̱*	*MD*	*NN*	*ṠṠ*	*NṠ*
	ka	*thā*	–	–	*ma*	*na*	*re*	–	*su*	*na*	*pu-*	*rā*	*ā-*	—	—	—
	x				2				0				3			
	ṆD	*PM*	*G̱R*	*SS*	*P*	*D*	*Ṇ*	–	*D*	*D*	*DP*	*G̱*	–	*G̱*	*RG̱*	*SR*
	—	—	—	—	*ma*	*na*	*re*	–	*su*	*na*	*pu-*	*rā*	–	*na*	*kī-*	—
	x				2				0				3			
4.	*P*	*P*	–	–	*RG̱*	*RM*	*PM*	*DṆ*	*DṠ*	*ṘṠ*	*ṘĠ̱*	*ṘṠ*	*RṠ*	*DṆ*	*DM*	*PM*
	ka	*thā*	–	–	*ā-*	—	—	—	—	—	—	—	—	—	—	—
	x				2				0				3			
	RG̱	*RS*	*RG̱*	*MP*	*P*	*D*	*Ṇ*	–	*D*	*D*	*DP*	*G̱*	*MD*	*NN*	*ṠṠ*	*NṠ*
	—	—	—	—	*ma*	*na*	*re*	–	*su*	*na*	*pu-*	*rā*	–	*na*	*kī-*	—
	x				2				0				3			
5.	*P*	*P*	–	–	*NS*	*G̱R*	*MG̱*	*RS*	*MP*	*DP*	*ṆD*	*PM*	*NṠ*	*ĠṘ*	*ṀG*	*ṘṠ*
	ka	*thā*	–	–	*ā-*	—	—	—	—	—	—	—	—	—	—	—
	x				2				0				3			
	ṆD	*PM*	*G̱R*	*SS*	*P*	*D*	*Ṇ*	–	*D*	*D*	*DP*	*G̱*	–	*G̱*	*RG̱*	*SR*
	—	—	—	—	*ma*	*na*	*re*	–	*su*	*na*	*pu-*	*rā*	–	*na*	*kī-*	—
	x				2				0				3			
	P	*P*	–	–	–											
	ka	*thā*	–	–	–											

tā.n-an.ta.rā									*M*	*M*	*P*	*D*	*N*	–	*Ṡ*	–
									su	*ta*	*va*	*ni*	*tā*	–	*ban*	–
	x				2				0				3			
1.	*ṘṘ*	*ṠṘ*	*ṠṈ*	*DP*	*DM*	*PD*	*NN*	*ṠṠ*	*M*	*M*	*P*	*D*	*N*	–	*Ṡ*	–
	ā-	--	--	--	--	--	--	--	*su*	*ta*	*va*	*ni*	*tā*	–	*ban*	–
	x				2				0				3			
2.	*ṠṈ*	*DP*	*MG̱*	*RR*	*SR*	*G̱S*	*RR*	*PP*	*M*	*M*	*P*	*D*	*N*	–	*Ṡ*	–
	ā-	--	--	--	--	--	--	--	*su*	*ta*	*va*	*ni*	*tā*	–	*ban*	–
	x				2				0				3			
3.	*NṠ*	*ĠṘ*	*ṀĠ*	*ṘṠ*	*ND*	*MP*	*NN*	*ṠṠ*	*M*	*M*	*P*	*D*	*N*	–	*Ṡ*	–
	ā-	--	--	--	--	--	--	--	*su*	*ta*	*va*	*ni*	*tā*	–	*ban*	–
	x				2				0				3			
4.	*NṠ*	*ṘĠ*	*Ṙ*	*Ṡ*	*Ṙ*	*N*	*Ṡ*	*Ṡ*	*ĠṘ*	*ṠĠ*	*ṘṠ*	*ĠṘ*	*ṠṈ*	*DP*	*ND*	*PṈ*
	dhu-	--	*ke*	–	*kā*	–	*ra*	*na*	*ā-*	--	--	--	--	--	--	--
	x				2				0				3			
	DP	*MG̱*	*RS*	*G̱R*	*SG̱*	*RS*	*RG̱*	*MP*	*M*	*M*	*P*	*D*	*N*	–	*Ṡ*	–
	--	--	--	--	--	--	--	--	*su*	*ta*	*va*	*ni*	*tā*	–	*ban*	–
	x				2				0				3			
	NṠ	*ṘĠ*	*Ṙ*	*Ṡ*	*Ṙ*	*N*	*Ṡ*	*Ṡ*	*N*	*N*	*Ṡ*	*Ṡ*	*N*	*N*	*Ṡ*	*Ṡ*
	dhu-	--	*ke*	–	*kā*	–	*ra*	*na*	*pa*	*ȧ*	*pa*	*ȧ*	*ja*	*na*	*ma*	*bi*
	x				2				0				3			
	NṠ	*ṘṈ*	*D*	*P*	*P*	*D*	*PD*	*Ṉ*	*D*	*D*	*DP*	*G̱*	–	*G̱*	*RG̱*	*SR*
	tī-	--	*tā*	–	*ma*	*na*	*re-*	–	*su*	*na*	*pu-*	*rā*	–	*na*	*kī-*	--
	x				2				0				3			
	P	*P*	–	–	–	–	–	–								
	ka	*thā*	–	–	–	–	–	–								
	x				2											

COMPOSITION 2

Rā.g Kā.fī, lak.ṣaṇ-gī.t, e.k-tā.l—medium tempo

Text[11]:

sthā.yī *gu.ni gā.va kā.fī rā.ga, kha.ra.ha.ra pri.ya me.la ja.ni.ta ko.ma.la ga ni uj.jva.la pa.ra su.ra pañ.ca.ma vā.dī sā.dha*

an.ta.rā *sa.ra.la sva.rū.pa vi.paś.ci.ta, mā.na.ta sa.ba su.dhi a.vi.ca.la, ā.śra.ya gu.ni ca.tu.ra ka.ha.ta ko.ma.la ga ni uj-jva.la pa.ra su.ra pañ.ca.ma vā.dī sā.dha*

Meaning: The learned singers sing *rā.g Kā.fī*. This *rā.g* belongs to the *Me.l kha.ra.ha.ra pri.ya*. The use of the notes *Ko.ma.la ga* and *ni* make this *rā.g* very melodious. The use of *pa as vā.dī* makes it sweeter. All experts are of the view that this melody is simple and sweet, and represents *thā.ṭ Kā.fī.*

[11]V.N. Bhatkhande, op. cit. (Hathras: Sangeet Karyalaya, 1954), vol. II, p. 320.

Composition 2: *Notation*

						sthā.yī					
						PD	*MP*	^{M}*G̱*	–	*RS*	*R*
						gu-	*ni-*	*gā*	–	*va-*	*ta*
						0		3		4	
^{M}*G̱*	–	*M*	*P*	–	*P*	*Ṡ*	*Ṙ*	*Ṡ*	*Ṉ*	*D*	*P*
kā	–	*fī-*	*rā*	–	*ga*	*kha*	*ra*	*ha*	*ra*	*pri*	*ya*
x		0		2		0		3		4	
^{M}*G̱*	–	*R*	*S*	*R*	*N*	*S*	–	*R*	*R*	^{M}*G̱*	^{M}*G̱*
me	–	*la*	*ja*	*ni*	*ta*	*ko*	–	*ma*	*la*	*ga*	*ni*
x		0		2		0		3		4	
M	–	*P*	*P*	*D*	*D*	*N*	*Ṡ*	*NṠ*	*ṘṠ*	*Ṉ*	*Ṉ*
u	–	*jjva*	*la*	*pa*	*ra*	*su*	*ra*	*pa-*	––	*ñca*	*ma*
x		0		2		0		3		4	
DP	*D*	^{P}*M*	*P*	–	*P*						
vā-	–	*dī*	*sā*	–	*dha*						
x		0		2							
						an.ta.rā					
						^{P}*M*	*M*	*P*	*P*	*N*	–
						sa	*ra*	*la*	*sva*	*rū*	–
						0		3		4	
Ṡ	*N*	*Ṡ*	*N*	*Ṡ*	*Ṡ*	*N*	*Ṡ*	*Ṙ*	*Ġ*	*Ṙ*	*Ṡ*
pa	*vi*	*pa*	–	*ści*	*ta*	*mā*	–	*na*	*ta*	*sa*	*ba*
x		0		2		0		3		4	
R	*N*	*Ṡ*	*N*	*Ṡ*	*Ṡ*	*Ṡ*	–	*Ṉ*	*D*	*M*	*P*
su	*dhi*	*a*	*vi*	*ca*	*la*	*ā*	–	*śra*	*ya*	*gu*	*ni*
x		0		2		0		3		4	
^{M}*G̱*	^{M}*G̱*	*R*	*S*	*R*	*N*	*S*	–	*R*	*R*	^{M}*G̱*	^{M}*G̱*
ca	*tu*	*ra*	*ka*	*ha*	*ta*	*ko*	–	*ma*	*la*	*ga*	*ni*
x		0		2		0		3		4	
M	–	*P*	*P*	*D*	*D*	*Ṉ*	*Ṡ*				
u	–	*jjva*	*la*	*pa*	*ra*	*su*	*ra*	sing further as in *sthā.yī.*			

COMPOSITION 3

Rā.g Kā.fī, tī.n-tā.l—medium tempo

Text[12]:

sthā.yī *jha.na.na jha.na.na mo.rī pā.ya.la bā.je, pi.yā se mi.la.na ko jā.ūṅ a.ba maiṅ*

an.ta.rā *di.na di.na mo.he cai.na nā ā.ye sa.ga.rī ra.ti.yāṅ bi.ra.hā sa.tā.ye, kai.se kai.se ḍhūṅ.ḍha.na ko jā.ūṅ a.ba maiṅ*

Meaning: My anklets are ringing. I am going to meet my beloved husband now. Days after days I feel restless and at night I am longing for him. How and where should I go to look for him.

[12]Nawab Ali Khan (Lakhimpur: 1954).

Notation

								sthā.yī							
								R	*G̱*	*R*	*S*	*R*	*M*	*P*	*D*
								jha	*na*	*na*	*jha*	*na*	*na*	*mo*	*rī*
								0				3			
Ṡ	–	*N̲*	*D*	*M*	*P*	*G̱*	*R*	*R*	*RD*	*D*	*D*	*DN̲*	*PD*	*Ṡ*	*Ṡ*
pā	–	*ya*	*la*	*bā*	–	*je*	–	*pi*	*yā-*	*se*	*mi*	*la-*	*na-*	*ko*	–
x				2				0				3			
N̲	*D*	*M*	–	*MN̲*	*P*	*G*	*R*								
jā	–	*ūṅ*	–	*a-*	*ba*	*maiṅ*									
x				2											
								an.ta.rā							
								D	*N̲*	*P*	*D*	*Ṡ*	–	*Ṡ*	*Ṡ*
								di	*na*	–	*di*	*na*	–	*mo*	*he*
								0				3			
DṠ	*ṘĠ*	*Ṙ*	*Ṡ*	*N̲*	*N̲*	*D*	*P*	*P*	*D*	*P*	*D*	*(Ṡ)*	*N̲*	*D*	*M*
cai-	*na*	*nā*	*ā*	–	*ye*	–	*sa*	*ga*	*rī*	*ra*	*ti*	*yāṅ*	–	–	–
x				2				0				3			
R	*M*	*RM̲*	*N̲P*	*G̱*	–	*R*	*S*	*R*	*G̱*	*R*	*S*	*R*	*M*	*P*	*D*
bi	*ra*	*hā-*	*sa-*	*tā*	–	*ye*	–	*kai*	*se*	*kai*	*se*	*ḍhūṅ*	*ḍha*	*na*	*ko*
x				2				0				3			
Ṡ	–	*N̲*	*DM*	*MN̲*	*P*	*G̱*	*R*								
jā	–	*ūṅ*	––	*a-*	*ba*	*maiṅ*	*N̲*								
x				2											

Rā.g Bhai.rav

Melodic pattern

ā.roh (ascent)	–	*Ṇ S G M ^{N}D̲, NṠ*
a.va.ro.h (descent)	–	*ṠN D̲ P, ^{S}M GR̲,Ṡ*[13]
vā.dī (prominent note)	–	*R̲*
sam.vā.dī (consonant of *vā.dī*)	–	*D̲*
sa.ma.y (time)	–	early morning, at sun rise
mu.khya svar saṅ.ga.ti (chief com. of notes)	–	*S GM ^{G}R̲ ^{G}R̲, GM ^{N}D̲P, M ^{G}R̲ ^{G}R̲ S*

Stage 1

muk.t ā.lā.p

1. *S ^{N}Ḍ̲ ^{N}Ḍ̲ ^{N}Ḍ̲ - N - S -, R̲ - R̲ S...*
2. *Ḍ̲ - Ṇ - S..., ^{G}R̲ - ^{G}R̲ -, G...M ^{G}R̲...S...*
3. *R̲R̲SNS - G - M - ^{M}P -..., P ^{P}G - - M R̲ - ^{G}R̲ - GMPGMR̲ - ^{G}R̲...S...*
4. *NSGM ^{N}D̲ - ^{N}D̲ - P..., P ^{P}D̲ M - M MP G - G GM R̲ - ^{G}R̲...S...*

[13]Pt. Onkar Nath Thakur, *Saṅgītāñjali* (Bombay: Onkar Nath Thakur Estate), pt. III, 52. It gives a clearer picture of *rā.g Bhai.rav.* According to Pt. Bhatkhande and Paluskara, the melodic pattern of *rā.g Bhai.rav* is *S R̲ G M, P ^{N}D, N Ṡ: Ṡ N D̲, P M G R̲, S.*

Stage 2

Composition 1

Text[14]:

sthā.yī *jā.go mo.ha.na pyā.re, sāṅ.va.rī sū.ra.ta mo.re ma.na bhā.ve sun.da.ra lā.la ha.mā.re*

an.ta.rā *prā.ta sa.ma.ya u.ṭha bhā.nu u.da.ya bha.yo, gvā.la bā.la bhū.pa.ti sa.ba ṭhā.rhe da.ra.śa.na ke sa.ba bhū.khe pyā.se, u.ṭhi.yo nan.da ki.śo.re*

Meaning: O, beloved Mohan (Krishna), please wake up. O, our pretty child, your lovley face enchants us. It is now morning and the sun has risen. The cowherds and the kings are all standing and desparately waiting for your holy appearance. O, beloved son of Nanda, please get up.

[14]Nawab Ali Khan (Lakhimpur: 1953). It is also mentioned in *Kramik Pustak Mālikā,* vol. I, 38 (Hathras: 1971) and *Rāga Vijñāna* (Pune: 1967), part III, 124.

COMPOSITION 1, *Notation* *Rā.g Bhai.rav, tī.n-tā.l*—medium tempo

								sthā.yī							
								^{M}G	*M*	*^{N}Ḏ*	–	*P*	–	*^{P}Ḏ*	*M*
								jā	–	*go*	–	*mo*	–	*ha*	*na*
x				2				0				3			
D̲D̲	*PM*	*P*	–	*M*	–	*G*	–	*^{P}G*	–	*M*	*^{M}G*	*^{G}Ṟ*	–	*G*	*P*
pya-	—	–	–	*re*	–	–	–	*sāṅ*	–	*va*	*ri*	*sū*	–	*ra*	*ta*
x				2				0				3			
^{G}M	*G*	*M*	*G*	*^{M}Ṟ*	–	*S*	–	*^{S}N*	*S*	*^{M}G*	*M*	*P*	*Ḏ*	*N*	*Ṡ*
mo	*re*	*ma*	*na*	*bhā*	–	*ve*	–	*sun*	–	*da*	*ra*	*lā*	–	*la*	*ha*
x				2				0				3			
^{Ṡ}Ṙ	*^{Ṡ}Ṙ*	*Ṡ*	*N*	*Ḏ*	*P*	*M*	*G*								
mā	–	–	–	–	–	*re*	–								
x				2											
								an.ta.rā							
								P	–	*P*	*P*	*^{N}Ḏ*	*Ḏ*	*N*	*N*
								prā	–	*ta*	*sa*	*ma*	*ya*	*u*	*ṭha*
x				2				0				3			
Ṡ	–	*Ṡ*	*Ṡ*	*N*	*Ṡ*	*Ṡ*	*Ṡ*	*Ḏ*	–	*Ḏ*	*N*	*Ṡ*	*Ṡ*	*Ṡ*	–
bhā	–	*nu*	*u*	*da*	*ya*	*bha*	*yo*	*gvā*	–	*la*	*bā*	–	*la*	*bhū*	–
x				2				0				3			
Ṟ̇	*Ṟ̇*	*Ṡ*	*Ṡ*	*N*	*Ṡ*	*Ḏ*	*P*	*^{P}G*	*M*	*P*	*Ḏ*	*^{Ḏ}Ṡ̱*	–	*^{N}Ḏ*	*P*
pa	*ti*	*sa*	*ba*	*thā*	–	*ṛhe*	–	*da*	*ra*	*śa*	*na*	*ke*	–	*sa*	*ba*
x				2				0				3			
M	*G*	*(M)*	*G*	*^{M}Ṟ*	–	*S*	–	*^{S}N*	*S*	*^{N}G*	*M*	*P*	*Ḏ*	*N*	*Ṡ*
bhū	–	*khe*	–	*pyā*	–	*se*	–	*u*	*ṭhi*	*yo*	–	*na*	–	*nda*	*ki*
x				2				0				3			
^{Ṡ}Ṙ	*^{Ṡ}Ṙ*	*Ṡ*	*N*	*Ḏ*	*P*	*M*	*G*								
śo	–	–	–	–	–	*re*	–								

Stage 3

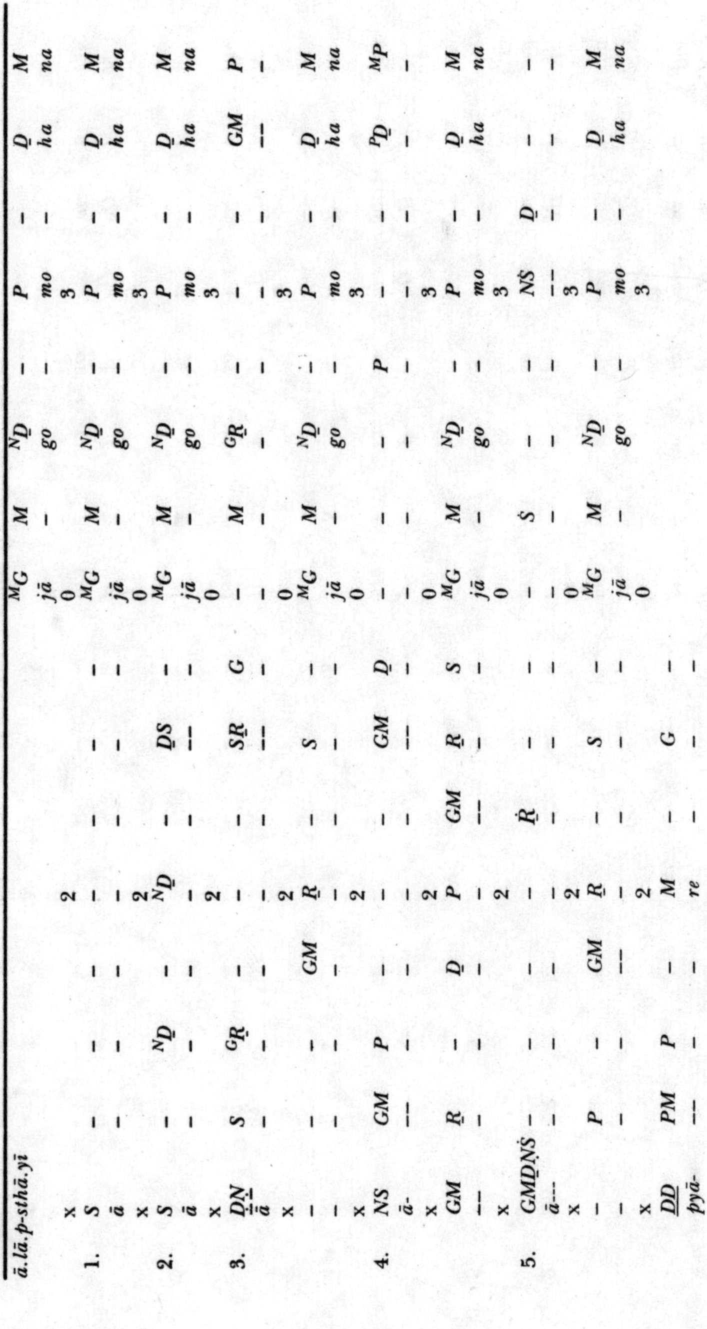

ā.lā.p-sthā.yī									^{M}G	M	^{N}Ḏ	–	P	–	Ḏ	M
									jā	–	go	–	mo	–	ha	na
	x				2				0				3			
1.	S	–	–	–	–	–	–	–	^{M}G	M	^{N}Ḏ	–	P	–	Ḏ	M
	ā	–	–	–	–	–	–	–	jā	–	go	–	mo	–	ha	na
	x				2				0				3			
2.	S	–	^{N}Ḏ	–	^{N}Ḏ	–	ḎS	–	^{M}G	M	^{N}Ḏ	–	P	–	Ḏ	M
	ā	–	–	–	–	–	––	–	jā	–	go	–	mo	–	ha	na
	x				2				0				3			
3.	ḎṈ	S	^{G}Ṟ	–	–	–	SṞ	G	–	M	^{G}Ṟ	–	–	–	GM	P
	ā̱	–	–	–	–	–	––	–	–	–	–	–	–	–	––	–
	x				2				0				3			
	–	–	–	GM	Ṟ	–	S	–	^{M}G	M	^{N}Ḏ	–	P	–	Ḏ	M
	–	–	–	–	–	–	–	–	jā	–	go	–	mo	–	ha	na
	x				2				0				3			
4.	NS	GM	P	–	–	–	GM	Ḏ	–	–	–	P	–	–	^{P}Ḏ	^{M}P
	ā-	––	–	–	–	–	––	–	–	–	–	–	–	–	–	–
	x				2				0				3			
	GM	Ṟ	–	Ḏ	P	GM	Ṟ	S	^{M}G	M	^{N}Ḏ	–	P	–	Ḏ	M
	––	–	–	–	–	––	–	–	jā	–	go	–	mo	–	ha	na
	x				2				0				3			
5.	GMḎṆṠ	–	–	–	–	Ṟ̇	–	–	–	Ṡ	–	–	NṠ	Ḏ	–	–
	ā---	–	–	–	–	–	–	–	–	–	–	–	––	–	–	–
	x				2				0				3			
	–	P	–	GM	Ṟ	–	S	–	^{M}G	M	^{N}Ḏ	–	P	–	Ḏ	M
	–	–	–	––	–	–	–	–	jā	–	go	–	mo	–	ha	na
	x				2				0				3			
	<u>DD</u>	PM	P	–	M	–	G	–								
	pyā-	––	–	–	re	–	–	–								
	x				2											

ā.lā.p-an.ta.rā									*P*	–	*P*	*P*	[N]*D̲*	[N]*D̲*	*N*	*N*
									prā	–	*ta*	*sa*	*ma*	*ya*	*u*	*ṭha*
	x				2				0				3			
1.	*Ṡ*	–	–	*ṠN*	*Ṙ̲*	[Ġ]*Ṙ̲*	*Ṡ*	–	*P*	–	*P*	*P*	[N]*D̲*	[N]*D̲*	*N*	*N*
	ā	–	–	––	–	–	–	–	*prā*	–	*ta*	*sa*	*ma*	*ya*	*u*	*ṭha*
	x				2				0				3			
2.	*D̲N*	*ṠṘ̲*	[G]*Ṙ̲*	–	*Ṡ*	–	–	–	*P*	–	*P*	*P*	[N]*D̲*	[N]*D̲*	*N*	*N*
	ā-	––	–	–	–	–	–	–	*prā*	–	*ta*	*sa*	*ma*	*ya*	*u*	*ṭha*
	x				2				0				3			
3.	*Ṡ*	–	*Ṡ*	*Ṡ*	*N*	*Ṡ*	*Ṡ*	*Ṡ*	*GM*	*D̲*	–	–	*P*	–	–	–
	bhā	–	*mu*	*u*	*da*	*ya*	*bha*	*yo*	*ā-*	–	–	–	–	–	–	–
	x				2				0				3			
	D̲	–	*N*	–	*Ṡ*	–	*Ṙ̲*	*Ṡ*	*P*	–	*P*	*P*	[N]*D̲*	[N]*D̲*	*N*	*N*
	–	–	–	–	–	–	–	–	*prā*	–	*ta*	*sa*	*ma*	*ya*	*u*	*ṭha*
	x				2				0				3			
4.	*Ṡ*	*Ṙ̲*	–	–	*ĠṀ*	*Ṙ̲*	–	*Ṡ*	–	*Ṡ*	[N]*D̲*	–	–	*P*	–	*M*
	ā	–	–	–	––	–	–	–	–	–	–	–	–	–	–	–
	x				2				0				3			
	P	[N]*D̲*	–	*N*	–	*N*	*Ṡ*	–	*P*	–	*P*	*P*	[N]*D̲*	[N]*D̲*	*N*	*N*
	–	–	–	–	–	–	–	–	*prā*	–	*ta*	*sa*	*ma*	*ya*	*u*	*ṭha*
	x				2				0				3			
5.	*Ṡ*	–	–	–	*ṠṘ̲*	*ĠṀ*	*Ṙ̲*	–	*Ṡ*	–	–	*N*	*D̲*	–	*P*	–
	ā	–	–	–	––	––	–	–	–	–	–	–	–	–	–	–
	x				2				0				3			
	–	*D̲*	–	–	*N*	*Ṡ*	–	–	*P*	–	*P*	*P*	[N]*D̲*	[N]*D̲*	*N*	*N*
	–	–	–	–	–	–	–	–	*prā*	–	*ta*	*sa*	*ma*	*ya*	*u*	*ṭha*
	x				2				0				3			
	Ṡ	–	*Ṡ*	*Ṡ*	*N*	*Ṡ*	*Ṡ*	*Ṡ*								
	bhā	–	*mu*	*u*	*da*	*ya*	*bha*	*yo*	sing the whole *an.ta.rā.*							
	x				2											

Stage 4 (increase your tempo a little)

tā.n-sthā.yī									^{M}*G*	*M*	^{N}*Ḏ*	–	*P*	–	^{P}*Ḏ*	*M*
									jā	–	*go*	–	*mo*	–	*ha*	*na*
	x				2				0				3			
1.	*SṞ*	*GM*	*PM*	*GM*	*D̲D̲*	*PM*	*GṞ*	*SS*	^{M}*G*	*M*	^{N}*Ḏ*	–	*P*	–	^{P}*Ḏ*	*M*
	ā-	--	--	--	--	--	--	--	*jā*	–	*go*	–	*mo*	–	*ha*	*na*
	x				2				0				3			
2.	*GM*	*PḎ*	*NṠ*	*Ṙ̲Ṡ̲*	*NḎ*	*PM*	*GṞ*	*SS*	^{M}*G*	*M*	^{N}*Ḏ*	–	*P*	–	^{P}*Ḏ*	*M*
	ā-	--	--	--	--	--	--	--	*jā*	–	*go*	–	*mo*	–	*ha*	*na*
	x				2				0				3			
3.	*Ṙ̲Ṙ̲*	*ṠṞ̇*	*Ṙ̲Ṡ̲*	*NḎ*	*PM*	*GM*	*GṞ*	*SS*	*G*	*M*	^{N}*Ḏ*	–	*P*	–	^{P}*Ḏ*	*M*
	ā-	--	--	--	--	--	--	--	*jā*	–	*go*	–	*mo*	–	*ha*	*na*
	x				2				0				3			
4.	*SṞ*	*GṞ*	*GM*	*GM*	*PM*	*PḎ*	*PḎ*	*NḎ*	*NṠ*	*NṠ*	*Ṙ̲Ṙ̲*	*ṠN*	*ḎN*	*ḎP*	*D̲D̲*	*PM*
	ā-	--	--	--	--	--	--	--	--	--	--	--	--	--	--	--
	x				2				0				3			
	PP	*MG*	*MM*	*GṞ*	*GM*	*PM*	*GṞ*	*SS*	^{M}*G*	*M*	^{N}*Ḏ*	–	*P*	–	^{P}*Ḏ*	*M*
	--	--	--	--	--	--	--	--	*jā*	–	*go*	–	*mo*	–	*ha*	*na*
	x				2				0				3			
5.	*SṞ*	*GM*	*MG*	*ṞS*	*GM*	*PḎ*	*ḎP*	*MG*	*PḎ*	*NṠ*	*ṠN*	*ḎP*	*NṠ*	*ṘĠ*	*ṀĠ*	*ṘṠ*
	ā-	--	--	--	--	--	--	--	--	--	--	--	--	--	--	--
	x				2				0				3			
	PḎ	*NṠ*	*NN*	*ḎP*	*MP*	*ḎP*	*MG*	*ṞS*	^{M}*G*	*M*	^{N}*Ḏ*	–	*P*	–	^{P}*Ḏ*	*M*
	--	--	--	--	--	--	--	--	*jā*	–	*go*	–	*mo*	–	*ha*	*na*
	x				2				0				3			
	D̲D̲	*PM*	*P*	–	*M*	–	*G*	–								
	pyā	–	–	–	*re*	–	–	–								

tā.n-an.ta.rā									*P*	–	*P*	*P*	^{N}*Ḏ*	^{N}*Ḏ*	*N*	*N*
									prā	–	*ta*	*sa*	*ma*	*ya*	*u*	*ṭha*
	x				2				0				3			
1.	*ṠṞ*	*ṠN*	*DP*	*MP*	*GM*	*PḎ*	*NN*	*ṠṠ*	*P*	–	*P*	*P*	^{N}*Ḏ*	^{N}*Ḏ*	*N*	*N*
	ā-	——	——	——	——	——	——	——	*prā*	–	*ta*	*sa*	*ma*	*ya*	*u*	*ṭha*
	x				2				0				3			
2.	*ṠN*	*ḎP*	*MG*	*ṞS*	*NS*	*GM*	*PḎ*	*NṠ*	*P*	–	*P*	*P*	^{N}*Ḏ*	^{N}*Ḏ*	*N*	*N*
	ā-	——	——	——	——	——	——	——	*prā*	–	*ta*	*sa*	*ma*	*ya*	*u*	*ṭha*
	x				2				0				3			
3.	*ṠṞ*	*ĠṞ*	*ṠN*	*ḎN*	*ṠN*	*DP*	*ḎN*	*ṠṠ*	*P*	–	*P*	*P*	^{N}*Ḏ*	^{N}*Ḏ*	*N*	*N*
	ā-	——	——	——	——	——	——	——	*prā*	–	*ta*	*sa*	*ma*	*ya*	*u*	*ṭha*
	x				2				0				3			
4.	*ṘṘ*	*ṠṞ*	*ṘṠ*	*ṘṘ*	*ṠN*	*ḎP*	*DD*	*PḎ*	*ḎP*	*DD*	*PM*	*GṞ*	*SṞ*	*GṞ*	*GM*	*GM*
	ā-	——	——	——	——	——	——	——	——	——	——	——	——	——	——	——
	x				2				0				3			
	PM	*PḎ*	*PḎ*	*NḎ*	*NṠ*	*NṠ*	*ṘṘ*	*ṠṠ*	*P*	–	*P*	*P*	^{N}*Ḏ*	^{N}*Ḏ*	*N*	*N*
	——	——	——	——	——	——	——	——	*prā*	–	*ta*	*sa*	*ma*	*ya*	*u*	*ṭha*
	x				2				0				3			
5.	*ṠN*	*DP*	*NḎ*	*PM*	*ḎP*	*MG*	*PM*	*GṞ*	*MG*	*ṞS*	*NS*	*GM*	*PP*	*GM*	*PḎ*	*NN*
	ā-	——	——	——	——	——	——	——	——	——	——	——	——	——	——	——
	x				2				0				3			
	PḎ	*NṠ*	*ṘṘ*	*ĠṀ*	*ĠṞ*	*ṠN*	*ḎN*	*ṠṠ*	*P*	–	*P*	*P*	^{N}*Ḏ*	^{N}*Ḏ*	*N*	*N*
	——	——	——	——	——	——	——	——	*prā*	–	*ta*	*sa*	*ma*	*ya*	*u*	*ṭha*
	x				2				0				3			
	Ṡ	–	*Ṡ*	*Ṡ*	*N*	*Ṡ*	*Ḏ*	–	*Ḏ*	–	*Ḏ*	*N*	*Ṡ*	*Ṡ*	*Ṡ*	–
	bhā	–	*nu*	*u*	*da*	*ya*	*bha*	*yo*	*gvā*	–	*la*	*bā*	–	*la*	*bhū*	–
	x				2				0				3			

Ṟ̇	Ṟ̇	Ṡ	Ṡ	N	Ṡ	Ḏ	P	^{P}G	M	P	Ḏ	^{D}Ṡ̱	–	^{N}Ḏ	P
pa	*ti*	*sa*	*ba*	*thā*	–	*rhe*	–	*da*	*ra*	*śa*	*na*	*ke*	–	*sa*	*ba*
x				2				0				3			
M	G	(M)	G	^{M}Ṟ	–	S	–	^{S}N	S	^{M}G	M	P	Ḏ	N	Ṡ
bhū	–	*khe*	–	*pyā*	–	*se*	–	*u*	*ṭhi*	*yo*	–	*na*	–	*nda*	*ki*
x				2				0				3			
^{Ṡ}Ṙ	^{S}Ṙ	Ṡ	N	Ḏ	P	M	G								
śo	–	–	–	–	–	*re*	–	sing the first line of *sthā.yī*				and conclude with the			
x				2				0				3			
following *ti.hā.ī:*								G	M	Ḏ	–	P	–	Ḏ	M
								jā	–	*go*	–	*mo*	–	*ha*	*na*
x				2				0				3			.
G	M	Ḏ	–	P	–	Ḏ	M	G	M	Ḏ	–	P	–	Ḏ	M
jā	–	*go*	–	*mo*	–	*ha*	*na*	*jā*	–	*go*	–	*mo*	–	*ha*	*na*
x				2				0				3			
<u>DD</u>	PM	P	–	M	–	G	–	M	Ṟ	–	S	–	–		
pyā	––	–	–	*re*	–	–	–	–	–	–	–	–	–		
x				2				0				3			

COMPOSITION 2

Rā.g Bhai.rav lak.ṣaṇ-gī.t-jhap.tā.l—medium tempo

Text[15]:

sthā.yī *bhai.ra.va ma.dhu.ra rā.ga, dha re ko.ma.la ga ma ni śud.dha, gā.va.ta ba.re bhā.ga*

an.ta.rā *dhai.va.ta ka.ra.ta vā.dī ri.sa.bha ka.re sam-vā-dī, san.dhi pra.kā.śa meṅ gā.va.ta gu.ni jā.ga*

Meaning: *Bhai.rav* is a sweet melody. The notes *dha* and *re* are flat and the rest are natural. The singers who can sing this, are the fortunate ones. Its *vā.dī* is *dha* and *sam.vā.dī* is *re*. The experts sing it at dawn.

[15] Nawab Ali Khan (Lakhimpur: 1953).

Notation — *ṭhe.kā-jhap.tāl*—10 beats

1	2	3	4	5	6	7	8	9	10
dhī	*nā*	*dhī*	*dhī*	*nā*	*tī*	*nā*	*dhī*	*dhī*	*nā*
x		2			0		3		
					sthā.yī				
Ṟ	–	*S*	*SṆ*	*S*	*ṆḎ*	*Ṇ*	*S*	–	*SṆ*
bhai	–	*ra*	*va-*	*ma*	*dhu-*	*ra*	*rā*	–	*ga-*
x		2			0		3		
M	*G*	*Ṟ*	*G*	*P*	*M*	*M*	*ᴳṞ*	*Ṟ*	*S*
dha	*re*	*ko*	*ma*	*la*	*ga*	*ma*	*ni-*	*śu*	*ddha*
x		2			0		3		
G	*M*	*Ḏ*	*PM*	*P*	*G*	*M*	*Ṟ*	–	*S*
gā	–	*va*	*ta-*	*ba*	*re*	–	*bhā*	–	*ga*
x		2			0		3		
					an.ta.rā				
M	*P*	*Ḏ*	*P*	*Ḏ*	*Ṡ*	*N*	*Ṡ*	–	*Ṡ*
dhai	–	*va*	*ta*	*ka*	*ra*	*ta*	*vā*	–	*dī*
x		2			0		3		
Ḏ	*Ḏ*	*N*	*Ṡ*	*Ṙ*	*Ṡ*	*N*	*Ḏ*	*P*	*M*
ri	*sa*	*bha*	*ka*	*re*	*sa*	*ma*	*vā*	–	*dī*
x		2			0		3		
G	*M*	*P*	–	*Ḏ*	*N*	*Ṡ*	*N*	*Ḏ*	*P*
saṅ	–	*dhi*	–	*pra*	*kā*	–	*śa*	*meṅ*	–
x		2			0		3		
G	*M*	*Ḏ*	*PM*	*P*	*G*	*M*	*Ṟ*	–	*S*
gā	–	*va*	*ta-*	*gu*	*ni*	–	*jā*	–	*ga*
x		2			0		3		

COMPOSITION 3

Rā.g Bhai.rav, tī.n-tā.l—medium tempo

Text:[16]

sthā.yī *gu.ru nā.thā sa.ba.na ke, ni.ta su.mi.re ma.na jī.vi.ta chi.na bhaṅ.gu.ra*

an.ta.rā *jo cā.he tū ca.ra su.kha sam.pa.da, maṅ.ga.la. nā.ma ka.ma.la mu.kha sam.va.da, jā.ki kri.pā sa.ba pū.ra.ta kā.ma*

Meaning: The great *gu.ru* belongs to everyone. Please remember Him everyday as this life will pass away in no time. If you want worldly pleasures and wealth then also remember Him. All desires are fulfilled by His grace.

[16] V.N. Bhatkhande, op. cit. (Hathras: Sangeet Karyalaya, 1971), vol. I, p. 37.

Notation

								sthā.yī							
						^{M}P	M	^{M}R̲	–	–	S	–	R̲	N	S
						gu	ru	nā	–	–	thā	–	sa	ba	na
x				2				0				3			
^{S}M	–	–	–	^{M}R̲	R̲	M	M	P	–	P	D̲	^{D}Ṡ̲	–	Ṡ	ṠN
ke	–	–	–	ni	ta	su	mi	re	–	ma	na	jī	–	vi	ta-
x				2				0				3			
D̲	N	D̲	P	^{G}M	R̲	$^{R̲}$P	M								
chi	na	bhan	–	gu	ra	gu	ru								
								an.ta.rā							
								^{G}M	–	P	–	^{N}D̲	–	N	N
								jo	–	cā	–	he	–	tū	ca
								0				3			
Ṡ	Ṡ	Ṡ	Ṡ	^{S}N	Ṡ	Ṡ	Ṡ	^{N}D̲	–	^{N}D̲	D̲	N	–	Ṡ	Ṡ
tu	ra	su	kha	sam	–	pa	da	maṅ	–	ga	la	nā	–	ma	ka
x				2				0				3			
Ṙ̲	Ṙ̲	Ṡ	Ṡ	^{S}N	Ṡ	D̲	P	^{M}G	M	P	D̲	^{D}Ṡ̲	–	Ṡ	ṠN
ma	la	mu	kha	sam	–	va	da	jā	–	ki	kri	pā	–	sa	ba-
x				2				0				3			
^{N}D̲	N	D̲	P	M	^{M}R̲	$^{R̲}$P	MG	^{M}R̲	–	–	S	–	R̲	N	S
pū	ra	ta	kā	–	ma,	gu	ru-	nā	–	–	thā	–	sa	ba	na

Rā.g Āsā.va.rī

Melodic pattern

ā.ro.h (ascent)	–	*S,R M P, D̲ Ṡ*
a.va.ro.h (descent)	–	*Ṡ N̲ D̲, P, M G̲, R S*
vā.dī (prominent note)	–	*D̲*
sam.vā.dī (consonant of *vā.dī*)	–	*G̲*
sa.ma.y (time)	–	forenoon

mu.kya svar saṅ.ga.ti (chief combinations of notes)—*RMP, <u>N̲D̲</u>P, D̲MPG̲–, ^{S}RS, D̲MPṠ*

Stage 1

muk.t ā.lā.p

1. *S..., ^{N}D̲-^{N}D̲-P..., ^{N}D̲-^{N}D̲-S...*
2. *RRSN̲ SR ^{N}D̲-^{N}D̲-^{S}N̲ S-, N̲S ^{M}R-^{P}M-^{MP}..., ^{P}M ^{P}M P G̲ ^{M}G̲-R-R...*
3. *SRMP ^{M}G̲-R ^{P}M ^{M}P..., ^{P}M ^{P}M P..., MP ^{N}D̲ ^{N}D̲ P-, D̲ M P-^{M}G̲-^{M}G̲-R-S...*
4. *SRMP ^{N}D̲-^{N}D̲-P-, PD̲MP ^{N}D̲ M P-D̲ M PD̲MP ^{M}G̲ ^{M}G̲ R-S-D̲-N̲-S...*

Stage 1

COMPOSITION 1

Text[17]:

sthā.yī *ma.dhu.ra ma.dhu.ra dhu.na mu.ra.lī ba.jā.ye, kuṅ.va.ra kan.hai.yā ḍhī.ṭha laṅ.ga.ra.vā*

an.ta.rā *dhu.na su.na sa.khi.yāṅ rī.jha.ta u.na pa.ra, gvā.la bā.la bhū.le sa.ba su.dhi ta.ja, ma.dhu.ba.na bī.ca ja.ba tā.n su.nā.ye*

Meaning: Krishna is playing enchanting melodies on his flute. He is our young and playful Kanhaiyā. The damsels (of Brij) are spellbound and the young cowherds lose all their senses when they hear Krishna's enchanting *tā.n* on the flute in Madhubana (an old forest near Mathura in Brij on the banks of the river Yamuna).

[17] Nawab Ali Khan (Lakhimpur: 1953).

Composition 1: *Notation*

Rā.g Āsā.va.rī, tī.n-tā.l—medium tempo

								sthā.yī							
								^{D}*M*	*M*	*P*	*Ṡ*	^{N}*Ḏ*	*P*	*PḎ*	*MP*
								ma	*dhu*	*ra*	*ma*	*dhu*	*ra*	*dhu-*	*na-*
								0				3			
^{M}*G̱*	^{M}*G̱*	*R*	*S*	^{G}*R*	^{P}*M*	*P*	–	^{M}*G̱*	^{M}*G̱*	*R*	*S*	*R*	–	*S*	–
mu	*ra*	*lī*	*ba*	*jā*	–	*ye*	–	*kuṅ*	*va*	*rạ*	*kan*	*hai*	–	*yā*	–
x				2				0				3			
Ṉ	–	*S*	*S*	*S*	*Ḏ*	^{N}*Ḏ*	*P*								
ḍhī	–	*ṭha*	*laṅ*	*ga*	*ra*	*vā*	–								
x				2											
								an.ta.rā							
								M	*M*	*P*	*P*	*Ḏ*	*Ḏ*	*Ḏ*	–
								dhu	*na*	*su*	*na*	*sa*	*khi*	*yān*	–
								0				3			
Ṡ	–	*Ṡ*	*Ṡ*	*R*	*N*	*Ṡ*	*Ṡ*	^{N}*Ḏ*	–	*Ḏ*	*Ḏ*	*Ṡ*	*Ṡ*	*Ṡ*	*R*
rī	–	*jha*	*ta*	*u*	*na*	*pa*	*ra*	*gvā*	–	*la*	*bā*	–	*la*	*bhū*	–
x				2				0				3			
ṠṘ	*Ġ*	*Ṙ*	*ṠṘ*	*Ṉ*	*Ṡ*	*Ḏ*	*P*	*Ḏ*	*Ḏ*	*P*	*P*	*G̱*	*G̱*	*R*	*S*
le-	–	*sa*	*ba-*	*su*	*dhi*	*ta*	*ja*	*ma*	*dhu*	*ba*	*na*	*bī*	*ca*	*ja*	*ba*
x				2				0				3			
Ṡ	*Ġ̱*	*Ṙ*	*Ṡ*	*ṠṘ*	*Ṉ*	*D*	*P*								
ta	–	*na*	*su*	*nā-*	–	*ye*	–								
x				2											

Stage 3

ā.lā.p-sthā.yī									$^{\underline{D}}M$	M	P	Ṡ	$^{N}\underline{D}$	P	P$\underline{D}$	MP
									ma	*dhu*	*ra*	*ma*	*dhu*	*ra*	*dhu-*	*na-*
	x				2				0				3			
1.	S	–	–	–	–	–	–	–	$^{\underline{D}}M$	M	P	Ṡ	$^{N}\underline{D}$	P	P$\underline{D}$	MP
	ā	–	–	–	–	–	–	–	*ma*	*dhu*	*ra*	*ma*	*dhu*	*ra*	*dhu-*	*na-*
	x				2				0				3			
2.	S	–	R	$\underline{N}$	$^{N}\underline{D}$	–	S	–	$^{\underline{D}}M$	M	P	Ṡ	$^{N}\underline{D}$	P	P$\underline{D}$	MP
	ā	–	–	–	–	–	–	–	*ma*	*dhu*	*ra*	*ma*	*dhu*	*ra*	*dhu-*	*na-*
	x				2				0				3			
3.	S	–	–	–	^{M}R	–	M	–	^{M}P	–	–	–	MP	$\underline{G}$	–	–
	ā	–	–	–	–	–	–	–	–	–	–	–	––	–	–	–
	x				2				0				3			
	R	–	$\underline{N}$	$\underline{D}$	–	S	–	–	$^{\underline{D}}M$	M	P	Ṡ	$^{N}\underline{D}$	P	PD	MP
	–	–	–	–	–	–	–	–	*ma*	*dhu*	*ra*	*ma*	*dhu*	*ra*	*dhu-*	*na-*
	x				2				0				3			
4.	SR	MP	$^{N}\underline{D}$	–	P	–	–	–	MP	$^{N}\underline{D}$	–	–	Ṡ	–	–	–
	ā	–	–	–	–	–	–	–	––	–	–	–	–	–	–	–
	x				2				0				3			
	Ṙ	$\underline{N}$	$\underline{D}$	M	P	–	–	$M^{\underline{D}}P$	$\underline{G}$	–	R	S	MM	PṠ	$\underline{D}$P	P$\underline{D}$MP
	–	–	–	–	–	–	–	–	–	–	–	–	*madhu*	*rama*	*dhura*	*dhu-na-*
	x				2				0				3			
5.	$^{M}\underline{G}$	$^{M}\underline{G}$	R	S	R	M	P	–	MP	$^{N}\underline{D}$	Ṡ	–	–	–	ṠṘ	$\underline{\dot{G}}$
	mu	*ra*	*lī*	*ba*	*jā*	–	*ye*	–	*ā*	–	–	–	–	–	––	–
	x				2				0				3			
	–	–	Ṙ	–	Ṡ	–	$\underline{D}$	P	$^{\underline{D}}M$	M	P	S	$^{N}\underline{D}$	P	P$\underline{D}$	MP
	–	–	–	–	–	–	–	–	*ma*	*dhu*	*ra*	*ma*	*dhu*	*ra*	*dhu-*	*na-*
	x				2				0				3			
	$^{M}\underline{G}$	$^{M}\underline{G}$	R	S	R	M	P	–								
	mu	*ra*	*lī*	*ba*	*jā*	–	*ye*	–								

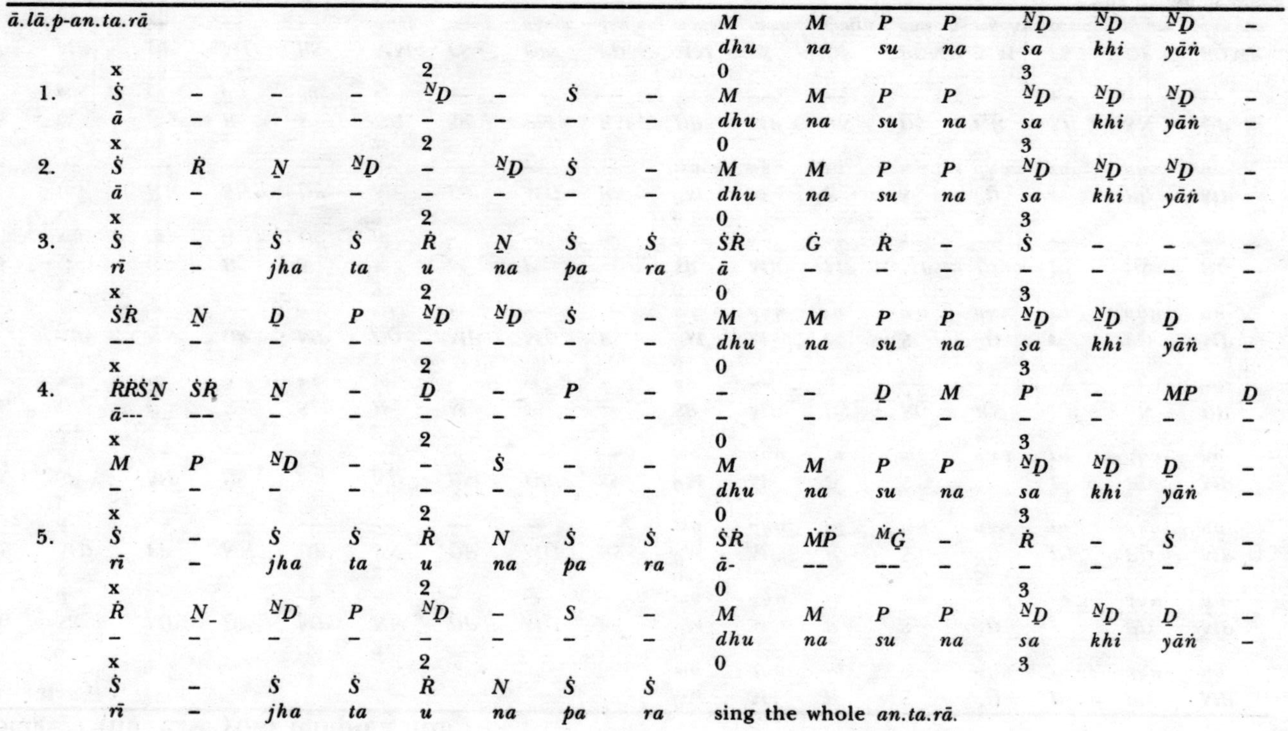

ā.lā.p-an.ta.rā																
									M	M	P	P	^{N}D̲	^{N}D̲	^{N}D̲	–
									dhu	*na*	*su*	*na*	*sa*	*khi*	*yāṅ*	–
	x				2				0				3			
1.	Ṡ	–	–	–	^{N}D̲	–	Ṡ	–	M	M	P	P	^{N}D̲	^{N}D̲	^{N}D̲	–
	ā	–	–	–	–	–	–	–	*dhu*	*na*	*su*	*na*	*sa*	*khi*	*yāṅ*	–
	x				2				0				3			
2.	Ṡ	Ṙ	N̲	^{N}D̲	–	^{N}D̲	Ṡ	–	M	M	P	P	^{N}D̲	^{N}D̲	^{N}D̲	–
	ā	–	–	–	–	–	–	–	*dhu*	*na*	*su*	*na*	*sa*	*khi*	*yāṅ*	–
	x				2				0				3			
3.	Ṡ	–	Ṡ	Ṡ	Ṙ	N̲	Ṡ	Ṡ	ṠṘ	Ġ	Ṙ	–	Ṡ	–	–	–
	rī	–	*jha*	*ta*	*u*	*na*	*pa*	*ra*	*ā*	–	–	–	–	–	–	–
	x				2				0				3			
	ṠṘ	N̲	D̲	P	^{N}D̲	^{N}D̲	Ṡ	–	M	M	P	P	^{N}D̲	^{N}D̲	D̲	–
	––	–	–	–	–	–	–	–	*dhu*	*na*	*su*	*na*	*sa*	*khi*	*yāṅ*	–
	x				2				0				3			
4.	ṘṘṠN̲	ṠṘ	N̲	–	D̲	–	P	–	–	–	D̲	M	P	–	MP	D̲
	ā---	––	–	–	–	–	–	–	–	–	–	–	–	–	–	–
	x				2				0				3			
	M	P	^{N}D̲	–	–	Ṡ	–	–	M	M	P	P	^{N}D̲	^{N}D̲	D̲	–
	–	–	–	–	–	–	–	–	*dhu*	*na*	*su*	*na*	*sa*	*khi*	*yāṅ*	–
	x				2				0				3			
5.	Ṡ	–	Ṡ	Ṡ	Ṙ	N	Ṡ	Ṡ	ṠṘ	ṀṖ	^{M}Ġ	–	Ṙ	–	Ṡ	–
	rī	–	*jha*	*ta*	*u*	*na*	*pa*	*ra*	*ā-*	––	––	–	–	–	–	–
	x				2				0				3			
	Ṙ	N̲_	^{N}D̲	P	^{N}D̲	–	S	–	M	M	P	P	^{N}D̲	^{N}D̲	D̲	–
	–	–	–	–	–	–	–	–	*dhu*	*na*	*su*	*na*	*sa*	*khi*	*yāṅ*	–
	x				2				0				3			
	Ṡ	–	Ṡ	Ṡ	Ṙ	N	Ṡ	Ṡ								
	rī	–	*jha*	*ta*	*u*	*na*	*pa*	*ra*	sing the whole *an.ta.rā.*							

Stage 4 (increase your tempo a little)

tā.n-sthā.yī									^{D}M	M	P	Ṡ	^{N}Ḍ	P	PḌ	MP
									ma	dhu	ra	ma	dhu	ra	dhu-	na-
	x				2				0				3			
1.	SR	MP	ḌP	MP	N̲N̲	ḌP	MG̣	RS	^{D}M	M	P	Ṡ	^{N}Ḍ	P	PḌ	MP
	ā-	--	--	--	--	--	--	--	ma	dhu	ra	ma	dhu	ra	dhu-	na-
	x				2				0				3			
2.	MḌ	PP	N̲N̲	ḌP	ṠṆ	ḌP	MG̣	RS	^{D}M	M	P	S	^{N}Ḍ	P	PḌ	MP
	ā-	--	--	--	--	--	--	--	ma	dhu	ra	ma	dhu	ra	dhu-	na-
	x				2				0				3			
3.	SR	MP	D̲Ṡ̲	ṘṠ	N̲D̲	PM	G̣R	SS	^{D}M	M	P	S	^{N}Ḍ	P	PḌ	MP
	ā-	--	--	--	--	--	--	--	ma	dhu	ra	ma	dhu	ra	dhu-	na-
	x				2				0				3			
4.	G	G̣	R	S	R	M	P	–	SR	MP	D̲Ṡ̲	ṘĠ̣	RṠ	RR	ṠṆ	ḌP
	mu	ra	lī	ba	jā	–	ye	–	ā-	--	--	--	--	--	--	--
	x				2				0				3			
	MP	N̲N̲	DP	MP	D̲D̲	MP	MG̣	RS	^{D}M	M	P	Ṡ	^{N}Ḍ	P	PḌ	MP
	--	--	--	--	--	--	--	--	ma	dhu	ra	ma	dhu	ra	dhu-	na-
	x				2				0				3			
5.	G̣	G̣	R	S	R	M	P	–	SR	MR	MP	MP	ḌP	D̲Ṡ̲	D̲Ṡ̲	ṘĠ̣
	mu	ra	lī	ba	jā	–	ye	–	ā-	--	--	--	--	--	--	--
	x				2				0				3			
	ṘṠ	ṘṘ	ṠṆ	ḌP	MP	ḌP	MG̣	RS	^{D}M	M	P	Ṡ	^{N}Ḍ	P	PḌ	MP
	--	--	--	--	--	--	--	--	ma	dhu	ra	ma	dhu	ra	dhu-	na-
	x				2				0				3			
6.	G̣	G̣	R	S	G̣R	SR	PM	RM	ḌP	MP	ṠṆ	D̲Ṡ̲	Ġ̲Ṙ̲	ṠṘ	SṆ	ḌP
	mu	ra	lī	ba	ā-	--	--	--	--	--	--	--	--	--	--	--
	x				2				0				3			
	MP	ḌP	MG̣	RS	MM	PṠ	ḌP	PḌMP	MM	PṠ	ḌP	PḌMP	MM	PṠ	ḌP	PḌMP
	--	--	--	--	madhu	rama	dhura	dhu-na-	madhu	rama	dhura	dhu-na-	madhu	rama	dhura	dhu-na-
	x				2				0				3	sing the whole line		

tā.n-an.ta.rā									M	M	P	P	^{N}Ḏ	^{N}Ḏ	^{N}Ḏ	–
									dhu	na	su	na	sa	khi	yāṅ	–
	x				2				0				3			
1.	PḎ	PṠ	ṘṠ	Ġ̱Ṙ	ṠṈ	ḎP	^{N}Ḏ^{N}Ḏ	ṠṠ	M	M	P	P	^{N}Ḏ	^{N}Ḏ	^{N}Ḏ	–
	ā-	—	—	—	—	—	—	—	dhu	na	su	na	sa	khi	yāṅ	–
	x				2				0				3			
2.	ṠṈ	ḎP	MG̱	RS	SR	MP	^{N}Ḏ^{N}Ḏ	ṠṠ	M	M	P	P	^{N}Ḏ	^{N}Ḏ	^{N}Ḏ	–
	ā-	—	—	—	—	—	—	—	dhu	na	su	na	sa	khi	yāṅ	–
	x				2				0				3			
3.	ṠṘ	Ġ̱Ṡ	ṘĠ̱	ṘṠ	ṘṘ	ṠṈ	^{N}Ḏ^{N}Ḏ	ṠṠ	M	M	P	P	^{N}Ḏ	^{N}Ḏ	^{N}Ḏ	–
	ā-	—	—	—	—	—	—	—	dhu	na	su	na	sa	khi	yāṅ	–
	x				2				0				3			
4.	MP	ḎM	PḎ	MP	ḎP	MG̱	RS	ṈS	ṠṘ	Ġ̱Ṡ	ṘĠ̱	ṠṘ	Ġ̱Ṙ	ṠṈ	ḎP	MP
	ā-	—	—	—	—	—	—	—	—	—	—	—	—	—	—	—
	x				2				0				3			
	SR	G̱S	RG̱	SR	MP	ḎP	D̳D̳	ṠṠ	M	M	P	P	^{N}Ḏ	^{N}Ḏ	^{N}Ḏ	–
	—	—	—	—	—	—	—	—	dhu	na	su	na	sa	khi	yāṅ	–
	x				2				0				3			
	Ṡ	–	Ṡ	Ṡ	Ṙ	Ṉ	Ṡ	Ṡ	^{N}Ḏ	–	Ḏ	Ḏ	Ṡ	Ṡ	Ṡ	Ṙ
	rī	–	jha	ta	u	na	pa	ra	gvā	–	la	bā	–	la	bhu	–
	x				2				0				3			
	ṠṘ	Ġ̱	Ṙ	ṠṘ	Ṉ	Ṡ	Ḏ	P	Ḏ	Ḏ	P	P	G̱	G̱	R	S
	le-	–	sa	ba-	su	dhi	ta	ja	ma	dhu	ba	na	bī	ca	ja	ba
	x				2				0				3			
	Ṡ	Ġ̱	Ṙ	Ṡ	ṠṘ	Ṉ	Ḏ	P	^{D}M	M	P	S	^{N}Ḏ	P	PḎ	MP
	tā	–	na	su	nā-	–	ye	–	ma	dhu	ra	ma	dhu	ra	dhu-	na-
	x				2				0				3			
	G̱	G̱	^{G}R	S	MM	PṠ	ḎP	PḎMP	MM	PṠ	ḎP	PḎMP	MM	PṠ	ḎP	PḎMP
	mu	ra	lī	ba	madhu	rama	dhura	dhu-ra-	madhu	rama	dhura	dhu-ra	madhu	rama	dhura	dhu-na-
	x				2	sing the first line of *sthā.yī* slowly and end the composition.										

COMPOSITION 2

Rā.g Āsā.va.rī lak.ṣaṇ-gī.t, tī.n-tā.l—medium tempo

Text[18]:

sthā.yī *kān.hā mo.he ā.sā.va.rī rā.ga su.nā.ye, ga ni ko a.dhi.ro.ha.na meṅ chu.pā.ye, sare mare mapa dhapa dhaga resa reni dhapa*

an.ta.rā *dhai.va.ta vā.dī ga sa.ma.vā.dī, ma.dhya.ma su.ra.ra gra.ha nyā.sa su.pañ.ca.ma a.va.ro.ha.na sam.pū.ra.na di.khā.va.ta, sare mare mapa dhapa dhaga resa reni dhapa*

Meaning: Krishna is playing *rā.g Ā.sā.va.rī.* He is deftfully hiding *ga* and *ni* in ascent. The melody he is playing has notes *sa re ma re ma pa dha ġa re ṡa re ni dha pa.*

The note *dha* is *vā.dī* and *ga* is *sam.vā.dī* and *ma* is also emphasized in this *rā.g. Pa* is a note on which melodic pieces are ended while improvising. The descent has all the seven notes.

[18]Nawab Ali Khan (Lakhimpur, 1953). It is also mentioned in *Hindustānī Saṅgīt Paddhati Kramik Pustak Mālikā* (Hathras: Sangeet Karyalaya, 1954), vol. II, pp. 359-60.

COMPOSITION 2: *Notation*

								sthā.yī							
								$^{\underline{D}}$M	PṠ	^{N}Ḏ	P	PḎ	M	^{M}PḎ	^{P}MP
								kā	*nhā*	*-mo*	*he*	*ā-*	*sā*	*va-*	*rī-*
								0				3			
^{M}G̱	–	$^{\underline{G}}$R	S	^{M}G̱	M	P	–	^{N}Ḏ	^{N}Ḏ	^{N}Ḏ	–	$^{\underline{D}}$Ṉ	Ḏ	P	ḎM
rā	–	*ga*	*su*	*nā*	–	*ye*	–	*ga*	*ni*	*ko*	–	*a*	*dhi*	*ro*	--
x				2				0				3			
^{P}M	P	^{M}PḎ	MP	^{M}G̱	–	^{S}R	S	S	R	M	R	M	P	Ḏ	P
ha	*na*	*meṅ-*	*chu-*	*pā*	–	*ye*	–	*sa*	*re*	*ma*	*re*	*ma*	*pa*	*dha*	*pa*
x				2				0				3			
^{N}Ḏ	$^{\underline{D}}$Ġ̱	Ṙ	Ṡ	Ṙ	Ṉ	Ḏ	P								
dha	*ga*	*re*	*sa*	*re*	*ni*	*dha*	*pa*								
x				2											
								an.ta.rā							
								^{P}M	–	P	^{M}P	^{N}Ḏ	–	^{N}Ḏ	–
								dhai	–	*va*	*ta*	*vā*	–	*dī*	–
								0				3			
$^{\underline{D}}$Ṡ̱	–	Ṡ	Ṡ	Ṙ	Ṉ	Ṡ	–	^{N}Ḏ	–	^{N}Ḏ	^{N}Ḏ	Ṡ	Ṡ	Ṡ	Ṡ
ga	–	*sam*	–	*vā*	–	*dī*	–	*ma*	–	*dhya*	*ma*	*su*	*ra*	*gra*	*ha*
x				2				0				3			
ṠṘ	^{M}Ġ̱	^{S}Ṙ	Ṡ	ṠṘ	Ṉ	Ḏ	P	M	P	^{P}Ṡ̱	–	^{N}Ḏ	P	^{M}PḎ	MP
nyā-	–	*sa*	*su*	*pañ*	–	*ca*	*ma*	*a*	*va*	*ro*	–	*ha*	*na*	*sa-*	--
x				2				0				3			
^{M}G̱	^{M}G̱	R	S	R	–	S	S	S	R	M	R	M	P	^{N}Ḏ	P
pu	*ra*	*na*	*di*	*khā*	–	*va*	*ta*	*sa*	*re*	*ma*	*re*	*ma*	*pa*	*dha*	*pa*
x				2				0				3			
^{N}Ḏ	$^{\underline{D}}$Ġ̱	Ṙ	Ṡ	Ṙ	Ṉ	D	P								
dha	*ga*	*re*	*sa*	*re*	*ni*	*dha*	*pa*								

COMPOSITION 3

Rā.g Āsā.va.rī, tī.n-tā.l—medium tempo

Text[19]:

sthā.yī *aṅ.khi.yāṅ lā.gī ra.ha.ta ni.sa.di.na, pyā.re ti.hā.re de.kh.na kā.hīṅ*

an.ta.rā *ghā.ri pa.la chi.na mo.he ju.ga sī bī.ta.ta ni.sa.di.na a.ca.pa.la lā.ga ra.ha.ta to.hīṅ*

Meaning: My eyes are desperate to see you day and night. A moment passes like an era for me, and I think about you constantly.

[19]V.N. Bhatkhande, op. cit. (Hathras: Sangeet Karyalaya, 1954), vol. II, pp. 360-61.

									sthā.yī			^{P}M	M	P	Ṡ
												aṅ	*khi*	*yāṅ*	–
x												3			
^{N}Ḏ	–	P	–	^{P}Ḏ	M	^{M}Ḏ^{P}Ḏ	PMP	^{M}G̱	–	^{S}R	S	^{G}R	S	S	R
lā	–	*gī*	–	*ra*	*ha*	*ta-*	*ni--*	*sa*	–	*di*	*na*	*pyā*	–	*re*	*ti*
x				2				0				3			
^{N}Ḏ	P	S	–	^{M}R	M	^{M}Ḏ^{P}Ḏ	PMP	^{M}G̱	–	^{S}R	S	^{G}R	S	S	R
hā	–	*re*	–	*de*	–	*kha-*	*na--*	*kā*	–	–	*hīṅ*				
x				2				0				3			
									an.ta.rā						
												^{P}M	P	^{N}Ḏ	^{N}Ḏ
												gha	*ri*	*pa*	*la*
												3			
Ṡ	Ṡ	Ṡ	Ṡ	Ṙ	Ġ̱	^{Ṡ}R	Ṡ	^{N}Ṡ̱	ṘṈ	Ḏ	P	^{M}P	^{P}Ġ̱	^{Ṡ}R	Ṡ
chi	*na*	*mo*	*he*	*ju*	*ga*	*sī*	–	*bī*	--	*ta*	*ta*	*ni*	*sa*	*di*	*na*
x				2				0				3			
Ṙ	Ṡ	^{N}Ḏ	P	M	P	^{P}Ḏ^{P}Ḏ	PMP	^{M}G̱	G̱	^{S}R	S				
a	*ca*	*pa*	*la*	*lā*	–	*ga-*	*ra--*	*ha*	*ta*	*to*	*hīṅ*				

Rā.g Bhai.ra.vī

Melodic Pattern

ā.ro.h (ascent)	–	*S R G M P D N Ṡ*
a.va.ro.h (descent)	–	*Ṡ N D P M G R S*
vā.dī (prominent note)	–	*S*
sam.vā.dī (consonant of *vā.dī*)	–	*P*
sa.ma.y (time)	–	morning

mu.khy svar saṅ.ga.ti (chief combinations of notes)—*NS, GMP, PMDP, DPMG, SRS*

Stage 1

muk.t ā.lā.p

1. *S..., ^{N}D-N-S..., S-R-^{R}G-S-*
2. *PDNS R-GR-S..., ^{S}N ^{R}S ^{M}G ^{P}MP..., P M G R-S...*
3. *NSGMP DP...,S G M D-P..., D M R..S R G S..DNS..*
4. *S...NSGMPDP...,M D P..., D M ^{G}R-S R G S -D N S..*

Stage 2

COMPOSITION 1

Text[20]:

sthā.yī *bha.vā.nī da.yā.nī ma.hā vā.ka.vā.nī, su.ra na.ra mu.ni.ja.na mā.nī sa.ka.la bu.dha jñā.nī*

an.ta.rā *ja.ga ja.na.nī ja.ga jā.nī, ma.hi.sā.su.ra ma.ra.di.nī, jvā.lā.mu.khī can.dī a.ma.ra.pa.da dānī*

Meaning: O, goddess Bhavānī (epithet of the Goddess Pārvatī, consort of God Śiva), You are kind-hearted. You are the great goddess of speech. You are esteemed by all the deities, human beings, seers, and wise people. You are the Mother of the world and the great seer. You are the slayer of the demon Mahiṣāsura. You are Jvālāmukhī (have the fierceness of volcanoes) and Caṇḍī (fierce form of the goddess Pārvatī). You are the giver of immortality.

[20] V.N. Bhatkhande, op. cit. (Hathras: Sangeet Karyalaya, 1954), vol. II, pp. 415-16.

COMPOSITION 1: *Notation* — *Rā.g Bhai.ra.vī, jhap-tā.l*—medium tempo

					sthā.yī				Ḏ
									bha
							3		
Ṡ	–	Ṡ	–	^{S}Ṟ̇	Ṡ	–	^{N}Ḏ	P	P
vā	–	*nī*	–	*da*	*yā*	–	*nī*	–	*ma*
x		2			0		3		
Ṉ	–	Ḏ	–	P	P	–	G̱	–	M
hā	–	*vā*	–	*ka*	*vā*	–	*nī*	–	*su*
x		2			0		3		
P	^{P}Ṉ	Ḏ	P	P	^{M}G̱	^{M}G̱	Ṟ	–	S
ra	*na*	*ra*	*mu*	*ni*	*ja*	*na*	*mā*	–	*nī*
x		2			0		3		
Ġ̱	Ġ̱	Ġ̱	Ṟ̇	Ṟ̇	Ṡ	–	^{N}Ḏ	–	Ṉ
sa	*ka*	*la*	*bu*	*dhu*	*jyā*	–	*nī*	–	*bha*
x		2			0		3		
					an.ta.rā				
^{P}Ḏ	M	Ḏ	Ḏ	Ṉ	Ṡ	Ṡ	Ṡ	–	Ṡ
ja	*ga*	*ja*	*na*	*nī*	*ja*	*ga*	*jā*	–	*nī*
x		2			0		3		
$^{\dot{S}}$Ṟ̇	Ṟ̇	Ṟ̇	–	Ṟ̇	Ġ̱	Ṟ̇	Ṟ̇	Ṡ	Ṡ
ma	*hi*	*sā*	–	*su*	*ra*	*ma*	*ra*	*di*	*nī*
x		2			0		3		
$^{\dot{S}}$Ġ̱	–	$^{\dot{R}}$Ġ̱	–	Ṁ	^{G}Ṟ	–	Ṡ	–	Ṡ
jvā	–	*lā*	–	*mu*	*khī*	–	*caṇ*	–	*ḍī*
x		2			0		3		
P	Ḏ	Ṉ	Ṡ	Ṟ̇	Ṡ	–	Ḏ	–	Ṉ
a	*ma*	*ra*	*pa*	*da*	*dā*	–	*nī*	–	*bha*

Stage 3

ā.lā.p-sthā.yī

										Ḏ
										bha
								3		
	Ṡ	–	Ṡ	–	$^{\dot{S}}\underline{\dot{R}}$	Ṡ	–	$^{N}\underline{D}$	*P*	–
	vā	–	*nī*	–	*da*	*yā*	–	*nī*	–	–
	x		2			0		3		
1.	*P*	–	*M*	G̱	–	$^{S}\underline{R}$	–	*S*	–	Ḏ
	ā	–	–	–	–	–	–	–	–	*bha*
	x		2			0		3		
	Ṡ	–	Ṡ	–	$^{\dot{S}}\underline{\dot{R}}$	Ṡ	–	$^{N}\underline{D}$	*P*	Ḏ
	vā	–	*nī*	–	*da*	*yā*	–	*nī*	–	*bha*
	x		2			0		3		
2.	Ṡ	–	Ṡ	–	$\underline{\dot{R}}$	*S*	Ḏ	–	–	–
	vā	–	*nī*	–	*da*	*ā*	–	–	–	–
	x		2			0		3		
	Ḏ	*M*	*P*	–	G̱	*M*	–	Ṟ*S*	–	Ḏ
	–	–	–	–	–	–	–	––	–	*bha*
	x		2			0		3		
	Ṡ	–	Ṡ	–	$^{\dot{S}}\underline{\dot{R}}$	Ṡ	–	$^{N}\underline{D}$	*P*	–
	vā	–	*nī*	–	*da*	*yā*	–	*nī*	–	–
	x		2			0		3		

3.	G̱M	Ḏ	Ṉ	–	–	–	Ṡ	–	–	–
	ā	–	–	–	–	–	–	–	–	–
	x		2			0		3		
	Ṟ̇	Ṡ	–	Ḏ	P	–	Ṉ	Ḏ	P	Ḏ
	–	–	–	–	–	–	–	–	–	bha
	x		2			0		3		
	Ṡ	–	Ṡ	–	$^{\dot{S}}$Ṟ̇	Ṡ	–	^{N}Ḏ	P	–
	vā	–	nī	–	da	yā	–	nī	–	–
	x		2			0		3		
4.	PḎ	N̲Ṡ̲	Ṙ̲Ġ̲	–	Ġ̱Ṁ	Ṟ̇	–	Ṡ	–	Ḏ
	ā	--	--	–	--	–	–	–	–	bha
	x		2			0		2		
	Ṡ	–	Ḏ	P	Ḏ	Ṡ	–	Ḏ	P	Ḏ
	vā	–	nī	–	bha	vā	–	nī	–	bha
	x		2			0		3		
	Ṡ	–	Ṡ	–	Ṟ̇	Ṡ	–	Ḏ	P	–
	vā	–	nī	–	da	yā	–	nī	–	–
	x		2			0		3		

ā.lā.p-an.ta.rā

	Ḏ	*M*	*Ḏ*	*Ḏ*	*Ṉ*	*Ṡ*	*Ṡ*	*Ṡ*	–	*Ṡ*
	ja	*ga*	*ja*	*na*	*nī*	*ja*	*ga*	*jā*	–	*nī*
	x		2			0		3		
1.	*Ṡ*	–	–	–	*Ṟ̇*	–	*Ḏ*	–	*Ṡ*	–
	ā	–	–		–	–		–		–
	x		2			0		3		
2.	^{P}*Ḏ*	*M*	*Ḏ*	*Ḏ*	*Ṉ*	*Ṡ*	–	*Ṟ̇*	–	*Ġ*
	ja	*ga*	*ja*	*na*	*nī*	*ā*	–	–	–	–
	x		2			0		3		
	–	–	–	*Ṟ̇*	–	^{N}*Ḏ*	^{N}*Ḏ*	*Ṡ*	–	–
	–	–	–	–	–	–	–	–	–	–
	x		2			0		3		
3.	^{P}*Ḏ*	*M*	*Ḏ*	*Ḏ*	*Ṉ*	*ṠṞ̇*	*Ġ*	–	*M*	^{G}*Ṟ̇*
	ja	*ga*	*ja*	*na*	*nī*	*ā*	–	–	–	–
	x		2			0		3		
	–	–	*Ṡ*	–	*Ṟ̇*	*Ṉ*	*Ḏ*	–	*Ṡ*	–
	–		–	–	–	–	–	–	–	–
	x		2			0		3		
	Ḏ	*M*	*Ḏ*	*Ḏ*	*Ṉ*	*Ṡ*	*Ṡ*	*Ṡ*	–	*Ṡ*
	ja	*ga*	*ja*	*na*	*nī*	*ja*	*ga*	*jā*	–	*nī*
	x		2			0		3		
	Ṟ̇	*Ṟ̇*	*Ṟ̇*	–	*Ṟ̇*	*Ġ*	*Ṟ̇*	*Ṟ̇*	*Ṡ*	*Ṡ*
	ma	*hi*	*sā*	–	*su*	*ra*	*ma*	*ra*	*di*	*nī*
	x		2			0		3		
	^{S}*Ġ*	–	^{R}*Ġ*	–	*Ṁ*	^{G}*Ṟ̇*	–	*Ṡ*	–	*Ṡ*
	jvā	–	*lā*	–	*mu*	*khī*	–	*caṇ*	–	*ḍī*
	x		2			0		3		
	P	*Ḏ*	*Ṉ*	*Ṡ*	*Ṟ̇*	*Ṡ*	–	*Ḏ*	–	*Ḏ*
	a	*ma*	*ra*	*pa*	*da*	*dā*	–	*nī*	–	*bha*
	x		2			0		3		

Stage 4 (increase your tempo a little)

tā.n-sthā.yī

									Ḏ	
										bha
	x		2			0		3		
	Ṡ	–	Ṡ	–	Ṟ̇	Ṡ	–	Ḏ	P	–
	vā	–	*nī*	–	*da*	*yā*	–	*nī*	–	–
	x		2			0		3		
1.	G̱M	PḎ	PM	G̱M	PḎ	ND	PM	GṞ	SS	Ḏ
	ā-	––	––	––	––	––	––	––	––	*bha*
	x		2			0		3		
2.	Ṡ	–	Ṡ	–	Ṡ	DD	MM	PP	MM	DD
	vā	–	*nī*	–	–	*ā-*	––	––	––	––
	x		2			0		3		
	PP	NN	ḎP	ṠṈ	ḎP	MP	ḎP	MG̱	ṞS	Ḏ
	––	––	––	––	––	––	––	––	––	*bha*
	x		2			0		3		
	Ṡ	–	Ṡ	–	ṠṞ̇	S	–	ᴺḎ	P	Ḏ
	vā	–	*nī*	–	*da-*	*yā*	–	*nī*	–	*bha*
	x		2			0		3		
3.	Ṡ	–	Ṡ	–	–	ĠĠ	ṘĠ	ĠṞ̇	ĠĠ	Ṟ̇Ṡ
	vā	–	*nī*	–	–	*ā-*	––	––	––	––
	x		2			0		3		
	ṘṘ	ṠṞ̇	Ṟ̇Ṡ	ṘṘ	ṠṈ	ḎP	G̱M	GṞ	SS	Ḏ
	––	––	––	––	––	––	––	––	––	*bha*
	x		2			0		3		
	Ṡ	–	Ṡ	–	Ṟ̇	Ṡ	–	Ḏ	P	–
	vā	–	*nī*	–	*da*	*yā*	–	*nī*	–	–
	x		2			0		3		

tā.n-an.ta.rā

	Ḏ	M	Ḏ	Ḏ	N̠	Ṡ	Ṡ	Ṡ	–	Ṡ
	ja	*ga*	*ja*	*na*	*nī*	*ja*	*ga*	*jā*	–	*nī*
	x		2			0		3		
1.	ṠṘ̠	ṠN̠	ṠN̠	D̲N̲	ḎP	ḎP	MP	G̠M	D̲N̲	ṠṠ
	ā-	––	––	––	––	––	––	––	––	––
	x		2			0		3		
	Ḏ	M	Ḏ	Ḏ	N̠	Ṡ	Ṡ	Ṡ	–	Ṡ
	ja	*ga*	*ja*	*na*	*nī*	*ja*	*ga*	*jā*	–	*nī*
	x		2			0		3		
2.	ṠN̠	ḎP	D̲N̲	ḎP	MG̠	R̠S	G̠M	D̲N̲	D̲N̲	ṠṠ
	ā-	––	––	––	––	––	––	––	––	––
	x		2			0		3		
	Ḏ	M	Ḏ	Ḏ	N̠	Ṡ	Ṡ	Ṡ	–	Ṡ
	ja	*ga*	*ja*	*na*	*nī*	*ja*	*ga*	*jā*	–	*nī*
	x		2			0		3		
3.	ṠṘ̠	G̠Ṁ	G̲Ṙ̲	ṠṘ̠	G̲Ṙ̲	ṠN̠	ḎP	G̠M	D̲N̲	ṠṠ
	ā-	––	––	––	––	––	––	––	––	––
	x		2			0		3		
	Ḏ	M	Ḏ	Ḏ	N̠	Ṡ	Ṡ	Ṡ	–	Ṡ
	ja	*ga*	*ja*	*na*	*nī*	*ja*	*ga*	*jā*	–	*nī*
	x		2			0		3		

sing the whole *an.ta.rā* and conclude with N̠ *bha*

							3		
Ṡ	–	Ṡ	–	Ṙ̠	Ṡ	N̲Ṡ̲	Ḏ	P	N̠
vā	–	*nī*	–	*da*	*yā*	––	*nī*	–	*bha*
x		2			0		3		
Ṡ	–	Ḏ	P	Ḏ	Ṡ	–	Ḏ	P	Ḏ
vā	–	*nī*	–	*bhu*	*vā*	–	*nī*	–	*bha*
x		2			0		3	sing the whole line.	

COMPOSITION 2

Text[21]: *Rā.g Bhai.ra.vī-Sar.gam, tīn-tā.l*—medium tempo

								sthā.yī							
								G̱	*G̱*	*Ṟ*	*S*	*Ṉ*	*S*	*Ḏ*	–
								0				3			
Ṉ	*Ḏ*	–	*G̱*	*M*	*Ḏ*	*M*	*P*	*G̱*	*M*	*G̱*	*Ṟ*	*S*	*Ṉ*	*Ḏ*	–
x				2				0				3			
M	*Ḏ*	*Ṉ*	*G̱*	–	*M*	*Ḏ*	–	*Ṉ*	*Ṡ*	–	*Ṟ̇*	*Ṡ*	*Ṉ*	*Ḏ*	*P*
x				2				0				3			
P	*Ṉ*	*Ḏ*	*P*	*M*	*G̱*	*Ṟ*	*S*								
x				2				0				3			
								an.ta.rā							
								Ṉ	*Ṉ*	*Ḏ*	*Ṉ*	*Ḏ*	*P*	*M*	*G̱*
								0				3			
M	*Ḏ*	*Ṉ*	*Ṡ*	*Ḏ*	*Ṉ*	*Ṡ*	–	*Ġ̱*	*Ṁ*	*Ġ̱*	*Ṟ̇*	*Ṡ*	*Ṉ*	*Ḏ*	*Ṉ*
x				2				0				3			
Ġ̱	–	*Ṡ*	–	*Ṟ̇*	*Ṉ*	*Ṡ*	–	*Ḏ*	–	*Ṉ*	*M*	–	*Ḏ*	*G̱*	–
x				2				0				3			
M	*Ṉ*	*Ḏ*	*P*	*M*	*G̱*	*Ṟ*	*S*								
x				2				0				3			

[21] V.N. Bhatkhande, op. cit. (Hathras: Sangeet Karyalaya, 1954), vol. II, p. 392.

Composition 2

Rā.g Bhai.ra.vī, tīn-tā.l—medium tempo

Text[22]:

sthā.yī *mu.ra.li.yā bā.je ā.ja ma.dhu.ba.na meṅ su.rī.lī ā.lī su.dha na ra.hī ta.na ma.na meṅ*

an.ta.rā *a.dha.ra ma.dhu.ra dhu.na mu.ra.lī ba.jā.ye, śyā.ma sun.da.ra sa.khī ni.ra.ta ka.ra.ta. kuñ.ja.na meṅ*

Meaning: (Krishna) is playing a sweet melody today in Madhubana (a forest in Brij). O my friend, it is so enchanting that I lost awarensess of my body and mind.

His lips are playing the sweet melody on the flute. O my friend, Śyāma Sundara (Krishna) is dancing in the groves.

[22] Nawab Ali Khan (Lakhimpur: 1954).

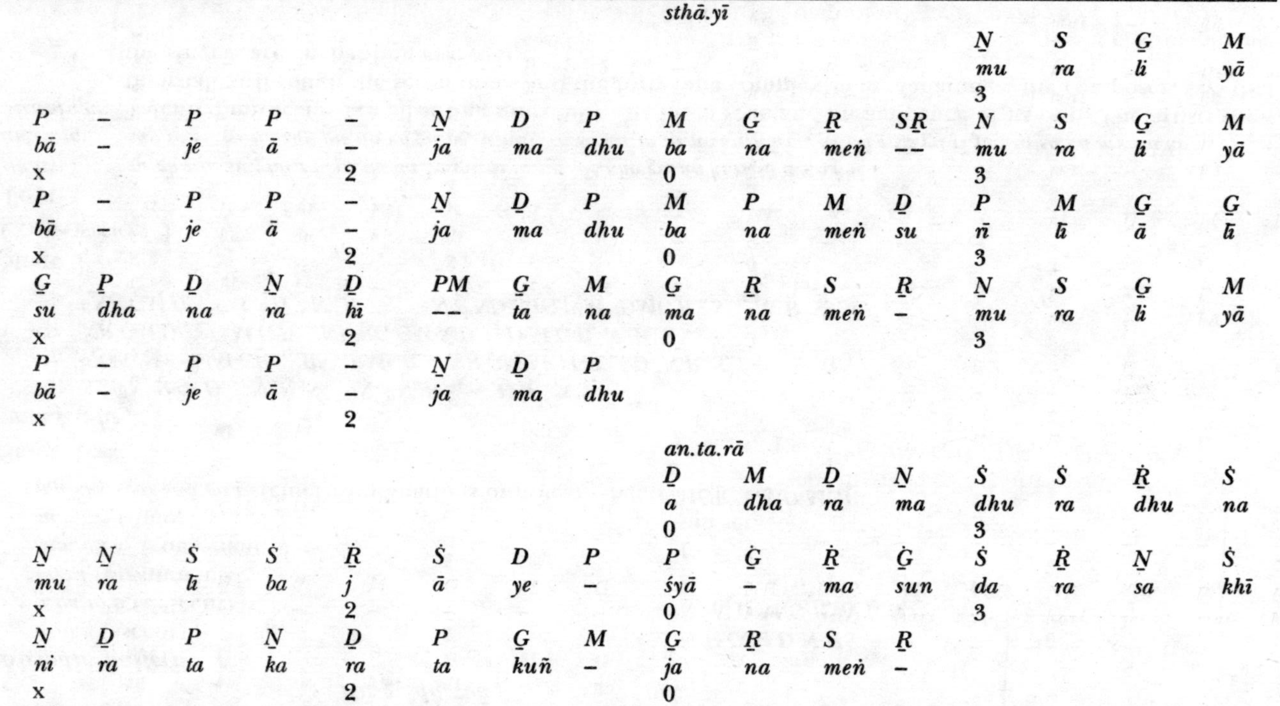

Notation

								sthā.yī							
												N̠	S	G̠	M
												mu	*ra*	*li*	*yā*
												3			
P	–	P	P	–	N̠	D	P	M	G̠	R̠	SR̠	N	S	G̠	M
bā	–	*je*	*ā*	–	*ja*	*ma*	*dhu*	*ba*	*na*	*meṅ*	––	*mu*	*ra*	*li*	*yā*
x				2				0				3			
P	–	P	P	–	N̠	D̠	P	M	P	M	D̠	P	M	G̠	G̠
bā	–	*je*	*ā*	–	*ja*	*ma*	*dhu*	*ba*	*na*	*meṅ*	*su*	*rī*	*lī*	*ā*	*lī*
x				2				0				3			
G̠	P̠	D̠	N̠	D̠	PM	G̠	M	G̠	R̠	S	R̠	N̠	S	G̠	M
su	*dha*	*na*	*ra*	*hī*	––	*ta*	*na*	*ma*	*na*	*meṅ*	–	*mu*	*ra*	*li*	*yā*
x				2				0				3			
P	–	P	P	–	N̠	D̠	P								
bā	–	*je*	*ā*	–	*ja*	*ma*	*dhu*								
x				2											
								an.ta.rā							
								D̠	M	D̠	N̠	Ṡ	Ṡ	Ṙ̠	Ṡ
								a	*dha*	*ra*	*ma*	*dhu*	*ra*	*dhu*	*na*
								0				3			
N̠	N̠	Ṡ	Ṡ	Ṙ̠	Ṡ	D	P	P	Ġ̠	Ṙ̠	Ġ̠	Ṡ	Ṙ̠	N̠	Ṡ
mu	*ra*	*lī*	*ba*	*j*	*ā*	*ye*	–	*śyā*	–	*ma*	*sun*	*da*	*ra*	*sa*	*khī*
x				2				0				3			
N̠	D̠	P	N̠	D̠	P	G̠	M	G̠	R̠	S	R̠				
ni	*ra*	*ta*	*ka*	*ra*	*ta*	*kuñ*	–	*ja*	*na*	*meṅ*	–				
x				2				0							

Rā.g Mā.rvā

Melodic pattern

- *ā.ro.h* (ascent) – *N R̲ G Ṁ D N Ṙ̲ Ṡ*
- *a.va.ro.h* (descent) – *Ṙ̲, N D M G R̲, N R̲ S*
- *vā.dī* (prominent) – *D*
- *sam.vā.dī* (consonant of *vā.dī*) – *R̲*
- *sa.ma.y* (time) – sun set
- *mu.khy svar saṅ.ga.ti* (chief combinations of notes)—*NR̲, GṀGR̲, GṀD-ṀGR̲-*

Stage 1

muk.t ā.lā.p

1. *S...,^{R}N̩, R̲..N̩D..., N̩..R̲..S..., ^{R}N̩..^{R}N̩..R̲..., N̩..D̩..R̲...S...*
2. *^{R}N̲R̲G^{D}M...MM GR̲..., RNGR̲ṀGR̲..., NR̲ GṀ ṀG GR̲..., D..N R̲..S...*
3. *NR̲ GṀ D..., D Ṁ G R̲...,NR̲ R̲G GṀ ṀD..., D Ṁ G R̲, N..R̲..S...*
4. *^{R}N̲R̲ GṀ D..., ^{D}Ṁ..^{N}D..^{R}N..Ṙ̲...Ṡ..., ^{R}N R̲ ND..ṀG., ^{D}M^{M}DṀG R̲...S..., N..R̲..S....*

Stage 2

COMPOSITION 1

Text[23]:

sthā.yī *su.gha.ra su.gha.ra bai.ṭhe sa.ba gu.ṇi ja.na, de.kho gu.na kī rī.ta a.no.khī*

an.ta.rā *sap.ta su.ra.na soṅ gu.ṇa ko gā.ve, u.nan.cā.sa kū.ta tā.na su.nā.ve, sa.dā.raṅ.ga rī.jha.ta sa.ba ma.na ko*

Meaning: Talented musicians are all sitting gracefully. Art has a style and an ambience of its own. The artists show their talent through the seven notes and the forty-nine complex *tā.ns*. Sadāraṅga, the composer, says that the singers are enchanting everyone.

[23] V.N. Bhatkhande, op. cit. (Hathras: Sangeet Karyalaya, 1954), vol. II, pp. 290-91.

Composition 1: *Notation*

Rā.g Mār.vā, tīn-tā.ƚ—medium tempo

								sthā.yī							
								D	*D*	*Ṁ*	*D*	*Ṁ*	*G*	*R̠*	–
								su	*gha*	*ra*	*su*	*gha*	*ra*	*bai*	–
								0				3			
SR̠	*G*	*G*	*Ṁ*	*G*	*R̠*	*S*	*S*	*M*	–	*D*	–	*S*	*S*	*S*	–
ṭhe-	–	*sa*	*ba*	*gu*	*ni*	*ja*	*na*	*de*	–	*kho*	–	*gu*	*ṇa*	*kā*	–
x				2				0				3			
SR̠	*G*	*G*	*Ṁ*	*G*	*R̠*	*S*	–								
rī	–	*ta*	*a*	*no*	–	*khī*	–								
x				2											
								an.ta.rā							
								Ṁ	–	*G*	*G*	^{D}*Ṁ*	*Ṁ*	*D*	–
								sa	–	*pta*	*su*	*ra*	*na*	*soṅ*	–
								0				3			
Ṁ	*Ṁ*	*Ṡ*	–	*Ṡ*	–	*Ṡ*	–	^{N}*Ṡ*	*Ṡ*	–	^{Ṡ}*N*	–	*Ṙ̠*	*N*	–
gu	*ṇa*	*ko*	–	*gā*	–	*ve*	–	*u*	*nan*	–	*cā*	–	*sa*	*ku*	–
x				2				0				3			
Ṙ̠	*N*	–	*DD*	*Ṁ*	*D*	*Ṁ*	*G*	*Ṁ*	*R̠*	–	*G*	–	*G*	^{D}*N*	^{D}*N*
ta	*tā*	–	*nasu*	*nā*	–	*ve*	–	*sa*	*dā*	–	*raṅ*	–	*ga*	*rī*	–
x				2				0				3			
D	*Ṁ*	*G*	*Ṁ*	*G*	*R̠*	*S*	–								
jha	*ta*	*sa*	*ba*	*ma*	*na*	*ko*									
x				2											

Stage 3

ā.lā.p-sthā.yī								*D*	*D*	*Ṁ*	*D*	*Ṁ*	*G*	*R̲*	–	
									su	*gha*	*ra*	*su*	*gha*	*ra*	*bai*	–
	x				2				0				3			
1.	*S*	–	*N*	*R̲*	–	–	*S*	–	*D*	*D*	*Ṁ*	*D*	*Ṁ*	*G*	*R̲*	–
	ā	–	–	–	–	–	–	–	*su*	*gha*	*ra*	*su*	*gha*	*ra*	*bai*	–
	x				2				0				3			
2.	*N*	*D*	–	–	*Ṁ*	*D*	*R̲*	*S*	*D*	*D*	*Ṁ*	*D*	*Ṁ*	*G*	*R̲*	–
	ā	–	–	–	–	–	–	–	*su*	*gha*	*ra*	*su*	*gha*	*ra*	*bai*	–
	x				2				0				3			
3.	*SR̲*	*G*	*G*	*Ṁ*	*G*	*R̲*	*S*	*S*	*NR̲*	*GṀ*	–	–	*ṀṀ*	*GR̲*	–	–
	ṭhe-	–	*sa*	*ba*	*gu*	*ni*	*ja*	*na*	*ā*	––	–	–	––	––	–	–
	x				2				0				3			
	N	*D*	–	–	*R̲*	–	*S*	–	*D*	*D*	*Ṁ*	*D*	*Ṁ*	*G*	*R̲*	–
	–	–	–	–	–	–	–	–	*su*	*gha*	*ra*	*su*	*gha*	*ra*	*bai*	–
	x				2				0				3			
4.	*NR̲*	*GṀ*	*D*	–	–	–	*ᴰṀ*	*ᴰṀ*	*D*	*Ṁ*	*G*	*R̲*	–	–	*Ṁ*	*ᴹ̇D*
	ā	–	–	–	–	–	–	–	–	–	–	–	–	–	–	–
	x				2				0				3			
	Ṁ	*G*	*R̲*	–	–	–	*S*	–	*D*	*D*	*Ṁ*	*D*	*Ṁ*	*G*	*R̲*	–
	–	–	–	–	–	–	–	–	*su*	*gha*	*ra*	*su*	*gha*	*ra*	*bai*	–
	x				2				0				3			
5.	*NR̲*	*GṀ*	*ᴺD*	*ᴿN*	*Ṙ̲*	–	–	–	*Ṡ*	–	–	–	*ᴿ̇N*	*ᴺṘ̲*	*N*	–
	ā-	—	–	–	–	–	–	–	–	–	–	–	–	–	–	–
	x				2				0				3			
	D	–	*Ṁ*	*G*	*R̲*	–	*S*	–	*DD*	*ṀṀ*	*DD*	*ṀṀ*	*DD*	*ṀD*	*ṀG*	*R̲S*
	–	–	–	–	–	–	–	–	*sugha*	*ra-*	*sugha*	*ra-*	*sugha*	*rasu*	*ghara*	*bai-*
	x				2				0				3			
	SR̲	*G*	*G*	*Ṁ*	*G*	*R̲*	*S*	*S*								
	ṭhe-	–	*sa*	*ba*	*gu*	*ni*	*ja*	*na*								

ā.lā.p-an.ta.rā									$^{D}\dot{M}$	–	*G*	*G*	$^{D}\dot{M}$	*Ṁ*	*D*	–
									sa	–	*pta*	*su*	*ra*	*na*	*soṅ*	–
	x				2				0				3			
1.	*Ṡ*	–	–	–	–	–	–	–	$^{D}\dot{M}$	–	*G*	*G*	$^{D}\dot{M}$	*Ṁ*	*D*	–
	ā	–	–	–	–	–	–	–	*sa*	–	*pta*	*su*	*ra*	*na*	*soṅ*	–
	x				2				0				3			
2.	$^{D}\dot{M}$	^{N}D	*Ṟ̇*	–	*Ṡ*	–	–	–	$^{D}\dot{M}$	–	*G*	*G*	$^{D}\dot{M}$	*Ṁ*	*D*	–
	ā	–	–	–	–	–	–	–	*sa*	–	*pta*	*su*	*ra*	*na*	*soṅ*	–
	x				2				0				3			
3.	*Ṁ*	*Ṁ*	*Ṡ*	–	*Ṡ*	–	*Ṡ*	–	*Ṡ*	–	*N*	*Ṟ̇*	–	–	*Ġ*	–
	gu	*ṇa*	*ko*	–	*gā*	–	*ve*	–	*ā*	–	–	–	–	–	–	–
	x				2				0				3			
	Ṟ̇	–	–	*N*	*Ṟ̇*	–	*Ṡ*	–	$^{D}\dot{M}$	–	*G*	*G*	$^{D}\dot{M}$	*Ṁ*	*D*	–
	–	–	–	–	–	–	–	–	*sa*	–	*pta*	*su*	*ra*	*na*	*soṅ*	–
	x				2				0				3			
4.	*D*	–	*Ṟ̇*	–	*Ṡ*	–	–	–	*N*	*Ṟ̇*	*N*	*D*	*Ṁ*	*D*	*Ṁ*	*G*
	ā	–	–	–	–	–	–	–	–	–	–	–	–	–	–	–
	x				2				0				3			
	$^{D}\dot{M}$	–	^{N}D	^{R}N	*Ṟ̇*	–	*Ṡ*	–	$^{D}\dot{M}$	–	*G*	*G*	$^{D}\dot{M}$	*Ṁ*	*D*	–
	–	–	–	–	–	–	–	–	*sa*	–	*pta*	*su*	*ra*	*na*	*soṅ*	–
	x				2				0				3			
5.	*Ṁ*	*Ṁ*	*Ṡ*	–	*Ṡ*	–	*Ṡ*	–	*N*	–	*Ṟ̇*	–	*Ġ*	*Ṁ*	–	*Ġ*
	gu	*ṇa*	*ko*	–	*gā*	–	*ve*	–	*ā*	–	–	–	–	–	–	–
	x				2				0				3			
	Ṟ̇	–	–	–	*Ṡ*	–	–	–	$^{D}\dot{M}$	–	*G*	*G*	$^{D}\dot{M}$	*Ṁ*	*D*	–
	–	–	–	–	–	–	–	–	*sa*	–	*pta*	*su*	*ra*	*na*	*soṅ*	–
	x				2				0				3			
	Ṁ	*Ṁ*	*Ṡ*	–	–	–	–	–	$^{N}\dot{S}$	*Ṡ*	–	$^{\dot{S}}N$	–	*Ṟ̇*	*N*	–
	gu	*ṇa*	*ko*	–	*gā*	–	*ve*	–	*u*	*nan*	–	*ca*	–	*sa*	*ku*	–
	x	sing the whole *an.ta.rā.*														

Stage 4 (increase your tempo a little)

tā.n-sthā.yī									*D*	*D*	*Ṁ*	*D*	*Ṁ*	*G*	*R̲*	–
									su	*gha*	*ra*	*su*	*gha*	*ra*	*bai*	–
	x				2				0				3			
1.	*NR̲*	*GṀ*	*DṀ*	*GṀ*	*DṀ*	*GṀ*	*GR̲*	*SS*	*D*	*D*	*Ṁ*	*D*	*Ṁ*	*G*	*R̲*	–
	ā-	––	––	––	––	––	––	––	*su*	*gha*	*ra*	*su*	*gha*	*ra*	*bai*	–
	x				2				0				3			
2.	*DN*	*R̲R̲*	*GṀ*	*DD*	*ṀD*	*ṀG*	*R̲R̲*	*SS*	*D*	*D*	*Ṁ*	*D*	*Ṁ*	*G*	*R̲*	–
	ā-	––	––	––	––	––	––	––	*su*	*gha*	*ra*	*su*	*gha*	*ra*	*bai*	–
	x				2				0				3			
3.	*SR̲*	*G*	*G*	*Ṁ*	*G*	*R̲*	*S*	*S*	*NR̲*	*GR̲*	*SS*	*GṀ*	*DṀ*	*GG*	*ṀD*	*ND*
	the	–	*sa*	*ba*	*gu*	*ni*	*ja*	*na*	*ā-*	––	––	––	––	––	––	––
	x				2				0				3			
	ṀṀ	*NR̲*	*GR̲*	*ṠṠ*	*ND*	*ṀG*	*R̲R̲*	*SS*	*D*	*D*	*Ṁ*	*D*	*Ṁ*	*G*	*R̲*	–
	––	––	––	––	––	––	––	––	*su*	*gha*	*ra*	*su*	*gha*	*ra*	*bai*	–
	x				2				0				3			
4.	*NR̲*	*GṀ*	*DD*	*ṀD*	*DṀ*	*DD*	*ṀG*	*Ṙ̲S*	*NR̲*	*GṀ*	*DN*	*ND*	*NN*	*DN*	*ND*	*ṀG*
	ā-	––	––	––	––	––	––	––	––	––	––	––	––	––	––	––
	x				2				0				3			
	Ṙ̲S	*NR̲*	*GṀ*	*DN*	*Ṙ̲N*	*DM*	*GR̲*	*SS*	*D*	*D*	*Ṁ*	*D*	*Ṁ*	*G*	*R̲*	–
	––	––	––	––	––	––	––	––	*su*	*gha*	*ra*	*su*	*gha*	*ra*	*bai*	–
	x				2				0				3			
5.	*SR̲*	*G*	*G*	*Ṁ*	*G*	*R̲*	*S*	*S*	*ṀG*	*ṀG*	*R̲S*	*DṀ*	*DṀ*	*GR̲*	*ND*	*ND*
	the	–	*sa*	*ba*	*gu*	*ni*	*ja*	*na*	*ā-*	––	––	––	––	––	––	––
	x				2				0				3			
	ṀG	*Ṙ̲N*	*Ṙ̲N*	*DṀ*	*GṀ*	*DṀ*	*GR̲*	*SS*	*D*	*D*	*Ṁ*	*D*	*Ṁ*	*G*	*R̲*	–
	––	––	––	––	––	––	––	––	*su*	*gha*	*ra*	*su*	*gha*	*ra*	*bai*	–
	x				2				0				3			
	SR̲	*G*	*G*	*Ṁ*	*G*	*R̲*	*S*	–								
	the	–	*sa*	*ba*	*gu*	*ni*	*ja*	*na*								

tā.n-an.ta.rā									ᴰṀ	–	G	G	ᴰṀ	Ṁ	D	–
									sa	–	*pta*	*su*	*ra*	*na*	*soṅ*	–
	x				2				0				3			
1.	NṚ	ND	ṀD	ṀG	GṀ	DN	Ṛ̲Ṛ̲	ṠṠ	ᴰṀ	–	G	G	ᴰṀ	Ṁ	D	–
	ā-	--	--	--	--	--	--	--	*sa*	–	*pta*	*su*	*ra*	*na*	*soṅ*	–
	x				2				0				3			
2.	DN	ND	NN	DṀ	GṀ	DN	Ṛ̲Ṛ̲	ṠṠ	ᴰM	–	G	G	ᴰṀ	Ṁ	D	–
	ā-	--	--	--	--	--	--	--	*sa*	–	*pta*	*su*	*ra*	*na*	*soṅ*	–
	x				2				0				3			
3.	NṚ	ĠṚ	NṚ	ND	ṀD	ṀG	DN	ṚS	ᴰM	–	G	G	ᴰṀ	Ṁ	D	–
	ā-	--	--	--	--	--	--	--	*sa*	–	*pta*	*su*	*ra*	*na*	*soṅ*	–
	x				2				0				3			
4.	Ṁ	Ṁ	Ṡ	–	Ṡ	–	Ṡ	–	NṚ	ND	MG	RS	NṚ	GṚ	GṀ	GṀ
	gu	*na*	*ko*	–	*gā*	–	*ve*	–	*ā-*	--	--	--	--	--	--	--
	x				2				0				3			
	DṀ	DN	DN	ṚN	ṘĠ	ṘĠ	ṀĠ	Ṛ̲Ṡ̲	ᴰṀ	–	G	G	ᴰṀ	Ṁ	D	–
	--	--	--	--	--	--	--	--	*sa*	–	*pta*	*su*	*ra*	*na*	*soṅ*	–
	x				2				0				3			
5.	Ṁ	Ṁ	Ṡ	–	Ṡ	–	Ṡ	–	NṚ	ND	ND	ṀD	ṀG	ṀG	ṚS	NṚ
	gu	*ṇa*	*ko*	–	*gā*	–	*ve*	–	*ā-*	--	--	--	--	--	--	--
	x				2				0				3			
	NṚ	GṚ	GṀ	GṀ	DṀ	DṀ	DN	ṠṠ	ᴰṀ	–	G	G	ᴰṀ	Ṁ	D	–
	--	--	--	--	--	--	--	--	*sa*	–	*pta*	*su*	*ra*	*na*	*soṅ*	–
	x				2				0				3			
	sing the whole *an.ta.rā* + the first line of *sthā.yī* and conclude with								D	D	Ṁ	D	Ṁ	G	Ṛ	–
									su	*gha*	*ra*	*su*	*gha*	*ra*	*bai*	–
									0				3			
	SṚ	G	G	Ṁ	DD	ṀD	ṀG	R̲R̲	DD	ṀD	ṀG	R̲R̲	DD	ṀD	ṀG	R̲R̲
	the	–	*sa*	*ba*	*sugha*	*rasu*	*ghara*	*bai-*	*sugha*	*rasu*	*ghara*	*bai-*	*sugha*	*rasu*	*ghara*	*bai-*
	x				2				0				3	sing the whole line		

COMPOSITION 2

Rā.g Mār.vā, lak.ṣaṇ-gī.t, jhap-tā.l—medium tempo

Text[24]:

sthā.yī *tī.va.ra ga ma dha ni su.ra me.la.na sa.ja.ta ma.dhu.ra, vi.ka.ra.ta ri.kha.ba bhī.ta.ra. mā.ra.vā ka.ha.ta ca.tu.ra*

an.ta.rā *rā.ga gā.va.ta su.ka.ra pañ.ca.ma. vi.vā.dī su.ra, sam.vā.da re dha bi.ca.ra as.ta di.na a.ti ru.ci.ra.*

Meaning: The notes *ga ma dha ni* which are natural in this *rā.g*, sound sweet. The composer, Catura says that the *rā.g Mā.ra.vā* has *re* flat. Only masters can sing this *rā.g* effortlessly. Note *pa* is used very seldom as *vi.vā.dī*.[25] The notes *dha* and *re* are *vā.dī* and *sam.vā.dī*. This *rā.g* is most pleasing when sung at dusk.

24 V.N. Bhatkhande, op. cit. (Hathras: Sangeet Karyalaya, 1954), vol. II, pp. 284-85.

25 *Vi.vā.dī* (literally means an enemy note). It is referred to as an omitted note in a *rā.g* yet may be occasionally used for creating a pleasing affect.

COMPOSITION 2: *Notation*

					sthā.yī				
^{S}D	–	Ṁ	Ṁ	D	Ṁ	D	Ṁ	G	R̠S
ū	–	*va*	*ra*	*ga*	*ma*	*dha*	*ni*	*su*	*ra-*
x		2			0		3		
SR̠	G	$^{\underline{R}}G$	G	Ṁ	G	R̠	G	R̠	S
me-	–	*la*	*na*	*sa*	*ja*	*ta*	*ma*	*dhu*	*ra*
x		2			0		3		
^{N}S	SN	R̠	R̠	R̠	$^{\underline{R}}N$	D	ṀD	S	S
vi	*ka-*	*ra*	*ta*	*ri*	*kha*	*ba*	*bhī-*	*ta*	*ra*
x		2			0		3		
SR̠	G	$^{\underline{R}}G$	G	Ṁ	G	R̠	G	R̠	S
mā-	–	*ra*	*vā*	*ka*	*ha*	*ta*	*ca*	*tu*	*ra*
x		2			0		3		
					an.ta.rā.				
G	–	$^{D}\dot{M}$	$^{D}\dot{M}$	D	$^{D}\dot{M}$	Ṡ	Ṡ	Ṡ	Ṡ
rā	–	*ga*	*gā*	–	*va*	*ta*	*su*	*ka*	*ra*
x		2			0		3		
$^{N}\dot{S}$	–	Ṙ̠	Ṙ̠	Ṙ̠	$^{\underline{R}}N$	Ṙ̠	N	D	D
pañ	–	*ca*	*ma*	*vi*	*vā*	–	*dā*	*su*	*ra*
x		2			0		3		
$^{D}\dot{M}$	D	Ṁ	G	R̠	Ṁ	G	R̠	R̠	S
sam	–	*vā*	–	*da*	*re*	*dha*	*bi*	*ca*	*ra*
x		2			0		3		
$^{S}\underline{R}$	–	Ṙ̠	Ṙ̠	Ṙ̠	$^{G}\underline{R}$	Ṙ̠	G	R̠	S
a	–	*sta*	*di*	*na*	*a*	*ti*	*ru*	*ci*	*ra*
x		2			0		3		

COMPOSITION 3

Rā.g Mār.vā, Ca.tu.ra.ṅg, tīn-tā.l—medium tempo

Text:[26]

sthā.yī *ca.ta.ra.ṅg sa.ba mi.la gā.i.ye, gā.i.ye ba.jā.i.ye au.ra ri.jhā.i.ye*

an.ta.rā *mo.ham.ma.da.śā va.ra kā.ja su.hā.ga nā.ca.ta sa.ba mi.la de de tā.rī, sa ga ma ga re sa.chom. cha.na.na.na.na*

chom.cha.na.na.na.na, ta.ka dhī ta.ka, dhī ta.ka ti.ra.ki.ta ta.ka dhī kṛṅā dhā dhā tī dhā dhā

Meaning: Let us all sing *ca.tu.ra.ṅg* together and enthrall everyone by it. The composer Mohammad Shah says this is a sacred occasion of wedding. Everybody is dancing while clapping and singing *sa ga ma ga re sa, chom.cha.na.na.na.na, ta.ka dhī ta.ka dhī ta.ka ti.ra.ki.ta ta.ka dhī kṛṅā dhā dhā tī dhā dhā.*

[26] R. Mehta, *Āgrā Gharānā: Paramparā Gāyakī aur Chīzen* (Baroda: Sayajirav Vishvavidyalaya, 1969), 99-100.

COMPOSITION 3: *Notation*

								sthā.yī							
								D	*Ṁ*	*D*	*Ṁ*	*G*	*Ṁ*	*D*	*Ṁ*
								ca	*ta*	*raṅ*	*ga*	*sa*	*ba*	*mi*	*la*
								0				3			
G	*Ṟ*	–	*Ṁ*	*G*	*Ṟ*	*S*	–	*N*	*Ṟ*	*G*	*Ṁ*	*G*	*Ṟ*	*S*	–
gā	–	–	*i*	*ye*	–	–	–	*gā*	*i*	*ye*	*ba*	*ja*	*i*	*ye*	–
x				2				0				3			
Ṁ	*D*	*Ṁ*	*D*	*Ṁ*	*G*	*Ṟ*	*S*								
au	–	*ra*	*ri*	*jhā*	*i*	*ye*	–								
x				2											
								an.ta.rā							
G	*G*	*G*	*G*	*Ṁ*	–	*D*	*D*	*Ṡ*	–	*Ṡ*	*Ṡ*	*ṠN*	*Ṟ*	*Ṡ*	*Ṡ*
mo	*ha*	*mma*	*da*	*śā*	–	*va*	*ra*	*kā*	–	*ja*	*su*	*hā-*	–	–	*ga*
x				2				0				3			
N	*Ṟ̇*	*N*	*D*	*N*	*D*	*Ṁ*	*G*	*Ṟ*	*G*	*G*	*Ṁ*	*G*	*Ṟ*	*S*	–
nā	–	*ca*	*ta*	*sa*	*ba*	*mi*	*la*	*de*	–	–	*de*	*tā*	–	*rī*	–
x				2				0				3			
S	*G*	–	*Ṁ*	*G*	*Ṟ*	*S*	–	*N*	–	*Ṟ̇*	*N*	*D*	*Ṁ*	*G*	*Ṟ*
sa	*ga*	–	*ma*	*ga*	*re*	*sa*	–	*cho*	–	–	*mcha*	*na*	*na*	*na*	*na*
x				2				0				3			
S	*G*	–	*Ṁ*	*G*	*Ṟ*	*S*	*S*	*SS*	*G*	*GG*	*G*	*ṀṀ*	*DD*	*DD*	*ṠṠ*
cho	–	*-m*	*cha*	*na*	*na*	*na*	*na*	*taka*	*dhī*	*taka*	*dhī*	*taka*	*tira*	*kita*	*taka*
x				2				0				3			
N	*N*	*Ṟ̇*	*N*	*D*	*Ṁ*	*G*	*Ṟ*								
dhī	*krāṅ*	–	*dhā*	*dhā*	*ti*	*dhā*	*dhā*								
x				2											

Rā.g Pūr.vī

Melodic pattern

ā.ro.h (ascent)	–	*N Ṟ G Ṁ Ḏ N Ṡ*
a.va.ro.h (descent)	–	*Ṡ N Ṟ̇ N Ḏ P, Ṁ G M G-Ṁ G Ṟ S*
vā.dī (prominent note)	–	*G*
sam.vā.dī (consonant of *vā.dī*)	–	*N*
sa.ma.y (time)	–	evening

mu.khy savr saṅ.ga.ti (chief combinations of notes)—*NṞGPṀḎP, PṀGM..^{R}G, NṞ̇NḎP, GṞMG*

Stage 1

muk.t ā.lā.p

1. *S..., ^{R}N^{D}ṆD...S..., N Ṟ G..., G M G..., Ṁ^{R}G.. Ṟ S...*
2. *R̲R̲ SṆ S..N Ṟ G..., G Ṟ M G..^{G}Ṟ^{G}Ṟ G.., M Ḏ P..^{D}Ṁ̱^{D}Ṁ̱ G M G..Ṟ M G..., G Ṟ S..*
3. *ṆṞ^{P}G^{G}P.., Ṁ Ḏ Ṁ P G M G.., G Ṟ M G.., Ṁ Ḏ P.., Ṁ Ḏ N..., Ḏ P.., P Ḏ Ṁ P G Ṁ G.., G Ṟ M G..^{S}Ṟ S..*
4. *ṆṞ GṀḎ..P.., ^{D}Ṁ̱^{D}ṀḎP.., ^{D}Ṁ̱ Ḏ N Ḏ^{Ṁ}P.., Ṁ Ḏ N Ḏ S..., ^{N}ṞNḎP., N Ṟ N Ḏ N S.., P Ḏ M P G M G..Ṟ M G..Ṟ S...*

Stage 2

COMPOSITION 1

Text[27]:

sthā.yī *ha.ri.ye ma.i.kā sa.ba su.kha dī.no, dū.dha pū.ta au.ra a.na dha.na la.cha.mī, ki.ra.pā.yo go.vin.da ra.ṅga dī.no*

an.ta.rā *a.dha.ma u.dhā.ra.na ja.sa vis.tā.ra.ṇa, kri.pā ka.ra.na du.kha ha.ra.na su.kha ka.ra.na, ā.ji.ja ke sa.ba lā.ya.ka kī.no*

Meaning: O Hari, please grant me all pleasures such as milk, children, food, money, and good fortune. Please dye me in the colour of Govind. You are known as the saviour of sinners, the giver of blessings, the remover of suffering, and the provider of all pleasures. Please make this devotee worthy of all your favours.

[27]Nawab Ali Khan (Lakhimpur: 1956). It is also mentioned in *Rāga Vijñāna,* pt. II, pp. 79-80 and *Hindustānī Saṅgīta Paddhati Kramik Pustak Mālikā,* vol. I, pp. 40-41. However, the next is a little different there.

Composition 1: *Notation*

Rā.g Pūr.vī, tīn-tā.l—medium tempo

								sthā.yī							
								^{S}Ṇ	Ṟ	^{M}G	P	P	–	P	–
								ha	*ri*	*ye*	–	*mai*	–	*kā*	–
								0				3			
^{P}Ṁ	Ḏ	Ṁ	PṀ	G	M	G	–	M	Ṟ	G	^{D}Ṁ	–	Ḏ	^{D}Ṁ	G
sa	*ba*	*su*	*kha-*	*dī*	–	*no*	–	*du*	–	*dha*	*pū*	–	*ta*	*au*	*ra*
x				2				0				3			
Ṁ	G	Ṁ	G	Ṟ	Ṟ	S	–	^{S}N	S	^{G}Ṟ	P	P	–	P	–
a	*na*	*dha*	*na*	*la*	*cha*	*mī*	–	*ki*	*ra*	*pā*	–	*yo*	–	*go*	–
x				2				0				3			
^{D}Ṁ	Ḏ	^{D}Ṁ	PṀ	G	M	G	–								
vin	*da*	*raṅ*	*ga-*	*dī*	–	*no*	–								
x				2											
								an.ta.rā							
								^{G}Ṁ	^{D}Ṁ	G	G	^{D}Ṁ	–	Ḏ	ṀḎ
								a	*dha*	*ma*	*u*	*dhā*	–	*ra*	*na-*
								0				3			
Ṡ	Ṡ	Ṡ	N	^{N}Ṟ̇	–	Ṡ	Ṡ	^{N}Ṡ	Ṡ	–	Ṡ	N	Ḏ	N	Ḏ
ja	*sa*	*vi*	–	*stā*	–	*ra*	*na*	*kri*	*pā*	–	*ka*	*ra*	*na*	*du*	*kha*
x				2				0				3			
^{Ṡ}N	^{Ṡ}NṞ̇	N	Ḏ	N	Ḏ	P	P	^{S}N	Ṟ	G	ṞG	P	–	P	P
ha	*ra-*	*na*	*su*	*kha*	*ka*	*ra*	*na*	*ā*	–	*ji*	*ja-*	*ke*	–	*sa*	*ba*
x				2				0				3			
PṀ	Ḏ	Ṁ	P	G	M	G	–								
lā-	–	*ya*	*ka*	*kī*	–	*no*	–								
x				2											

Stage 3

ā.lā.p-sthā.yī

									N	Ṟ	^{M}G	P	P	–	P	–
									ha	ri	ye	–	mai	–	kā	–
	x				2				0				3			
1.	S	–	–	–	N	Ṟ	S	–	N	Ṟ	^{M}G	P	P	–	P	–
	ā	–	–	–	–	–	–	–	ha	ri	ye	–	mai	–	kā	–
	x				2				0				3			
2.	N	Ṟ	G	–	^{Ṟ}G	Ṟ	S	–	N	Ṟ	^{M}G	P	P	–	P	–
	ā	–	–	–	–	–	–	–	ha	ri	ye	–	mai	–	kā	–
	x				2				0				3			
3.	^{P}Ṁ	Ḏ	Ṁ	PṀ	G	M	G	–	NṞ	^{Ṁ}G	P	–	Ṁ	Ḏ	Ṁ	P
	sa	ba	su	kha-	dī	–	no	–	a	–	–	–	–	–	–	–
	x				2				0				3			
	G	M	G	–	^{G}Ṟ	G	Ṟ	S	N	Ṟ	^{M}G	P	P	–	P	–
	–	–	–	–	–	–	–	–	ha	ri	ye	–	mai	–	kā	–
	x				2				0				3			
4.	^{D}Ṁ	–	Ḏ	^{N}Ḏ	P	–	Ṁ	Ḏ	N	Ḏ	–	P	–	Ḏ	Ṁ	P
	ā	–	–	–	–	–	–	–	–	–	–	–	–	–	–	–
	x				2				0				3			
	Ṁ	G	M	G	–	Ṟ	–	S	N	Ṟ	^{M}G	P	P	–	P	–
	–	–	–	–	–	–	–	–	ha	ri	ye	–	mai	–	kā	–
	x				2				0				3			
5.	NṞ	GṀ	Ḏ	–	P	–	Ṁ	Ḏ	N	–	Ṡ	–	–	–	N	Ṙ
	ā	——	–	–	–	–	–	–	–	–	–	–	–	–	–	–
	x				2				0				3			
	N	Ḏ	P	Ṁ	G	M	G	–	NṞ	^{M}GP	NṞ	^{M}GP	NṞ	^{M}GP	P-	P-
	–	–	–	–	–	–	–	–	hari	ye-	hari	ye-	hari	ye-	mai-	kā-
	x				2				0				3			
	^{P}Ṁ	Ḏ	Ṁ	PṀ	G	M	G	–								
	sa	ba	su	kha-	dī	–	no	–								

ā.lā.p-an.ta.rā									*Ṁ*	*Ṁ*	*G*	*G*	*Ṁ*	–	*D*	*ṀḌ*
									a	*dha*	*ma*	*u*	*dhā*	–	*ra*	*na-*
	x				2				0				3			
1.	*Ṡ*	–	–	–	*N*	*Ṛ̇*	*Ṡ*	–	*Ṁ*	*Ṁ*	*G*	*G*	*Ṁ*	–	*Ḍ*	*ṀḌ*
	ā	–	–	–	–	–	–	–	*a*	*dha*	*ma*	*u*	*dhā*	–	*ra*	*na-*
	x				2				0				3			
2.	*Ṛ̇Ṛ̇*	*ṠN*	*Ṡ*	–	*ᴺḌ*	*ᴺḌ*	*Ṡ*	–	*Ṁ*	*Ṁ*	*G*	*G*	*Ṁ*	–	*Ḍ*	*ṀḌ*
	ā	––	–	–	–	–	–	–	*a*	*dha*	*ma*	*u*	*dhā*	–	*ra*	*na-*
	x				2				0				3			
3.	*Ṡ*	*Ṡ*	*Ṡ*	*N*	*Ṛ̇*	–	*Ṡ*	*Ṡ*	*Ṇ*	*Ṛ*	*N*	*Ḍ*	*P*	–	*Ṁ*	*G*
	ja	*sa*	*vi*	–	*stā*	–	*ra*	*na*	*ā*	–	–	–	–	–	–	–
	x				2				0				3			
	Ṁ	–	*Ḍ*	–	*N*	*Ṡ*	–	–	*Ṁ*	*Ṁ*	*G*	*G*	*Ṁ*	–	*Ḍ*	*ṀḌ*
	–	–	–	–	–	–	–	–	*a*	*dha*	*ma*	*u*	*dhā*	–	*ra*	*na-*
	x				2				0				3			
4.	*Ṡ*	–	–	–	*N*	*Ṛ̇*	*Ġ*	–	*Ġ*	*Ṁ*	*Ġ*	–	*ᴿĠ*	*Ṛ̇*	*Ṡ*	*N*
	ā	–	–	–	–	–	–	–	–	–	–	–	–	–	–	–
	x				2				0				3			
	Ṛ	–	*Ṡ*	–	*ṀṀ*	*GG*	*Ṁ-*	*DD*	*ṀṀ*	*GG*	*Ṁ-*	*DD*	*ṀṀ*	*GG*	*Ṁ-*	*DD*
	–	–	–	–	*adha*	*mau*	*dhā-*	*rana*	*adha*	*mau*	*dhā-*	*rana*	*adha*	*mau*	*dhā-*	*rana*
	x				2				0				3			
	Ṡ	*Ṡ*	*Ṡ*	*N*	*Ṛ̇*	–	*Ṡ*	*Ṡ*	*Ṁ*	*Ṁ*	*G*	*G*	*Ṁ*	–	*Ḍ*	*ṀḌ*
	ja	*sa*	*vi*	–	*stā*	–	*ra*	*na*	*a*	*dha*	*ma*	*u*	*dhā*	–	*ra*	*na-*
	x				2				0				3			
5.	*NṚ̇*	*Ġ*	–	–	*ᴳP*	–	–	*Ṁ*	*Ġ*	*Ṁ*	*Ġ*	–	*Ṛ̇*	–	*Ṡ*	–
	ā	–	–	–	–	–	–	–	–	–	–	–	–	–	–	–
	x				2				0				3			
	N	*Ṛ*	*N*	*Ḍ*	–	*Ṡ*	–	–	*Ṁ*	*Ṁ*	*G*	*G*	*Ṁ*	–	*Ḍ*	*ṀḌ*
	–	–	–	–	–	–	–	–	*a*	*dha*	*ma*	*u*	*dhā*	–	*ra*	*na-*
	x				2				0				3	sing the whole *an.ta.rā*		

Stage 4 (increase your tempo a little)

tā.n-sthā.yī									*Ṇ*	*R̲*	*G*	*P*	*P*	–	*P*	–
									ha	*ri*	*ye*	–	*mai*	–	*kā*	–
	x				2				0				3			
1.	*NR̲*	*GṀ*	*PṀ*	*GM*	*GR̲*	*SN*	*R̲R̲*	*SS*	*Ṇ*	*R̲*	*G*	*P*	*P*	–	*P*	–
	ā	--	--	--	--	--	--	--	*ha*	*ri*	*ye*	–	*mai*	–	*kā*	–
	x				2				0				3			
2.	*PṀ*	*D̲P*	*ND̲*	*PṀ*	*GM*	*GR̲*	*GR̲*	*SS*	*Ṇ*	*R̲*	*G*	*P*	*P*	–	*P*	–
	ā	--	--	--	--	--	--	--	*ha*	*ri*	*ye*	–	*mai*	–	*kā*	–
	x				2				0				3			
3.	*NR̲*	*GR̲*	*GṀ*	*GṀ*	*PṀ*	*GṀ*	*GR̲*	*SS*	*Ṇ*	*R̲*	*G*	*P*	*P*	–	*P*	–
	ā	--	--	--	--	--	--	--	*ha*	*ri*	*ye*	–	*mai*	–	*kā*	–
	x				2				0				3			
4.	*Ṁ*	*D̲*	*Ṁ*	*PṀ*	*G*	*M*	*G*	–	*ṆR̲*	*GṀ*	*PD̲*	*NN*	*D̲P*	*ṀD̲*	*NṘ̲*	*ND̲*
	sa	*ba*	*su*	*kha-*	*dī*	–	*no*	–	*ā*	--	--	--	--	--	--	--
	x				2				0				3			
	PṀ	*D̲M̲*	*PṀ*	*GM*	*GR̲*	*GR̲*	*NR̲*	*SS*	*Ṇ*	*R̲*	*G*	*P*	*P*	–	*P*	–
	--	--	--	--	--	--	--	--	*ha*	*ri*	*ye*	–	*mai*	–	*kā*	–
	x				2				0				3			
5.	*NR̲*	*GG*	*R̲G*	*R̲S*	*GṀ*	*PP*	*ṀP*	*ṀG*	*PD̲*	*NN*	*D̲N*	*D̲P*	*NṘ̲*	*GG*	*Ṙ̲G*	*Ṙ̲Ṡ*
	ā	--	--	--	--	--	--	--	--	--	--	--	--	--	--	--
	x				2				0				3			
	NN	*D̲P*	*ṀP*	*D̲Ṁ̲*	*PṀ*	*GM*	*GR̲*	*SS*	*N*	*R̲*	*G*	*P*	*P*	–	*P*	–
	--	--	--	--	--	--	--	--	*ha*	*ri*	*ye*	–	*mai*	–	*kā*	–
	x				2				0				3			
	Ṁ	*D̲*	*Ṁ*	*PṀ*	*G*	*M*	*G*	–								
	sa	*ba*	*su*	*kha-*	*dī*	–	*no*	–								
	x				2											

tā.n-an.ta.rā

									Ṁ	*Ṁ*	*G*	*G*	*Ṁ*	–	*D*	*ṀD̲*
									a	*dha*	*ma*	*u*	*dhā*	–	*ra*	*na-*
	x				2				0				3			
1.	*NṘ̲*	*ṠN*	*D̲N*	*D̲P*	*ṀG*	*ṀD̲*	*NṘ̲*	*ṠṠ*	*Ṁ*	*Ṁ*	*G*	*G*	*Ṁ*	–	*D*	*ṀD̲*
	ā-	––	––	––	––	––	––	––	*a*	*dha*	*ma*	*u*	*dhā*	–	*ra*	*na-*
	x				2				0				3			
2.	*ṠN*	*D̲P*	*ṀG*	*R̲S*	*NR̲*	*GṀ*	*D̲N*	*ṠṠ*	*Ṁ*	*Ṁ*	*G*	*G*	*Ṁ*	–	*D̲*	*ṀD̲*
	ā-	––	––	––	––	––	––	––	*a*	*dha*	*ma*	*u*	*dhā*	–	*ra*	*na-*
	x				2				0				3			
3.	*NṘ̲*	*ĠṘ̲*	*ĠṀ*	*ĠṘ̲*	*ṠN*	*D̲P*	*MD*	*ṠṠ*	*Ṁ*	*Ṁ*	*G*	*G*	*Ṁ*	–	*D̲*	*ṀD̲*
	ā-	––	––	––	––	––	––	––	*a*	*dha*	*ma*	*u*	*dhā*	–	*ra*	*na-*
	x				2				0				3			
4.	*Ṡ*	*Ṡ*	*Ṡ*	*N*	*Ṙ̲*	–	*Ṡ*	*Ṡ*	*Ṙ̲Ṙ̲*	*ṠN*	*D̲P*	*ṀD̲*	*PṀ*	*GM*	*GR̲*	*SS*
	ja	*sa*	*vi*	–	*sta*	–	*ra*	*na*	*ā*	––	––	––	––	––	––	––
	x				2				0				3			
	NR̲	*GR̲*	*GṀ*	*PṀ*	*PD̲*	*ND̲*	*NN*	*ṠṠ*	*Ṁ*	*Ṁ*	*G*	*G*	*Ṁ*	–	*D̲*	*ṀD̲*
	––	––	––	––	––	––	––	––	*a*	*dha*	*ma*	*u*	*dhā*	–	*ra*	*na-*
	x				2				0				3			
5.	*NṘ̲*	*ĠP*	*ṀĠ*	*ṀĠ*	*Ṙ̲Ṡ*	*NṘ̲*	*ND̲*	*PṀ*	*D̲P*	*ṀG*	*GM*	*R̲G*	*R̲N̲*	*R̲G*	*R̲G*	*ṀG*
	ā-	––	––	––	––	––	––	––	––	––	––	––	––	––	––	––
	x				2				0				3			

ṀḎ	*ṀḎ*	*NḎ*	*NṞ*	*ĠĠ*	*ṞṠ*	*NṞ*	*ṠṠ*	*ṀṀ*	*GG*	*ṀṀ*	*GG*	*ṀṀ*	*GG*	*Ṁ-*	*Ḏ-ṀḎ*
--	--	--	--	--	--	--	--	*adha*	*mau*	*adha*	*mau*	*adha*	*mau*	*dhā*	*rana-*
x				2				0				3			
Ṡ	*Ṡ*	*Ṡ*	*N*	*Ṟ*	–	*Ṡ*	*Ṡ*	*Ṡ*	*Ṡ*	–	*Ṡ*	*N*	*Ḏ*	*N*	*Ḏ*
ja	*sa*	*vi*	–	*stā*	–	*ra*	*na*	*kri*	*pā*	–	*ka*	*ra*	*ṇa*	*du*	*kha*
x				2				0				3			
sing the whole *an.ta.rā*				and conclude with *ti.hā.ī*				*Ṉ*	*Ṟ*	*G*	*P*	*P*	–	*P*	–
								ha	*ri*	*ye*	–	*mai*	–	*kā*	–
x				2				0				3			
Ṁ	*Ḏ*	*Ṁ*	*PṀ*	*G*	*M*	*G*	–	*Ṁ*	*Ḏ*	*Ṁ*	*PṀ*	*G*	*M*	*G*	–
sa	*ba*	*su*	*khā-*	*dī*	–	*no*	–	*sa*	*ba*	*su*	*khā-*	*dī*	–	*no*	–
x				2				0				3			
Ṁ	*Ḏ*	*Ṁ*	*PṀ*	*G*	–	*M*	–	*G*	–	–	–				
sa	*ba*	*su*	*khā-*	*dī*	–	–	–	*no*	–	–	–				
x				2				0							

COMPOSITION 2

Rā.g Pūr.vī lak.ṣaṇ-gī.t, tīn-tā.l—medium tempo

Text[28]:

sthā.yī *pū.ra.vī ke su.ra gā.ya gu.nī.va.ra, gare gama padha mapa gare gama gare sa nini sare ga ja.hān aṅ.ga ma.no.ha.ra*

an.ta.rā *vā.dī gan.dhā.ra ni.śā.da su.sa.ha.ca.ra, ma.dhya.ma jo.ga di.khā.va.ta sun.da.ra, san.dhi pra.kā.śa sa.ma.ya ka.ha.ta ca.tu.ra*

Meaning: The accomplished singers are singing the melody of *rā.g Pūr.vī.* The combination of the notes *gare gama padha mapa gare gama gare sasa nini sare,* and *ga* is very sweet. The *vā.dī* note of this melody is *ga* and consonant of *vā.dī* is *ni.* The presence of the note *ma* makes it very enchanting. Poet Catura says that this *rā.g* is best sung at dusk.

[28]V.N. Bhatkhande, op. cit. (Hathras: Sangeet Karyalaya, 1954), vol. II, pp. 237-38.

Composition 2: *Notation*

								sthā.yī							
								$^{\dot{M}}$*P*	*Ḏ*	*Ṁ*	*PṀ*	*G*	*M*	*G*	*Ṟ*
								pū	–	*ra*	*vī-*	*ke*	–	*su*	*ra*
								0				3			
G	–	*N*	*Ṟ*	*G*	*M*	*G*	*G*	*G*	*Ṟ*	*G*	*Ṁ*	*P*	*Ḏ*	*Ṁ*	*P*
gā	–	*ya*	*gu*	*nī*	–	*va*	*ra*	*ga*	*re*	*ga*	*ma*	*pa*	*dha*	*ma*	*pa*
x				2				0				3			
$^{\dot{M}}$*G*	*Ṟ*	*G*	*Ṁ*	*G*	*Ṟ*	*S*	–	*N*	*N*	*S*	*Ṟ*	*G*	–	^{D}*Ṁ*	*Ḏ*
ga	*re*	*ga*	*ma*	*ga*	*re*	*sa*	–	*ni*	*ni*	*sa*	*re*	*ga*	–	*ja*	*hān*
x				2				0				3			
^{D}*Ṟ̇*	*N*	*Ḏ*	*N*	^{D}*Ṁ*	–	*GM*	*G*								
aṅ	–	*ga*	*ma*	*no*	–	*ha-*	*ra*								
x				2											
								an.ta.rā							
								^{D}*Ṁ*	–	*G*	*G*	^{D}*Ṁ*	–	*Ḏ*	*ṀḎ*
								vā	–	*dī*	*gan*	*dhā*	–	*ra*	*ni-*
								0				3			
^{D}*Ṡ*	–	*Ṡ*	*Ṡ*	^{N}*Ṡ*	*Ṟ̇*	*Ṡ*	*Ṡ*	^{N}*Ṡ*	–	*Ṡ*	*Ṡ*	*N*	–	*Ḏ*	*Ḏ*
śā	–	*da*	*su*	*sa*	*ha*	*ca*	*ra*	*ma*	–	*dhya*	*ma*	*jo*	–	*ga*	*di*
x				2				0				3			
N	*Ṟ̇*	*N*	*Ḏ*	*N*	*Ḏ*	*P*	*P*	^{S}*Ṇ*	–	*S*	*Ṟ*	*G*	–	*Ṁ*	*Ḏ*
khā	–	*va*	*ta*	*sun*	–	*da*	*ra*	*san*	–	*dhi*	*pra*	*kā*	–	*śa*	*sa*
x				2				0				3			
^{D}*Ṟ̇*	*N*	*Ḏ*	*N*	*ḎP*	*PṀ*	*GM*	*G*								
ma	*ya*	*ka*	*ha*	*ta-*	*ca-*	*tu-*	*ra*								
x				2											

COMPOSITION 3

Rā.g Pūr.vī, ta.rā.nā, ek-tā.l—fast tempo

Text[29]:

meaningless syllables

sthā.yī *ta.na.na tā.n. de.re nā ta.na.na.na.na.na de.re n̠ā ta.de.re ta.de.re dā.nī dā.nī*

an.ta.rā *nā.dir dir ta.na.na tom ta.na.na.na tom ta.na.ṅa.na ta.na.na.na.na.na.nā.ta.nā.ta.ka dhi.dān dhi.da na.ga ta.ka kṛāṅ dha dha dha dha*

Notation

						sthā.yī					
N	*D̠*	*P*	*P*	–	*Ṁ*	*G*	*M*	*R̠*	*G*	–	*G*
ta	*na*	*na*	*tā*	–	*na*	*de*	*re*	–	*nā*	–	*na*
x		0		2		0		3		4	
Ṁ	*D̠*	*P*	*Ṁ*	*G*	*R̠*	*G*	*Ṙ̠*	–	*S*	–	*S*
ta	*na*	*na*	*na*	*na*	*na*	*de*	*re*	–	*nā*	–	*na*
x		0		2		0		3		4	
R̠	*R̠*	*G*	*Ṁ*	*Ṁ*	*D̠*	*N*	*Ṙ̠*	*N*	*D̠*	*P*	*P*
ta	*de*	*re*	*ta*	*de*	*re*	*dā*	–	*nī*	*dā*	–	*nī*
x		0		2		0		3		4	

[29]V.N. Patvardhan, *Rāga Vijñāna* (Pune: Sangit Gaurav Granthamala, 1961), pt. II, pp. 84-85.

							an.ta.rā				
Ṁ	*G*	*G*	*Ṁ*	*Ṁ*	*Ḏ*	–	*ᴺṠ*	*N*	*Ṟ*	*Ṡ*	*Ṡ*
nā	*dir*	*dir*	*ta*	*na*	*na*	–	*tom*	*ta*	*na*	*na*	*na*
x		0		2		0		3		4	
Ṟ̇	*G*	–	*Ṟ̇*	*Ṡ*	*N*	*Ḏ*	*N*	*N*	*Ḏ*	*P*	*Ṁ*
na	*na*	*tom*	*ta*	*na*	*na*	*to*	–	*om*	*ta*	*na*	*na*
x		0		2		0		3		4	
N	*Ḏ*	*P*	*Ṁ*	*G*	*M*	*Ṟ*	*G*	–	*Ṟ*	*S*	*S*
na	*na*	*na*	*na*	*na*	*na*	*ta*	*nā*	–	*ta*	*na*	*na*
x		0		2		0		3		4	
GG	*GG*	*G*	*ṀṀ*	*ṀṀ*	*D̲D̲*	*Ṟ̇*	*Ṟ*	*N*	*Ḏ*	*P*	*Ṁ*
taka	*dhīdhā*	*an*	*dhīdhā*	*naga*	*taka*	*krā*	*-ṅ*	*dha*	*dha*	*dha*	*dha*
x		0		2		0		3		4	

Rā.g To.ṛī

Melodic pattern

(According to Pt. Onkar Nath Thakur and V.N. Patavardhan), this is more popular.

ā.ro.h (ascent)	–	*N R̲ G̲ Ṁ D̲, N S*
a.va.ro.h (descent)	–	*S N D̲ P, Ṁ D̲ Ṁ G̲, R̲ G̲ R̲ S̱*
according to Bhatkhande		
ā.ro.h (ascent)	–	*S, R̲ G̲, Ṁ P, D̲ N S*
a.va.ro.h (descent)	–	*S N D̲ P, Ṁ G̲, R̲ S*
vā.dī (prominent note)	–	*D̲*
sam.vā.dī (consonant of *vā.dī*)	–	*G̲*
sa.ma.y (time)	–	noon

mu.khy svar saṅ.ga.ti (chief combinations of notes)—^{N}*D̲, N<u>R̲G̲</u>, ^{Ṁ}<u>R̲G̲</u>, ^{Ṁ}R̲S*

Note: In this *rā.g G* (E flat) is a little lower than the usual *G* (E flat).

Stage 1

muk.t ā.lā.p

1. *S..., NSR̲S, ^{N}D̲..^{N}D̲..^{S}N..^{R}D̲ S..., D̲N SR̲.., ^{G}R̲^{G}R̲ N D̲ ..^{N}D̲^{R}D̲ S...,*
2. *N R̲^{G}R̲ G̲..., Ṁ G̲..^{G}R̲..G̲ R̲ G̲.., G̲.. R̲ N D N R̲ G̲ ..^{G}R̲. ^{G}R̲ N D̲^{R}D̲ S*
3. *NR̲ <u>GM</u>.. Ṁ R̲^{R}G̲.., P.., Ṁ D̲ P.., ^{D}Ṁ D̲ N D̲..., N D̲...,^{Ṁ}P..Ṁ D̲..D̲ Ṁ Ṁ G̲.. ^{G}R̲^{R}G̲ R̲...*
4. *N R̲ G̲ Ṁ D̲..., D̲ Ṁ <u>GR</u> G̲ Ṁ D̲.., Ṁ ^{N}D̲ ^{S}N^{R}D̲ Ṡ..., Ṡ Ṙ̲Ṡ N^{N}D̲ N D̲ ^{M}P..., Ṁ D̲.., D̲ Ṁ Ṁ G̲..., ^{Ṁ}R̲ G̲ R̲.., ^{N}S...*

Stage 2

COMPOSITION 1[30]

Rā.g To.ṛī, tīn-tā.l—medium tempo

Text:

sthā.yī *pi.yā saṅ.ga khe.la.ta pyā.rī, jo.va.na kī ma.ta.vā.rī,*

an.ta.rā *mri.ga ma.da au.re ke.sa.ra ḍo.re, bhī.ja.ta raṅ.ga sā.rī*

Meaning: A comely damsel is playing with colours with her beloved. She is intoxicated by her youth. She is delirious with joy like a deer. The strings in her eyes have become as yellow as saffron and her *sā.rī* is getting drenched with colour.

[30]V.N. Bhatkhande, op.cit. (Hathras: Sangeet Karyalaya, 1954), vol. II, pp. 441-42.

COMPOSITION 1: *Notation*

Rā.g To.ṛī, tīn-tā.l—medium tempo

								sthā.yī							
								^{G}*Ṟ*	^{R}*G̱*	*R*	*R*	*S*	–	*Ḏ*	*N*
								pi	*yā*	*saṅ*	*ga*	*khe*	–	*la*	*ta*
								0				3			
S	–	–	*Ṟ*	*G̱*	–	*G̱Ṁ*	*P*	*Ṁ*	*G̱*	*Ṟ*	*Ṟ*	*S*	–	*Ḏ*	*N*
pyā	–	–	–	*rī*	–	––	–	*pi*	*yā*	*saṅ*	*ga*	*khe*	–	*la*	*ta*
x				2				0				3			
S	–	–	*Ṟ*	*G̱*	–	–	–	*G̱*	–	*Ṁ*	*Ṁ*	*P*	–	*Ṁ*	*Ḏ*
pyā	–	–	–	*rī*	–	–	–	*jo*	–	*va*	*na*	*kī*	–	*ma*	*ta*
x				2				0				3			
^{D}*N*	^{D}*N*	*Ḏ*	*P*	*Ṁ*	*G̱*	*G̱Ṁ*	*Ḏ*	*Ṁ*	*G̱*	*Ṟ*	*Ṟ*	*S*	–	*Ḏ*	*N*
vā	–	–	–	*rī*	–	––	–	*pi*	*yā*	*saṅ*	*ga*	*khe*	–	*la*	*ta*
x				2				0				3			
								an.ta.rā							
								P	*Ṁ*	*P*	*Ḏ*	*Ṁ*	*G̱*	*Ṁ*	*Ḏ*
								mri	*ga*	*ma*	*da*	*au*	–	*re*	–
								0				3			
^{N}*Ṡ*	–	*Ṡ*	*N*	*Ṟ̇*	–	*Ṡ*	–	^{S}*N*	–	*Ṡ*	*Ġ̱*	*Ṟ̇*	–	*Ṡ*	–
ke	–	*sa*	*ra*	*do*	–	*re*	–	*bhī*	–	*ja*	*ta*	*raṅ*	–	*ga*	–
x				2				0				3			
^{P}*Ḏ*	^{P}*Ḏ*	*Ṡ*	*N*	*Ḏ*	*P*	^{M}*P*	*G̱*	*Ṁ*	*G̱*	*Ṟ*	*R*	*S*	–	*Ḏ*	*N*
sā	–	–	–	–	–	*rī*	–	*pi*	*yā*	*saṅ*	*ga*	*khe*	–	*la*	*ta*
x				2				0				3			

Stage 3

ā.lā.p-sthā.yī									^{G}Ṟ	^{B}G̱	Ṟ	Ṟ	S	–	Ḏ	N
									pi	yā	saṅ	ga	khe	–	la	ta
	x				2				0				3			
1.	S	–	–	–	^{B}Ḏ	–	S	–	^{G}Ṟ	^{B}G̱	Ṟ	Ṟ	S	–	Ḏ	N
	ā	–	–	–	–	–	–	–	pi	yā	saṅ	ga	khe	–	la	ta
	x				2				0				3			
2.	Ḏ	–	S	Ṟ	G̱	–	Ṟ	S	^{G}Ṟ	^{B}G̱	Ṟ	Ṟ	S	–	Ḏ	N
	ā	–	–	–	–	–	–	–	pi	yā	saṅ	ga	khe	–	la	ta
	x				2				0				3			
3.	S	–	NSṞS	Ḏ	–	N	S	Ṟ	G̱	–	–	–	^{G}Ṟ	^{G}Ṟ	G̱	–
	ā	–	----	–	–	–	–	–	–	–	–	–	–	–	–	–
	x				2				0				3			
	G̱	Ṟ	N	Ḏ	^{N}Ḏ	S	–	–	^{G}Ṟ	^{B}G̱	Ṟ	Ṟ	S	–	Ḏ	N
	–	–	–	–	–	–	–	–	pi	yā	saṅ	ga	khe	–	la	ta
	x				2				0				3			
4.	S	–	–	–	N	–	SṞ	G̱	–	Ṁ	G̱	–	P	–	–	–
	pyā	–	–	–	ā	–	--	–	–	–	–	–	–	–	–	–
	x				2				0				3			
	Ṁ	Ḏ	P	–	Ṁ	G̱	Ṟ	S	^{G}Ṟ	^{B}G̱	Ṟ	Ṟ	S	–	Ḏ	N
	–	–	–	–	–	–	–	–	pi	yā	saṅ	ga	khe	–	la	ta
	x				2				0				3			
5.	NṞG̱Ṁ	Ḏ	–	N	Ḏ	P	–	Ṁ	Ḏ	N	Ḏ	Ṡ	–	–	Ṡ	Ṟ̇Ṡ
	ā--	–	–	–	–	–	–	–	–	–	–	–	–	–	–	--
	x				2				0				3			
	N	Ḏ	–	P	–	ṀG̱	Ṟ	S	RG	RR	RG	RR	RG	RR	S-	ḎN
	–	–	–	–	–	--	–	–	piyā	saṅga	piyā	saṅga	piyā	saṅga	khe-	lata
	x				2				0				3			
	S	–	–	Ṟ	G̱	–	G̱Ṁ	D								
	pyā	–	–	–	rī	–	--	–								

ā.lā.p-an.ta.rā									*P*	*Ṁ*	*P*	*Ḏ*	*Ṁ*	*G̱*	*Ṁ*	*Ḏ*
									mri	*ga*	*ma*	*da*	*au*	–	*re*	–
	x				2				0				3			
1.	*Ṡ*	–	–	*Ḏ*	*Ṟ̇*	–	*Ṡ*	–	*P*	*Ṁ*	*P*	*Ḏ*	*Ṁ*	*G̱*	*Ṁ*	*Ḏ*
	ā	–	–	–	–	–	–	–	*mri*	*ga*	*ma*	*da*	*au*	–	*re*	–
	x				2				0				3			
2.	*Ṡ*	*Ṟ̇*	*Ġ̱*	–	*Ṟ̇*	–	*Ḏ*	*Ṡ*	*P*	*Ṁ*	*P*	*Ḏ*	*Ṁ*	*G̱*	*Ṁ*	*Ḏ*
	ā	–	–	–	–	–	–	–	*mri*	*ga*	*ma*	*da*	*au*	–	*re*	–
	x				2				0				3			
3.	*Ṡ*	–	*Ṡ*	*N*	*Ṟ̇*	–	*Ṡ*	–	*M*	*Ḏ*	*Ṡ*	–	*ᴳṞ̇*	*ᴳṞ̇*	*Ġ̱*	–
	ke	–	*sa*	*ra*	*do*	–	*re*	–	*ā*	–	–	–	–	–	–	–
	x				2				0				3			
	Ṟ̇	*Ṟ̇*	*Ṡ*	*N*	*Ḏ*	–	*Ṡ*	*Ṡ*	*P*	*Ṁ*	*P*	*Ḏ*	*Ṁ*	*G̱*	*Ṁ*	*Ḏ*
	–	–	–	–	–	–	–	–	*mri*	*ga*	*ma*	*da*	*au*	–	*re*	–
	x				2				0				3			
4.	*N*	–	*Ṡ*	–	*NṞ̇*	*Ġ̱*	*M*	*Ġ̱*	*Ṟ̇*	*Ṟ̇*	*N*	*Ḏ*	*Ṁ*	*P*	–	–
	ā	–	–	–	––	–	–	–	–	–	–	–	–	–	–	–
	x				2				0				3			
	M	*Ḏ*	*N*	–	*Ṡ*	–	–	–	*P*	*Ṁ*	*P*	*Ḏ*	*Ṁ*	*G̱*	*Ṁ*	*Ḏ*
	–	–	–	–	–	–	–	–	*mri*	*ga*	*ma*	*da*	*au*	–	*re*	–
	x				2				0				3			
	ᴺṠ	–	*Ṡ*	*N*	*Ṟ̇*	–	*Ṡ*	–	*ˢN*	–	*Ṡ*	*Ġ̱*	*Ṟ̇*	–	*Ṡ*	–
	ke	–	*sa*	*ra*	*do*	–	*re*	–	*bhi*	–	*ja*	*ta*	*raṅ*	–	*ga*	–
	x				2				0				3			
	ᴾḎ	*ᴾḎ*	*Ṡ*	*N*	*Ḏ*	*P*	*ᴹ̇P*	*G̱*								
	sā	–	–	–	–	–	*rī*	–								
	x				2											

Stage 4 (increase your tempo a little)

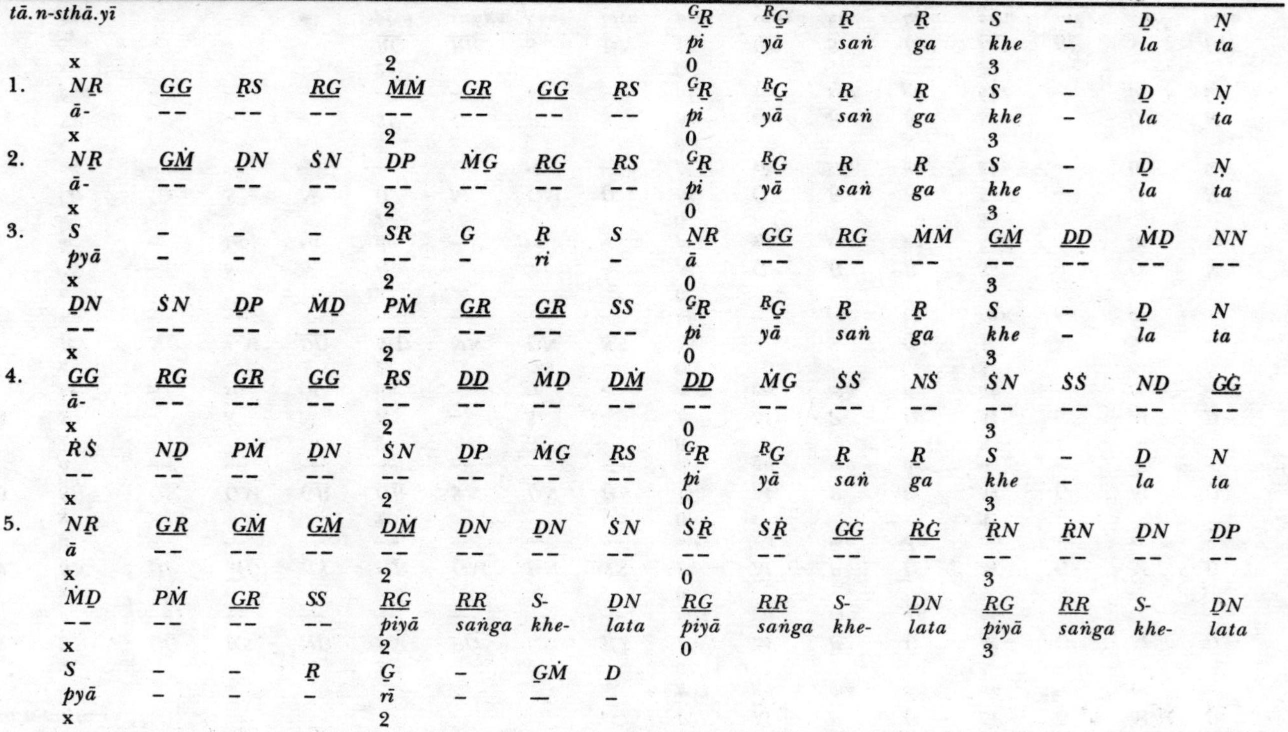

tā.n-sthā.yī									^{G}Ṟ	^{R}G̱	Ṟ	Ṟ	S	–	Ḏ	Ṇ
									pi	*yā*	*saṅ*	*ga*	*khe*	–	*la*	*ta*
	x				2				0				3			
1.	NṞ	GG	ṞS	ṞG	ṀṀ	GṞ	GG	ṞS	^{G}Ṟ	^{R}G̱	Ṟ	Ṟ	S	–	Ḏ	Ṇ
	ā-	--	--	--	--	--	--	--	*pi*	*yā*	*saṅ*	*ga*	*khe*	–	*la*	*ta*
	x				2				0				3			
2.	NṞ	GṀ	ḎN	ṠN	ḎP	ṀG̱	ṞG	ṞS	^{G}Ṟ	^{R}G̱	Ṟ	Ṟ	S	–	Ḏ	Ṇ
	ā-	--	--	--	--	--	--	--	*pi*	*yā*	*saṅ*	*ga*	*khe*	–	*la*	*ta*
	x				2				0				3			
3.	S	–	–	–	SṞ	G̱	Ṟ	S	NṞ	GG	ṞG	ṀṀ	GṀ	DD	ṀḎ	NN
	pyā	–	–	–	--	–	*ri*	–	*ā*	--	--	--	--	--	--	--
	x				2				0				3			
	ḎN	ṠN	ḎP	ṀḎ	PṀ	GṞ	GṞ	SS	^{G}Ṟ	^{R}G̱	Ṟ	Ṟ	S	–	Ḏ	N
	--	--	--	--	--	--	--	--	*pi*	*yā*	*saṅ*	*ga*	*khe*	–	*la*	*ta*
	x				2				0				3			
4.	GG	ṞG	GṞ	GG	ṞS	DD	ṀḎ	DṀ	DD	ṀG̱	ṠṠ	NṠ	ṠN	ṠṠ	NḎ	ĠĠ
	ā-	--	--	--	--	--	--	--	--	--	--	--	--	--	--	--
	x				2				0				3			
	ṘṠ	NḎ	PṀ	ḎN	ṠN	ḎP	ṀG̱	ṞS	^{G}Ṟ	^{R}G̱	Ṟ	Ṟ	S	–	Ḏ	N
	--	--	--	--	--	--	--	--	*pi*	*yā*	*saṅ*	*ga*	*khe*	–	*la*	*ta*
	x				2				0				3			
5.	NṞ	GṞ	GṀ	GṀ	DṀ	ḎN	ḎN	ṠN	ṠṞ	ṠṞ	ĠĠ	ṘĠ	ṘN	ṘN	ḎN	ḎP
	ā	--	--	--	--	--	--	--	--	--	--	--	--	--	--	--
	x				2				0				3			
	ṀḎ	PṀ	GṞ	SS	ṞG	ṞṞ	S-	ḎN	ṞG	ṞṞ	S-	ḎN	ṞG	ṞṞ	S-	ḎN
	--	--	--	--	*piyā*	*saṅga*	*khe-*	*lata*	*piyā*	*saṅga*	*khe-*	*lata*	*piyā*	*saṅga*	*khe-*	*lata*
	x				2				0				3			
	S	–	–	Ṟ	G̱	–	G̱Ṁ	D								
	pyā	–	–	–	*rī*	–	—	–								
	x				2											

tā.n-an.ta.rā									*P*	*Ṁ*	*P*	*D̲*	*Ṁ*	*G̲*	*Ṁ*	*D̲*
									mri	*ga*	*ma*	*da*	*au*	–	*re*	–
	x				2				0				3			
1.	*ṠṘ̲*	*Ġ̲Ġ̲*	*Ṙ̲Ṡ*	*ND̲*	*PṀ*	*PD̲*	*NṠ*	*Ṙ̲Ṡ*	*P*	*Ṁ*	*P*	*D̲*	*Ṁ*	*G̲*	*Ṁ*	*D̲*
	ā	--	--	--	--	--	--	--	*mri*	*ga*	*ma*	*da*	*au*	–	*re*	–
	x				2				0				3			
2.	*ṠN*	*D̲P*	*ṀĠ̲*	*R̲S*	*NR̲*	*G̲Ṁ*	*D̲N*	*ṠṠ*	*P*	*Ṁ*	*P*	*D̲*	*Ṁ*	*G̲*	*Ṁ*	*D̲*
	ā	--	--	--	--	--	--	--	*mri*	*ga*	*ma*	*da*	*au*	–	*re*	–
	x				2				0				3			
3.	*ṠṘ̲*	*Ġ̲Ṙ̲*	*Ġ̲Ṁ*	*Ġ̲Ṙ̲*	*Ġ̲Ṙ̲*	*ṠN*	*D̲N*	*Ṙ̲Ṡ*	*P*	*Ṁ*	*P*	*D̲*	*Ṁ*	*G̲*	*Ṁ*	*D̲*
	ā	--	--	--	--	--	--	--	*mri*	*ga*	*ma*	*da*	–	–	–	–
	x				2				0				3			
4.	*Ṡ*	–	*Ṡ*	*N*	*Ṙ̲*	–	*Ṡ*	–	*P*	*Ṁ*	*P*	*D̲*	*Ṁ*	*G̲*	*Ṁ*	*D̲*
	ke	–	*sa*	*ra*	*do*	–	*re*	–	*mri*	*ga*	*ma*	*da*	*au*	–	*re*	–
	x				2				0				3			
	R̲S	*NR̲*	*G̲Ṁ*	*D̲D̲*	*ṀD̲*	*NN*	*D̲N*	*ṠṠ*	^{Ṡ}*N*	–	*Ṡ*	*Ġ̲*	*Ṙ̲*	–	*Ṡ*	–
	--	--	--	--	--	--	--	--	*bhī*	–	*ja*	*ta*	*raṅ*	–	*ga*	–
	x				2				0				3			
	^{N}*Ṡ*	–	*Ṡ*	*N*	*Ṙ̲*	–	*Ṡ*	–	*Ṁ*	*G̲*	*R̲*	*R̲*	*S*	–	*D̲*	*Ṇ*
	ke	–	*sa*	*ra*	*do*	–	*re*	–	*pi*	*yā*	*saṅ*	*ga*	*khe*	–	*la*	*ta*
	x				2				0				3			
	^{P}*D̲*	^{P}*D̲*	*Ṡ*	*N*	*D̲*	*Ṁ*	*G̲Ṁ*	*D̲*	*Ṁ*	*G̲*	*R̲*	*R̲*	*S*	–	*D̲*	*Ṇ*
	sā	–	–	–	–	–	*rī*	–	*pi*	*yā*	*saṅ*	*ga*	*khe*	–	*la*	*ta*
	x				2				0				3			
	S	–	–	–	*SR̲*	*G̲*	*R̲*	*S*	*Ṁ*	*G̲*	*R̲*	*R̲*	*S*	–	*D̲*	*N*
	pyā	–	–	–	--	–	*ri*	–	*pi*	*yā*	*saṅ*	*ga*	*khe*	–	*la*	*ta*
	x				2				0				3			
	S	–	–	–	*R̲G̲*	*R̲R̲*	*S-*	*D̲N*	*R̲G̲*	*R̲R̲*	*S-*	*D̲N*	*R̲G̲*	*R̲R̲*	*S-*	*D̲N*
	pyā	–	–	–	*piyā*	*saṅga*	*khe-*	*lata*	*piyā*	*saṅga*	*khe-*	*lata*	*piyā*	*saṅga*	*khe-*	*lata*

COMPOSITION 2

Rā.g To.ṛī, lak.ṣaṇ-gī.t, ek-tā.l—medium tempo

Text[31]:

sthā.yī *vi.kri.ta ja.ba dha ga re ka.ra.ta, ma ni tī.va.ra su.ra saṅ.ga.ta su.ga.ma sa.ra.la sam.pū.ra.na gu.nī to.rī ko ba.ra.na.ta*

an.ta.rā *dha.i.va.ta ja.hāṅ aṅ.śa ra.ha.ta, ri.ga su.ra ta.hāṅ sa.ha.ca.ra ma.ta pañ.ca.ma ko.u al.pa ka.ha.ta, ha.ra.ra.ṅga ko ma.ta a.bhi.ma.ta*

Meaning: When the notes *dha, ga, re* are flat, *ma* is sharp and *ni* is natural and when all the seven notes are used, the experts describe it as *rā.g To.ṛī.* The note *dha* is an important note of this *rā.g* and *re* and *ga* are the consonants to *dha.* According to the composer Hararaṅg, the note *pa* should be used sparingly and his view is broadly accepted.

[31] V.N. Bhatkhande, op. cit., vol. II, pp. 433-34. The text is a little different there. The word *vikrit* is stated in the book as *bikarita.*

Composition 2: *Notation*

						sthā.yī					
^{S}R̲	^{R}G̲	R̲	R̲	S	S	^{N}D̲	D̲	N	S	R̲	G̲
vi	–	*kri*	*ta*	*ja*	*ba*	*dha*	*ga*	*re*	*ka*	*ra*	*ta*
x		0		2		0		3		4	
Ṁ	P	ṀP	D̲	Ṁ	G̲	R̲	G̲	R̲	–	S	S
ma	*ni*	*tī-*	–	*va*	*ra*	*su*	*ra*	*saṅ*	–	*ga*	*ta*
x		0		2		0		3		4	
^{S}N	SR̲	G̲	G̲	$^{D̲}$Ṁ	Ṁ	D̲	–	D̲	–	D̲	D̲
su	*ga-*	*ma*	*sa*	*ra*	*la*	*saṅ*	–	*pū*	–	*ra*	*na*
x		0		2		0		3		4	
^{P}D̲	N	^{N}D̲	N	$^{D̲}$Ṁ	G̲	$^{G̲}$R̲	G̲	R̲	R̲	S	S
gu	*nī*	*to*	–	*rī*	–	*ko*	–	*va*	*ra*	*na*	*ta*
x		0		2		0		3		4	
						an.ta.rā					
$^{D̲}$Ṁ	G̲	$^{D̲}$Ṁ	Ṁ	D̲	D̲	^{Ṡ}N	–	Ṡ	N	Ṡ	Ṡ
dhai	–	*va*	*ta*	*ja*	*hāṅ*	*aṅ*	–	*śa*	*ra*	*ha*	*ta*
x		0		2		0		3		4	
^{S}N	N	ṠṘ̲	Ġ̲	Ṙ̲	Ṡ	N	N	^{N}Ṙ̲	N	D̲	P
re	*ga*	*su-*	*ra*	*ta*	*hāṅ*	*sa*	*ha*	*ca*	*ra*	*ma*	*ta*
x		0		2		0		3		4	
$^{D̲}$Ṁ	D̲	N	Ṡ	N	D̲	$^{D̲}$Ṁ	G̲	R̲	^{R}G̲	R̲	S
pan	–	*ca*	*ma*	*ko*	*u*	*a*	–	*lpa*	*ka*	*ha*	*ta*
x		0		2		0		3		4	
^{S}R̲	R̲	Ṙ̲	^{Ṙ}Ġ̲	Ṙ̲	Ṡ	^{G}R̲	R̲	^{R}G̲	R̲	S	S
ha	*ra*	*raṅ*	*ga*	*ko*	–	*ma*	*ta*	*a*	*bhi*	*ma*	*ta*
x		0		2		0		3		4	

Composition 3

Rā.g To.ṛī, tīn-tā.l—medium tempo

Text[32]:

sthā.yī *mo.ha.na gha.na śyā.ma ā.ye mo.re dvā.re, ta.na kī ta.pa.na ga.ī mo.rī*
an.ta.rā *śu.bha di.na śu.bha hai ā.ja kī gha.rī, bhāga kī mo.re, sa.khī.rī*
Meaning: Mohan Ghanaśyāma (Krishna), has come to my doorstep. All my suffering has gone away now. It is my great luck, O my friend.

Composition 3: *Notation*

sthā.yī

															N
															mo
x				2				0				3			
D̠	P	ᴹG̱	Ṁ	D̠	–	D̠	Ṁ	–	G̱	R̠	G̱	R̠	–	S	–
ha	*na*	*gha*	*na*	*śyā-*	*ma*	*ā*	–	*ye*	*mo*	*re*	*dvā*	–	*re*	–	–
x				2				0				3			
S	R̠	G̱	Ṁ	D̠	N	Ṡ	Ṡ	D̠N	ṠR̠	<u>ĠR̠</u>	ṠN	D̠P	ṀG̱	R̠S	,N
ta	*na*	*kī*	*ta*	*pa*	*na*	*ga*	*ī*	*mo-*	--	--	--	*rī-*	--	--	*,mo*
x				2				0				3			

[32]N.L. Gune, *Saṅgīta Prabhākara Darśikā* (Allahabad: Pt. Narayan Lakhaman Gune, 1984), pp. 157-58.

							an.ta.rā								
												Ṁ	*G̱*	*Ṁ*	*Ḏ*
												śu	*bha*	*di*	*na*
x				2				0				3			
Ṡ	*Ṡ*	*Ṡ*	–	*Ṡ*	–	*Ṡ*	*Ṡ*	–	*Ṟ̇*	*Ṡ*	–	*Ṡ*	*Ṟ̇*	*Ġ̱*	*Ṟ̇*
śu	*bha*	*hai*	–	*ā*	–	*ja*	*kī*	–	*gha*	*rī*	–	*bhā*	–	*ga*	*kī*
x				2				0				3			
Ġ̱	*Ṟ̇*	*Ṡ*	–	*Ṁ*	*Ṁ*	*ḎN*	*ṠN,*	*ḎP*	*ṀG̱*	*ṞS*	*,N*	*Ḏ*	*P*	*Ṁ*	*G̱*
–	*mo*	*re*	–	*sa*	*khī*	*rī-*	--	--	--	--	*,mo*	*ha*	*na*	*gha*	*na*
x				2				0				3			

Appendix

Transcriptions of the Ten Basic *rā.gs* in Staff Notation

Key to Reading the Transcription of the *Rā.gs*

1. The tonic *Sa* (*S*) is always = note c' (= do' or ut')
2. Fixed flats (♭, *ko.mal*) and sharps (#, *tī.vr*) are put after the clef. Alterations are put before the notes.
3. The sections between two vertical lines represent one *vi.bhā.g* (division of the time-cycle).
4. One crotchet (quarter note ♩) represents one beat in the time-cycle.
5. Each cycle starts with *sa.m* (x) at the beginning of a (five-line)-system.
6. Embellishments = examples and interpretation:

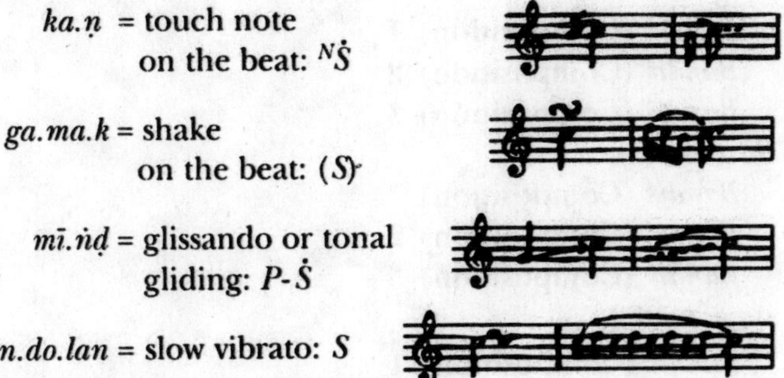

ka.ṇ = touch note on the beat: $^{N}\dot{S}$

ga.ma.k = shake on the beat: (*S*)

mī.ṅḍ = glissando or tonal gliding: *P*-$\dot{S}$

ān.do.lan = slow vibrato: *S*

7. Differences appearing in repetitions of the first line of *sthā.yī* and *an.ta.rā* are indicated by the word "varied" or "var".
8. The lines between the syllables of the text correspond to the beats in the cycle. They are not used as in Western

music to unite the syllables which belong to one word. In this transcription, the syllables constituting one word are united by straight horizontal brackets.

The Transcriptions

Rā.g Bi.lā.val

STAGE 1
mukt ālāp (improvisation in slow tempo without rhythm)
1.
2.
3.
4.
STAGE 2
bandiś 1 (composition 1)
1 2 3 4 5 6 7 8 9 10 11 12 13 14 15 16
tīntāl
dhā dhiṅ dhiṅ dhā dhā dhiṅ dhiṅ dhā dhā tiṅ tiṅ tā tā dhiṅ dhiṅ dhā
x 2 0 3
sthāyī (1st part)
tū - hī a
dhā - ra sa ka la tri bhu va na ko- — pā - la ka-
sa ca rā - ca ra bhū - ta na ko- —
repeat the 1st
line of sthāyī and then sing antarā:
antarā (2nd part)
tū - hī -
vi - ṣṇu - tū - nā - rā - ya na kā - ra na
tū - pa ra bra - hma ja- ga ta ko- —
repeat the 1st line of sthāyī and start ālāp sthāyī:

STAGE 3

ālāp sthāyī

tū – hī a

1. dhā – ra sa ka la tri bhu va na ko— ā – – –

– – – – – – – – – – – – tū – hī a

2. ā – – – – – – – – – – – – – tū – hī a

3. dhā ra sa ka la tri bhu va na ko— ā– – – —

– – – – – – – – – – – – – – – tū – hī a

4. ā— – – – – – – – – – – – – tū – hī a

5. ā– – – – – – – – – – – – – – – –

tihāī

– – – – – – – – – – – – – tu– hīa tū– hīa tu– hīa

dhā – ra sa ka la tri bhu va na ko— repeat the 1st line of sthāyī + the 1st line of antarā and start baddha ālāp antarā:

ālāp antarā

tū – hī –

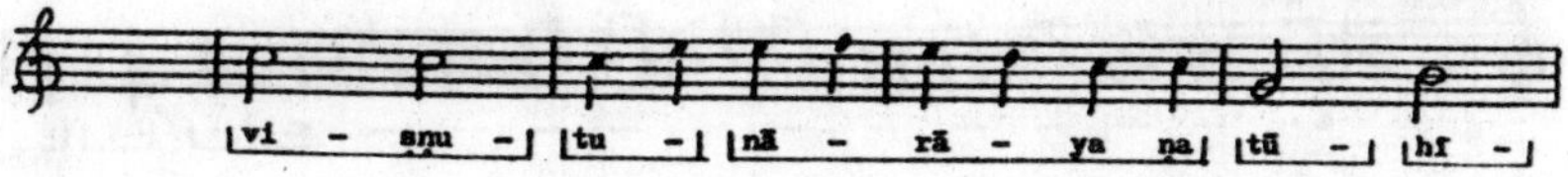

vi – ṣṇu – tu – nā – rā – ya na tū – hī –

1.
a – – – ā – – – – – – – – – – tū – hī –
2.
tū – hī –
3.
vi – smu – ā – – – – – – – – – – – – –
tū – hī –
4.
vi – smu – ā – – – – – – – – – – – –
tū – hī –
5.
vi – smu – ā – – – – – – – – – – – –
tū – hī –
sing the whole antarā + 1st line of sthāyī; increase the tempo of sthāyī and start tān sthāyī:
tān sthāyī
tū – hī a
STAGE 4
1.
dhā – ra sa – – – – – – – – – – tū – hī a
2.
ā – – – – – – – – – – – – – – tū – hī a
3.
ā – – – – – – – – – – – – – – tū – hī a

4.
ā
tihāī
tu- hi̱a dhar tu- hi̱a dhar tu- hi̱a
dhā - ra sa ka la tri bhu va na ko- tū - hī -
tān antarā
vi - ṣnu - tū - nā - rā - ya ṇa tū - hī -
1.
vi - ṣnu - ā tū - hī -
2.
vi - ṣnu - ā tū - hī -
3.
vi - ṣnu - ā tū - hī -
4.
antarā var.
ā tū - hī -
var. var.
vi - ṣnu - tū - nā - rā - ya na kā - ra na
var.
tihāī-sthāyī
tu - pa ra bra - hma ja- ga ta ko- tū - hī a
dhā - - ra tū - hī a dhā - - ra tū - hī a
dhā - - ra tū - hī a dhā - - -

bandiś 2
1 2 3 4 5 6 7 8 9 10 11 12 13 14 15 16
tīntāl
dhā dhiṅ dhiṅ dhā dhā dhiṅ dhiṅ dhā dhā tiṅ tiṅ tā tā dhiṅ dhiṅ dhā
x 2 0 3
sthāyī
ta ba ka ha ta bi lā - va- la
bhe - da ca tu- ra ja ba me- - - la mi- lā - va ta
śu - ddha su ra- na- ko - prā - ta sa ma ya ni ta
pra tha ma pra ha- ra ta ba
antarā
dhai - va- ta vā - dī -
ga - sa ma vā- - - dī - a - ṣṭa bhe - da sa ba
gā - - - ya ma- dhu ra ta ba

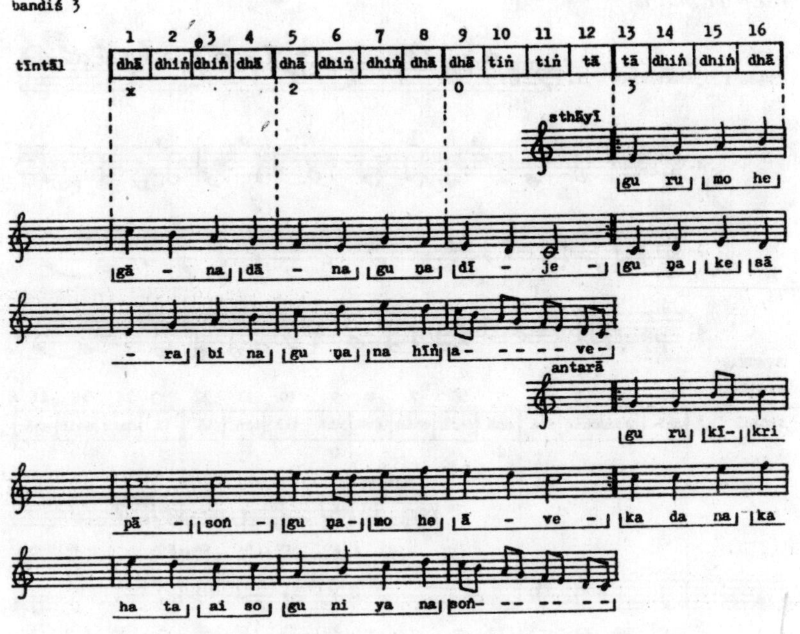
bandiś 3
tīntāl
1 2 3 4 5 6 7 8 9 10 11 12 13 14 15 16
dhā dhiṅ dhiṅ dhā dhā dhiṅ dhiṅ dhā dhā tiṅ tiṅ tā tā dhiṅ dhiṅ dhā
x 2 0 3
sthāyī
gu ru mo he
gā – na dā – na gu ṇa dī – je – gu ṇa ke sā
– ra bi na gu ṇa na hīṅ a – – – – – ve –
antarā
gu ru kī – kri
pā – soṅ – gu ṇa – mo he ā – ve – ka da na ka
ha ta ai so gu ni ya na soṅ – – – – – – –

Rā.g Ya.ma.n

STAGE 1 mukt ālāp 1.
F-1
2.
3.
4.
STAGE 2
bandiś 1
tīntāl
1 2 3 4 5 6 7 8 9 10 11 12 13 14 15 16
dhā dhiṅ dhiṅ dhā dhā dhiṅ dhiṅ dhā dhā tiṅ tiṅ tā tā dhiṅ dhiṅ dhā
x 2 0 3
sthāyī
gu ru bi na kai - se -
gu na gā - ve - - - gu ru na mā - ne to -
gu na na— hīṅ ā - ve - gu ni ya na meṅ - be -
gu nī - ka hā - ve
repeat the 1st line of sthāyī
and then sing antarā:
antarā
mā - ne - to - ri -
jhā - ve - sa ba ko - ca ra na ga he - sā -
de - pa na se - ja ba ā - ve - a ca pa la
tā — — — — — la— su ra
repeat the 1st line of sthāyī
and start ālāp sthāyī:

ālāp sthāyī
STAGE 3
gu ru bi na kai - se -
1.
ā
gu ru bi na kai - se -
2.
ā
gu ru bi na kai - se -
3.
ā
gu ru bi na kai - se -
4.
ā
repeat the 1st line of sthāyī +
the 1st line of antarā
and start ālāp antarā:
ālāp antarā
mā - ne - to - ri -
1.
ā
mā - ne - to - ri -
2.
ā

mā - ne - to - ri -
3.
jhā - ve - sa ba ko - ā
sing the whole antarā + the 1st line of sthāyī; increase the tempo of sthāyī and start tān sthāyī:
STAGE 4
tān sthāyī
gu ru bi na kai - se -
1.
ā - gu ru bi na kai - se -
2.
ā - gu ru bi na kai - se -
3.
ā - gu ru bi na kai - se -
4.
ā -
ā -
repeat the 1st line of sthāyī + the 1st line of antarā and start tān antarā:
tān antarā
mā - ne - to - ri -
1.
ā - mā - ne - to - ri -

2.
ā - - - - - - - - - mā - ne - to - ri -
3.
ā - - - - - - - - - mā - ne - to - ri -
4.
ā - - - - - - - - - - - - - - - - -
sing the whole antarā + the 1st line of sthāyī and conclude with tihāī:
tihāī
gu ru bi na kai - se -
gu ru bi na kai - se - gu ru bi na kai - se . -
gu - na - ga - - - ve - - -

bandiś 2
ektāl
1 2 3 4 5 6 7 8 9 10 11 12
dhiṅ dhiṅ dha ge tirakiṭ tu na ka ta dha ge tirakiṭ dhiṅ na
x 0 5 0 9 11
sthāyī
sa ba gu ni– ja na ya ma na gā – ta
tī – va ra su ra ka ra ta sā – – dha
sa sa re re ga ga ma ma pa pa dha dha
ni ni re re ga re sa re sa ni dha pa

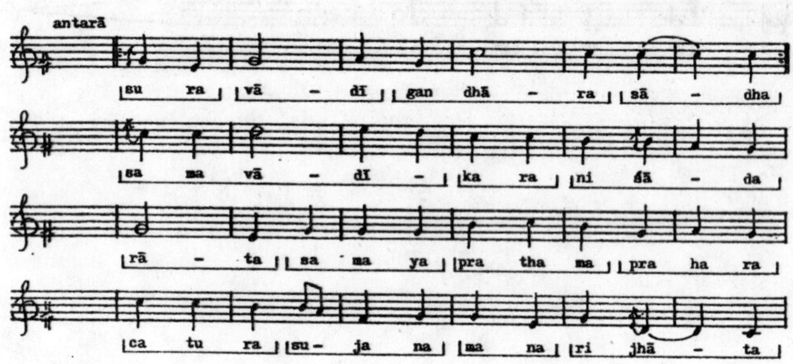
antarā
su ra vā – dī gan dhā – ra sā – dha
sa ma vā – dī – ka ra ni śā – da
rā – ta sa ma ya pra tha ma pra ha ra
ca tu ra su– ja na ma na ri jhā – ta

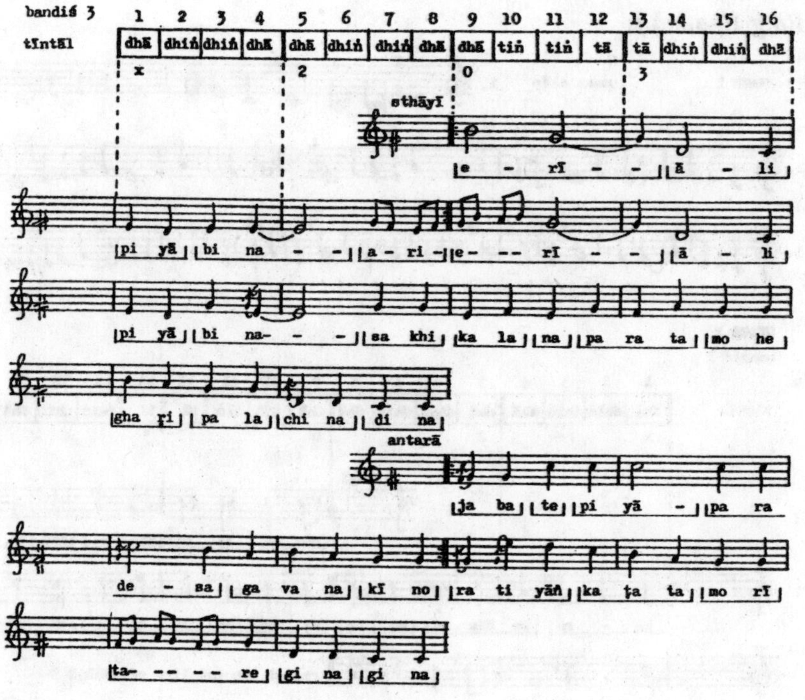
bandiś 3
tīntāl
1 2 3 4 5 6 7 8 9 10 11 12 13 14 15 16
dhā dhiṅ dhiṅ dhā dhā dhiṅ dhiṅ dhā dhā tiṅ tiṅ tā tā dhiṅ dhiṅ dhā
x 2 0 3
sthāyī
e - rī - - ā - li
pi yā bi na - - a - ri - e - -- rī - - ā - li
pi yā bi na- - - sa khi ka la na pa ra ta mo he
gha ṛi pa la chi na di na
antarā
ja ba te pi yā - pa ra
de - sa ga va na kī no ra ti yāṅ ka ṭa ta mo rī
ta- -- -- re gi na gi na

Rā.g Kha.mā.j

STAGE 1
mukt ālāp
1.
2.
3.
STAGE 2
bandiś 1
1 2 3 4 5 6 7 8 9 10 11 12 13 14 15 16
tintāl
dhā dhiṅ dhiṅ dhā dhā dhiṅ dhiṅ dhā dhā tiṅ tiṅ tā tā dhiṅ dhiṅ dhā
x 2 0 3
sthāyī
nū- - pu ra kī- - jha na
kā - ra ma dhu ra mṛ du ma na ha ra nī - ma ta
vā - rī - pyā- - rī -
repeat the 1st line of sthāyī
and then sing antarā:
antarā
saṅ ga meṅ - sa khi yāṅ -
bī - ca ka nhai - yā - bhū - le - dhu na- su na
sa ba na ra nā- - rī -
repeat the 1st line of sthāyī
and start ālāp sthāyī:

the 1st line of antarā and then start ālāp antarā:

ālāp antarā
saṅ ga meṅ - sa khi yaṅ -
1.
ā
saṅ ga meṅ - sa khi yaṅ -
2.
ā
saṅ ga meṅ - sa khi yaṅ -
3.
ā
saṅ ga meṅ - sa khi yaṅ -
4.
bī - ca ka nhai - yā - ā-
saṅ ga meṅ - sa khi yaṅ -
5.
ā
antarā
saṅ ga meṅ - sa khi yaṅ -
bī - ca ka nhai - yā - bhū - le - dhu na su na
sa ba na ra nā- - rī -
repeat the 1st line of sthāyī;
increase the tempo of sthāyī
and start tān sthāyī:

STAGE 4
tān sthāyī
nū- - pu ra kī- - jha na
1.
ā - - - - - - - - -
nū- - pu ra kī- - jha na
2.
ā - - - - - - - - -
nū- - pu ra kī- - jha na
3.
kā - ra ma dhu ra mṛ du ā - - - - - - - - -
- - - - - - - - -
nū- - pu ra kī- - jha na
4.
kā - ra ma dhu ra mṛ du ā - - - - - - - - -
- - - - - - - - -
nū- - pu ra kī- - jha na
5.
ā - - - - - - - - - - - - - - - - -
tihāī-sthāyī
- - - - nū— pura kī— jhana nū— pura kī— jhana nū— pura kī— jhana
kā - ra ma dhu ra mṛ du
repeat the 1st line of sthāyī +
the 1st line of antarā
and start tān antarā:
tān antarā
saṅ ga meṅ - sa khi yāṅ -
1.
- - - - - - - - -
saṅ ga meṅ - sa khi yāṅ -

2.
ā — — — — — — — — — sań ga meń - sa khi yāń -
3.
bī - ca ka nhai - yā - ā — — — — — — — — —
— — — — — — — — — sań ga meń - sa khi yāń -
4.
ā- — — — — — — — — — — — — — — —
antarā
— — — — — — — — — sań ga meń - sa khi yāń -
bī - ca ka nhai - yā - bhū - le - dhu na- su na
1st line sthāyī
sa ba na ra nā- - rī - nū- - pu ra kī- - jha na
tihāī-sthāyī
kā - ra ma dhu ra mr du nū- - pu ra kī- - jha na
nū- - pu ra kī- - jha na nū- - pu ra kī- - jha na
kā - ra ma dhu - ra - mr - du -

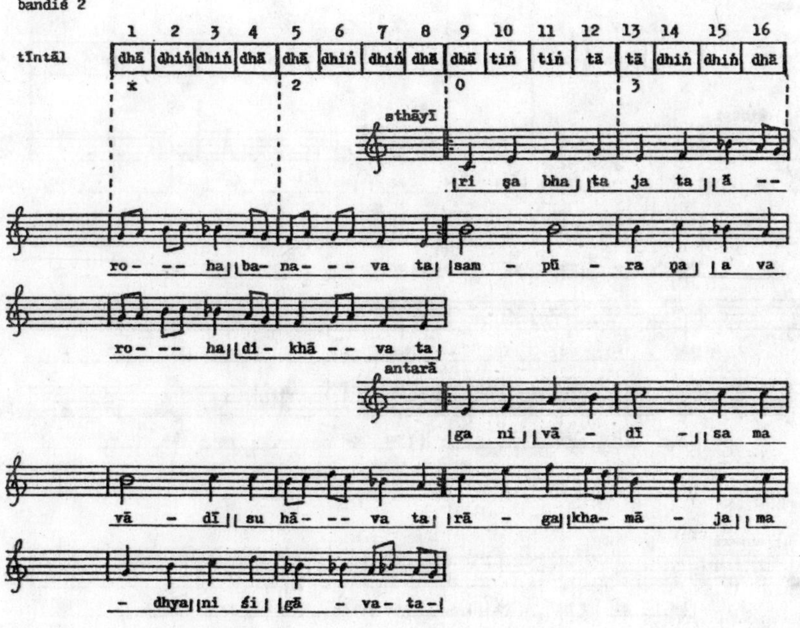
bandiś 2
1 2 3 4 5 6 7 8 9 10 11 12 13 14 15 16
tīntāl
dhā dhiṅ dhiṅ dhā dhā dhiṅ dhiṅ dhā dhā tiṅ tiṅ tā tā dhiṅ dhiṅ dhā
x 2 0 3
sthāyī
ri ṣa bha ta ja ta ā --
ro- -- ha ba- na- -- va ta sam - pū - ra ṇa a va
ro- -- ha di - khā -- va ta
antarā
ga ni vā - dī - sa ma
vā - dī su hā- -- va ta rā - ga kha- mā - ja ma
- dhya ni śi gā - va- ta-

bandiś 3
1 2 3 4 5 6 1 2 3 4 5 6
dādrā
dha din na dha tin na dha din na dha tin na
x 0 x 0
sthāyī
ā - ja śyā - ma mo - ha li - yo
bāṅ - su rī - - ba jā - ya ke - -
bāṅ - su rī - ba jā - ya kā nhā -
mu - ra lī - - su nā - ya ke - -

antarā
ha ri ha ri sa ba ka ra ta jā - ta
gā - ga ra si ra dha ra ta jā - ta
nī - ra nā - ra bha ra na ca lī -
su - dha - na ra hi - śa rī - ra kī - -

Rā.g Kā.fī

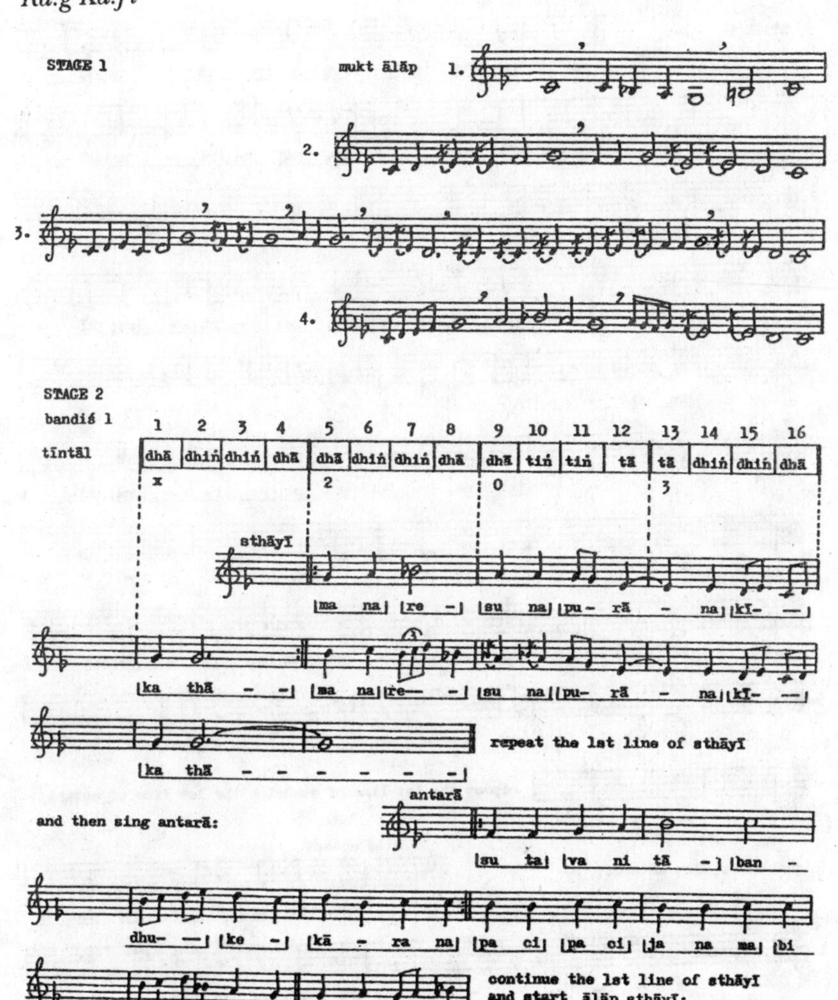
STAGE 1
mukt ālāp
1.
2.
3.
4.
STAGE 2
bandiś 1
tīntāl
1 2 3 4 5 6 7 8 9 10 11 12 13 14 15 16
dhā dhiṅ dhiṅ dhā dhā dhiṅ dhiṅ dhā dhā tiṅ tiṅ tā tā dhiṅ dhiṅ dhā
x 2 0 3
sthāyī
ma na re – su na pu- rā – na kī- —
ka thā – – ma na re— – su na pu- rā – na kī- —
ka thā – – – – – – –
repeat the 1st line of sthāyī
and then sing antarā:
antarā
su ta va ni tā – ban –
dhu- — ke – kā – ra na pa ci pa ci ja na ma bi
ti- — tā – ma na re- –
continue the 1st line of sthāyī
and start ālāp sthāyī:

STAGE 3
ālāp sthāyī
ma na re – su na pu- rā – na kī- –
1.
ā – – – – – – – – su na pu- rā – na kī – –
2.
ka thā – – ā – – – – – – – – – – – – –
– – – – ma na re – su na pu- rā – na kī- –
3.
ka thā – – ā – –– – – – – – – – – – – – –
– – – – ma na re – su na pu- rā – na kī- –
4.
ā – – – – – – – – – – – – – – –
– – – – ma na re – su na pu- rā – na kī- –
5.
ā – – – – – – – – – – – – – – –
– – – –
repeat the 1st line of sthāyī + the 1st line of antarā
and start ālāp antarā:
ālāp antarā
su ta va ni tā – ban –
1.
ā – – – – – – – su ta va ni tā – ban –

2.
ā - - - - - - - - - - - - su ta va ni tā - ban -
3.
dhu- — ke - kā - ra na ā - - - - - - - - - -
- - - - - — — — — su ta va ni tā - ban -
4.
ā - — — - - - - - - - - - - - - - - - -
- - - - - - - - -
sing the whole antarā
and then:
ma na re- -
continue the 1st line of sthāyī;
increase the tempo of sthāyī and
and start tān sthāyī:
tān sthāyī
STAGE 4
1.
ma na re - su na pu- rā ā- — — — —
2.
— — — — ma na re - su na pu- rā ā- — — —
— — — — — — — — su na pu- rā - na kī- —
3.
ka thā - - ma na re - su na pu- rā ā- — — —
— — — — ma na rē - su na pu- rā - na kī- —
4.
ka thā - - ā- — — — — — — — — — — — — — —

ma na re — su na pu— rā — na kī— —
5.
ka thā — — ā-
repeat the 1st line of sthāyī + the 1st line of antarā
tān antarā
and start tān antarā:
su ta va ni tā — ban —
1.
ā-
su ta va ni tā — ban —
2.
ā-
su ta va ni tā — ban —
3.
ā-
su ..ta va ni tā — ban —
4.
dhu— ke — kā — ra na ā-
sing the whole antarā and
conclude with:
ma na re— su na pu— rā — na kī— —
ka thā — — — — — —

bandiś 2
1 2 3 4 5 6 7 8 9 10 11 12
ektāl
dhiṅ dhiṅ dha ge tirakiṭ tu na ka ta dha ge tirakiṭ dhiṅ na
x 0 5 0 9 11
sthāyī
gu - ni - gā - va - ta
kā - fī rā - ga kha ra ha ra pri ya
me - la ja ni ta ko - ma la ga ni
u - jjva la pa ra su ra pa - - ñca ma
va - - dī sā - dha
antarā
sa ra la sva rū
pa vi pa - ści ta mā - na ta sa ba
su dhi a vi ca la ā - śra ya gu ni
ca tu ra ka ha ta ko - ma la ga ni
u - jjva la pa ra su ra pa - - ñca ma
vā - - dī sā - dha

bandiś 3
tīntāl
1 2 3 4 5 6 7 8 9 10 11 12 13 14 15 16
dhā dhiṅ dhiṅ dhā dhā dhiṅ dhiṅ dhā dhā tiṅ tiṅ tā tā dhiṅ dhiṅ dhā
x 2 0 3
sthāyī
jha na na jha na na mo rī
pā - ya la bā - je - pi yā - se mi la - na - ko -
jā - ūṅ - a - ba maiṅ -
antarā
di na - di na - mo he
cai - - - na nā ā - ye - sa ga rī ra ti yāṅ - -
bi ra hā - - sa tā - ye - kai se kai se dhūṅ dha na ko
jā - ūṅ - - a - ba maiṅ -

Rā.g Bhai.rav

STAGE 1
mukt ālāp
1.
2.
3.
4.

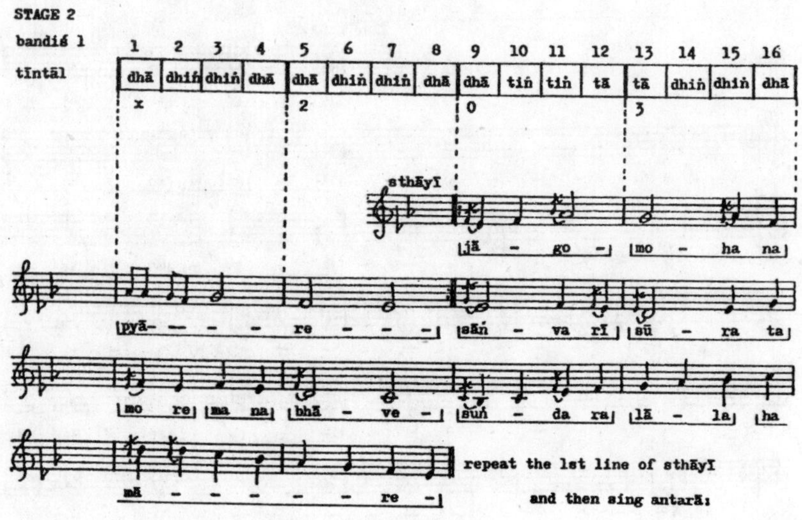
STAGE 2
bandiś 1
tīntāl
1 2 3 4 5 6 7 8 9 10 11 12 13 14 15 16
dhā dhiṅ dhiṅ dhā dhā dhiṅ dhiṅ dhā dhā tiṅ tiṅ tā tā dhiṅ dhiṅ dhā
x 2 0 3
sthāyī
jā - go - mo - ha na
pyā- - - - re - - - sāṅ - va rī sū - ra ta
mo re ma na bhā - ve - suṅ - da ra lā - la ha
mā - - - - - re -
repeat the 1st line of sthāyī
and then sing antarā:

antarā
prā - ta sa ma ya u tha
bhā - nu u da ya bha yo gvā - la bā - la bhū -
pa ti sa ba thā - rhe - da ra śa na ke - sa ba
bhū - khe - pyā - se - u thi yo - nā - nda ki
śo - - - - - - re -
repeat the 1st line of sthāyī and start ālāp sthāyī:
ālāp sthāyī
STAGE 3
jā - go - mo ha na
1.
ā - - - - - - - - jā - go - mo - ha na
2.
ā - - - - - - - - jā - go - mo - ha na
3.
ā
jā - go - mo - ha na
4.
ā
jā - go - mo - ha na

5.
ā
repeat the 1st line of sthāyī +
the 1st line of antarā
and start ālāp antarā:
ālāp antarā
prā - ta sa ma ya u tha
1.
ā
prā - ta sa ma ya u tha
2.
ā
prā - ta sa ma ya u tha
3.
bhā - nu u da ya bha yo ā
prā - ta sa ma ya u tha
4.
ā
prā - ta sa ma ya u tha
5.
ā
sing the whole antarā + 1st line
of sthāyī; increase the tempo of
sthāyī and start tān sthāyī:

STAGE 4
tān sthāyī
jā - go - mo - ha na
1.
ā - jā - go - mo - ha na
2.
ā - jā - go - mo - ha na
3.
ā - jā - go - mo - ha na
4.
ā -
jā - go - mo - ha na
5.
ā -
repeat the 1st line of sthāyī +
the 1st line of antarā
and start tān antarā:
tān antarā
prā - ta sa ma ya u tha
1.
ā - prā - ta sa ma ya u tha
2.
ā - prā - ta sa ma ya u tha
3.
ā - prā - ta sa ma ya u tha

4.
ā-
prā - ta sa ma ya u tha
5.
ā-
sing the whole antarā + the lst
line of sthāyī and conclude with tihāī:
tihāī
jā - go - mo - ha na
jā - go - mo - ha na jā - go - mo - ha na
pyā- re

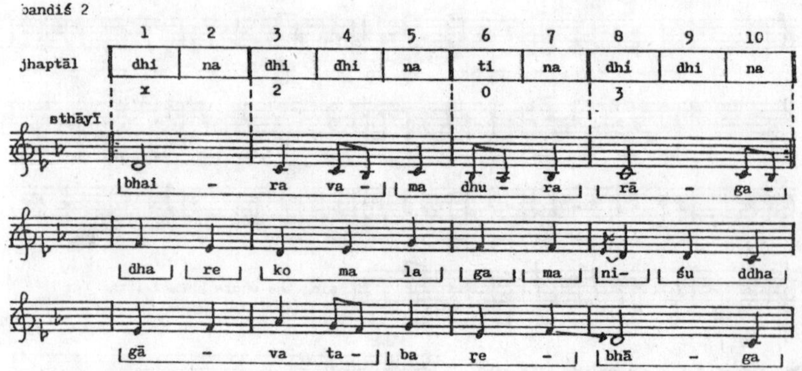
bandiś 2
1 2 3 4 5 6 7 8 9 10
jhaptāl
dhi na dhi dhi na ti na dhi dhi na
x 2 0 3
sthāyī
bhai - ra va - ma dhu - ra rā - ga -
dha re ko ma la ga ma ni- śu ddha
gā - va ta - ba re - bhā - ga

antarā
dhai - va ta ka ra ta vā - dī
ri ga bha ka re sa ma vā - dī
san - dhi - pra kā - śa meṅ -
gā - va ta - gu ni - ja - ga

bandiś 3
1 2 3 4 5 6 7 8 9 10 11 12 13 14 15 16
tīntāl
dhā dhiṅ dhiṅ dhā dhā dhiṅ dhiṅ dhā dhā tiṅ tiṅ tā tā dhiṅ dhiṅ dhā
x 2 0 3
sthāyī
gu ru nā - - thā - sa ba na
ke - - - ni ta su mi re - ma na jī - vi ta -
chi na bhan - gu ra gu ru
antarā
jo - cā - he - tū ca
tu ra su kha sam - pa da maṅ - ga la nā - ma ka
ma la mu kha sam - va da jā - ki kri pā - sa ba -
pū ra ta kā - ma gu ru - nā - - thā - sa ba na

Rā.g Āsā.va.rī

STAGE 1
mukt ālāp 1.
2.
3.
4.
STAGE 2
bandiś 1
1 2 3 4 5 6 7 8 9 10 11 12 13 14 15 16
tīntāl
dhā dhiṅ dhiṅ dhā dhā dhiṅ dhiṅ dhā dhā tiṅ tiṅ tā tā dhiṅ dhiṅ dhā
x 2 0 3
sthāyī
ma dhu ra ma dhu ra dhu- na -
mu ra li ba jā - ye - kuṅ va ra ka ṅhai - yā -
dhī - tha laṅ ga ra vā -
repeat the 1st line of sthāyī
and then sing antarā:
antarā
dhu na su na sa khi yāṅ -
rī - jha ta u na pa ra gvā - la bā - la bhū -
le- - sa ba- su dhi ta ja ma dhu ba na bī ca ja ba
tā - na su nā- - ye -
repeat the 1st line of sthāyī
and start ālāp sthāyī:

STAGE 3
ālāp sthāyī
ma dhu ra ma dhu ra dhu- na-
1.
ā
ma dhu ra ma dhu ra dhu- na-
2.
ā
ma dhu ra ma dhu ra dhu- na-
3.
ā
ma dhu ra ma dhu ra dhu- na-
4.
ā
var. in 1st line
madhu rama dhuradhuna
5.
mu ra li ba jā - ye -
ā
sing the 1st line of sthāyī
dhu ra dhu - na-
var. var. var.
sing the 1st line of antarā varied
mu ra li ba jā - ye -
sa khi yāṅ -
continue and start ālāp antarā:
ālāp antarā
dhu na su na sa khi yāṅ -
1.
ā
dhu na su na sa khi yāṅ -

2.
ā - - - - - - - - dhu na su na sa khi yāṅ -
3.
rī - jha ta u na pa ra ā- - - - - - - - -
- - - - - - - - - - dhu na su na sa khi yāṅ -
4.
ā— — - - - - - - - - - - - - - - - — -
- - - - - - - - - - dhu na su na sa khi yāṅ -
5.
rī - jha ta u na pa ra ā- — - - - - - - - -
- - - - - - - - -
sing the whole antarā varied
var. var.
sa khi yāṅ -
continue antarā
gvā - la bā
continue antarā
le- - sa ba su dhi ta ja
sing the rest of antarā and after that
the 1st line of sthāyī increasing the tempo:
ma dhu ra ma dhu ra dhu- na-
var. var.
mu ra li ba jā - ye -
and start tān sthāyī:

continue the 1st line of antarā and start tān antarā:

tān antarā
dhu na su na sa khi yāṅ -
1.
ā- - - - - - - - -
dhu na su na sa khi yāṅ -
2.
ā- - - - - - - - -
dhu na su na sa khi yāṅ -
3.
ā- - - - - - - - -
dhu na su na sa khi yāṅ -
4.
ā - - - - - - - - - - - - - - - -
sing the whole
antarā varied
var. var. var.
sa khi yāṅ -
contimue antarā
var.
gvā - la bā
contimue antarā
var.
le- - sa ba
sing the rest of antarā and after that the 1st line of
sthāyī combined with tihāī:
ma dhu ra ma dhu ra dhu- na-
mu ra li ba madhura ma dhura dhuna madhura ma dhura dhuna madhura ma dhura dhuna
mu ra li ba jā - - - - ye - - - -

bandiś 2

tīntāl
1 2 3 4 5 6 7 8 9 10 11 12 13 14 15 16
dhā dhiṅ dhiṅ dhā dhā dhiṅ dhiṅ dhā dhā tiṅ tiṅ tā tā dhiṅ dhiṅ dhā
x 2 0 3
sthāyī
kā nhā– mo he ā – sā va– rī–
rā – ga su nā – ye – ga ni ko – a dhi ro – –
ha na meṅ– chu– pā – ye – sa re ma re ma pa dha pa
dha ga re sa re ni dha pa
antarā
dhai – va ta vā – di –
ga – sa ma vā – dī – ma – dhya ma su ra gra ha
nyā– – sa su pan– – ca ma a va ro – ha na sam– – –
pu ra na di khā – va ta sa re ma re ma pa dha pa
dha ga re sa re ni dha pa

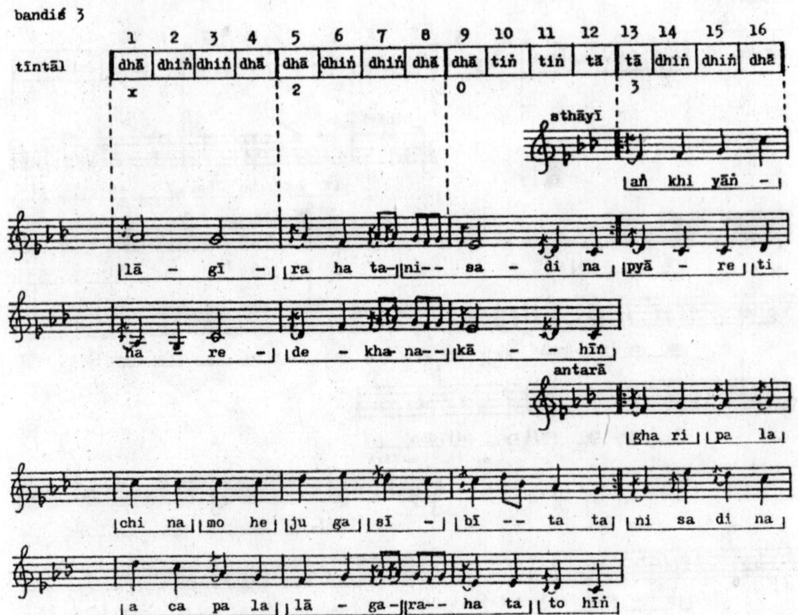
bandiś 3
1 2 3 4 5 6 7 8 9 10 11 12 13 14 15 16
tīntāl
dhā dhiṅ dhiṅ dhā dhā dhiṅ dhiṅ dhā dhā tiṅ tiṅ tā tā dhiṅ dhiṅ dhā
x 2 0 3
sthāyī
aṅ khi yāṅ -
lā - gī - ra ha ta- ni-- sa - di na pyā - re ti
na - re - de - kha- na-- kā - - hīṅ
antarā
gha ri pa la
chi na mo he ju ga sī - bī -- ta ta ni sa di na
a ca pa la lā - ga- ra-- ha ta to hīṅ

Rā.g Bhai.ra.vī

antarā
ja ga ja na nī ja ga jā – nī
ma hi ṣā – su ra ma ra da nī
jvā – lā – mu khī – caṇ – dī
a ma ra pa da dā – nī bha
ālāp sthāyī
repeat the 1st line of sthāyī and start ālāp sthāyī:
bha
STAGE 3
vā – nī – da yā – nī – –
1.
ā – – – – – – – – bha
vā – nī – da yā – nī – bha
2.
vā – nī – da ā – – – –
– – – – – – – – – bha
vā – nī – da yā – nī – –
3.
ā – – – – – – – – – –

repeat the 1st line of sthāyī + the 1st line of antarā and start ālāp antarā:

sing the whole antarā + the 1st line of sthāyi;
increase the tempo of sthāyī and start tān sthāyī:
STAGE 4
tān sthāyī
bha
vā - nī - da yā - nī - -
1.
ā -
bha
2.
vā - nī - ā
bha
vā - nī - da yā - nī - bha
3.
vā - nī - - ā -
bha
vā - nī - da yā - nī - -
repeat the 1st line of sthāyī + the 1st line of antarā and start tan antarā:
tān antarā
ja ga ja na nī ja ga jā - nī
1.
ā -

ja ga ja na nī ja ga jā - nī
2.
ā - -- -- -- -- -- -- -- -- --
ja ga ja na nī ja ga jā - nī
3.
ā - -- -- -- -- -- -- -- -- --
ja ga ja na nī ja ga jā - nī
sing the whole antarā and conclude with:
bha
vā - nī - da yā - nī - bha
vā - nī - bha vā - nī - bha
vā - - - nī - - -

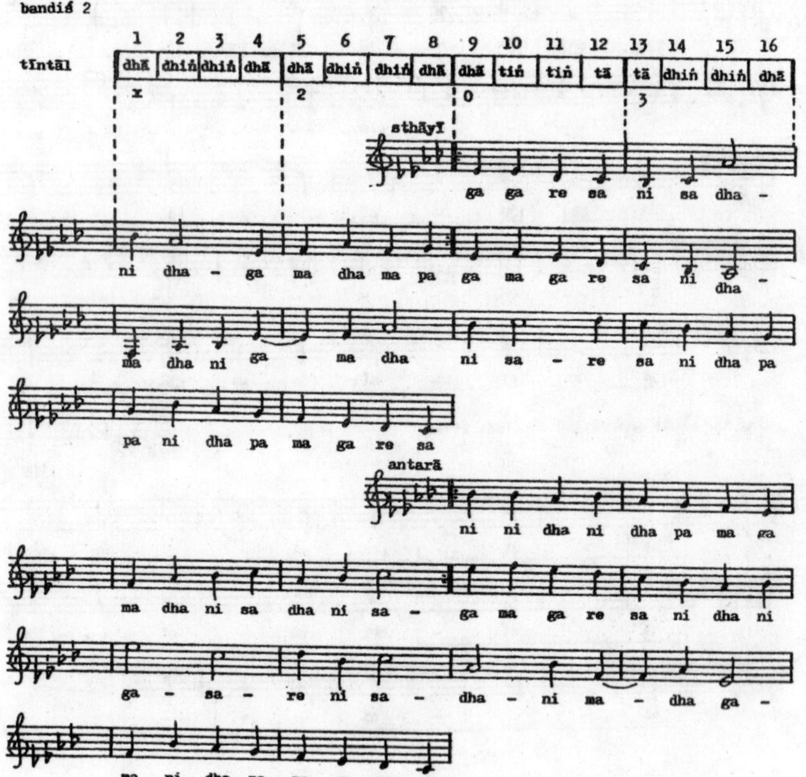
bandiś 2
1 2 3 4 5 6 7 8 9 10 11 12 13 14 15 16
tīntāl dhā dhiṅ dhiṅ dhā dhā dhiṅ dhiṅ dhā dhā tiṅ tiṅ tā tā dhiṅ dhiṅ dhā
x 2 0 3
sthāyī
ga ga re sa ni sa dha –
ni dha – ga ma dha ma pa ga ma ga re sa ni dha –
ma dha ni ga – ma dha ni sa – re sa ni dha pa
pa ni dha pa ma ga re sa
antarā
ni ni dha ni dha pa ma ga
ma dha ni sa dha ni sa – ga ma ga re sa ni dha ni
ga – sa – re ni sa – dha – ni ma – dha ga –
ma ni dha pa ma ga re sa

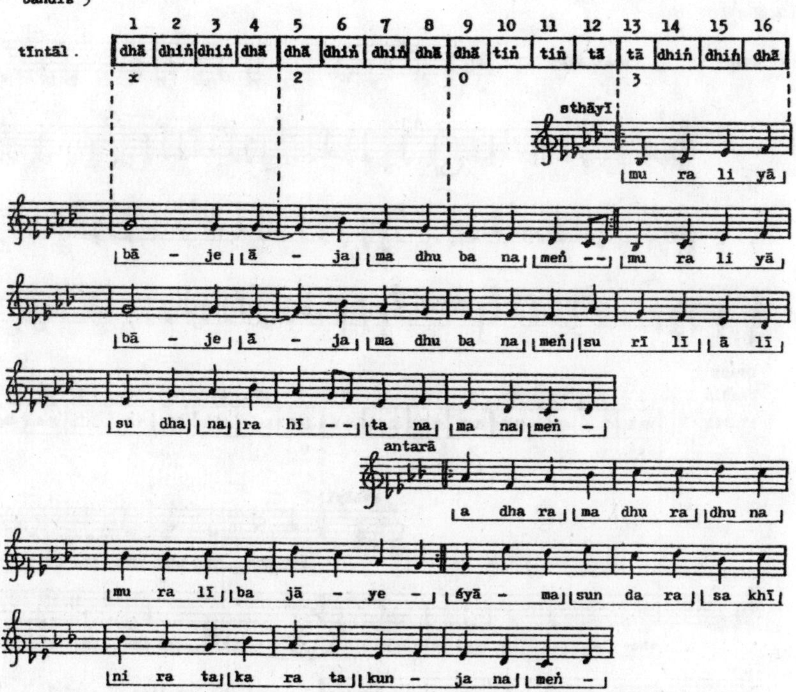
bandiś 3
tīntāl.
1 2 3 4 5 6 7 8 9 10 11 12 13 14 15 16
dhā dhiṅ dhiṅ dhā dhā dhiṅ dhiṅ dhā dhā tiṅ tiṅ tā tā dhiṅ dhiṅ dhā
x 2 0 3
sthāyī
mu ra li yā
bā – je ā – ja ma dhu ba na meṅ – – mu ra li yā
bā – je ā – ja ma dhu ba na meṅ su rī lī ā lī
su dha na ra hī – – ta na ma na meṅ –
antarā
a dha ra ma dhu ra dhu na
mu ra lī ba jā – ye – śyā – ma sun da ra sa khī
ni ra ta ka ra ta kun – ja na meṅ –

Rā.g Mār.vā

STAGE 1
mukt ālāp 1.
2.
3.
4.
STAGE 2
bandiś 1
tīntāl
1 2 3 4 5 6 7 8 9 10 11 12 13 14 15 16
dhā dhiṅ dhiṅ dhā dhā dhiṅ dhiṅ dhā dhā tiṅ tiṅ tā tā dhiṅ dhiṅ dhā
x 2 0 3
sthāyī
su gha ra su gha ra bai -
the- - sa ba gu nī ja na de - kho - gu na kī -
rī - ta a no - khī -
repeat the 1st line of sthāyī
and then sing antarā:
antarā
sa - pta su ra na soṅ -
gu na ko - gā - ve - u nan - cā - sa kū -
ta tā - na su nā - ve - sa dā - raṅ - ga rī -
jha ta sa ba ma na ko -
repeat the 1st line of sthāyī
and start ālāp sthāyī:

STAGE 3
ālāp sthāyī
su gha ra su gha ra bai -
1.
ā - - - - - - - -
su gha ra su gha ra bai -
2.
ā - - - - - - -
su gha ra su gha ra bai -
3.
the- sa ba gu ni ja na ā - - - - - - - - -
su gha ra su gha ra bai -
4.
ā - - - - - - - - - - - - - - - - - -
su gha ra su gha ra bai -
5.
ā - - - - - - - - - - - - - - - - -
tihāī
sugha ra- sugha ra- sugha ra sughara bai-
the- sa ba gu ni ja na
repeat the 1st line of sthāyī + the 1st line of antarā and start ālāp antarā:
ālāp antarā
sa - pta su ra na soṅ -
1.
ā - - - - - - - -
sa - pta su ra na soṅ -

2.
ā - - - - - - - - sa - pta su ra na soṅ -
3.
gu na ko - gā - ve - ā - - - - - - - -
- - - - - - - - - sa - pta su ra na soṅ -
4.
ā - - - - - - - - - - - - - - -
- - - - - - - - - sa - pta su ra na soṅ -
5.
gu na ko - gā - ve - ā - - - - - - - -
sing the whole antarā + the 1st line
of sthāyī; increase the tempo of sthāyī
and start tān sthāyī:
STAGE 4
tān sthāyī
su gha ra su gha ra bai -
1.
ā - - - - - - - - su gha ra su gha ra bai -
2.
ā - - - - - - - - su gha ra su gha ra bai -
3.
the- - sa ba gu ni ja na ā - - - - - - - -
- - - - - - - - su gha ra su gha ra bai -

4.
ā-
su gha ra su gha ra bai -
5.
the- sa ba gu ni ja na ā-
repeat the 1st line of sthāyī +
the 1st line of antarā
and start tān antarā:
tān antarā
sa - pta su ra na soṅ -
1.
ā-
sa - pta su ra na soṅ -
2.
ā-
sa - pta su ra na soṅ -
3.
ā-
sa - pta su ra na soṅ -
4.
gu na ko - gā - ve - ā-
sa - pta su ra na soṅ -
5.
gu na ko - gā - ve - ā-
sing the whole antarā + the 1st

line of sthāyī and conclude with:

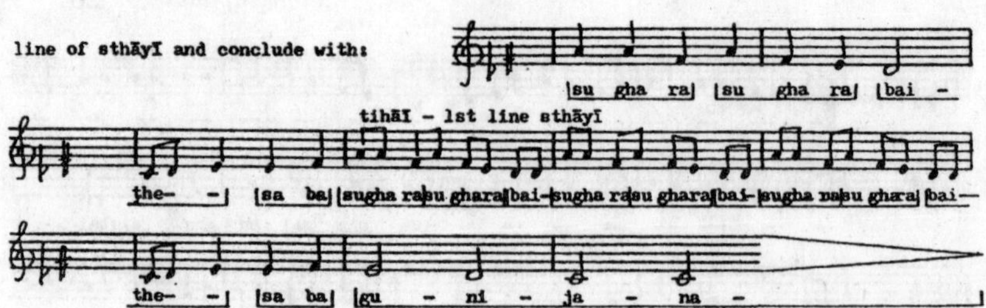

bandiś 2

1 2 3 4 5 6 7 8 9 10
jhaptāl
dhi na dhi dhi na ti na dhi dhi na
x 2 0 3
sthāyī
tī – va ra ga ma dha ni su ra –
me – – la na sa ja ta ma dhu ra
vi ka – ra ta ri kha ba bhī – ta ra
mā – – ra vā ka ha ta ca tu ra

antarā
rā – ga gā – va ta su ka ra
pañ – ca ma vi vā – dī su ra
sam – vā – da re dha bi ca ra
a – sta di na a ti ru ci ra

bandiś 3
1 2 3 4 5 6 7 8 9 10 11 12 13 14 15 16
tīntāl
dhā dhiṅ dhiṅ dhā dhā dhiṅ dhiṅ dhā dhā tiṅ tiṅ tā tā dhiṅ dhiṅ dhā
x 2 0 3
sthāyī
ca ta raṅ ga sa ba mi la
gā – – i ye – – – gā i ye ba jā i ye –
au – ra ri jhā i ye –
antarā
mo ha mma da śā – va ra kā – ja su hā– – – ga
nā – ca ta sa ba mi la de – – de tā – rī –
sa ga – ma gā re sa – cho – – mcha na na na na
cho – – mcha na na na na taka dhi– taka dhi– taka tira kiṭa taka
dhī krāṅ – dhā dhā ti dhā dhā

Rā.g Pū.rvī

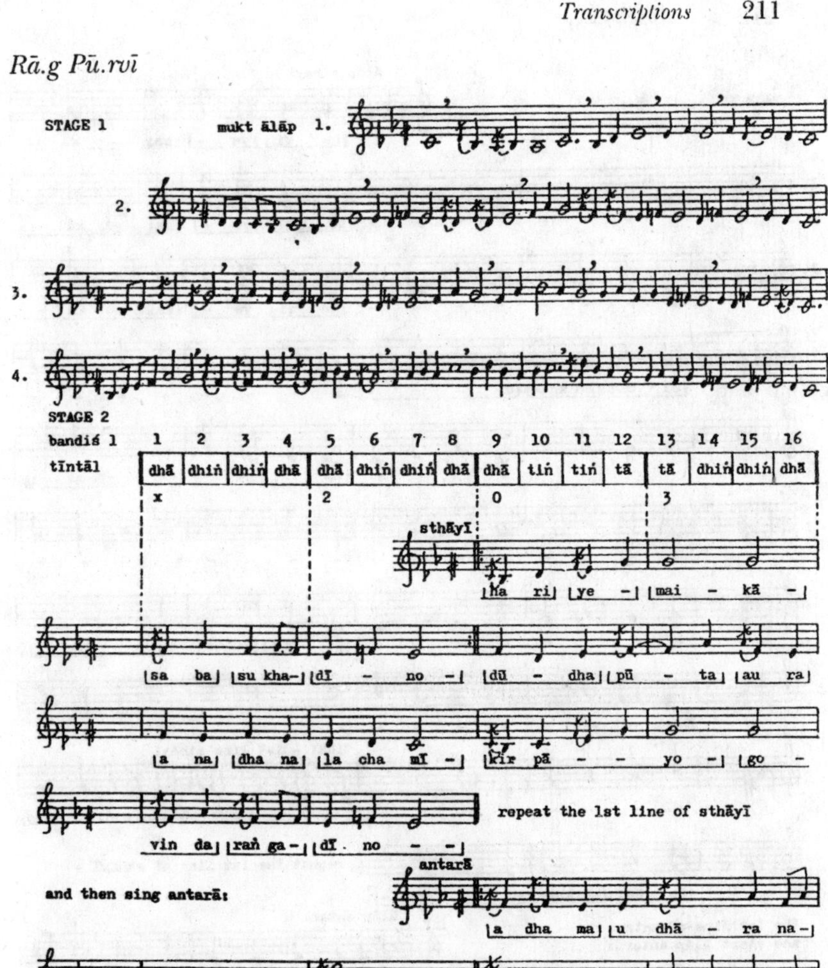
STAGE 1
mukt ālāp 1.
2.
3.
4.
STAGE 2
bandiś 1
tīntāl
1 2 3 4 5 6 7 8 9 10 11 12 13 14 15 16
dhā dhiṅ dhiṅ dhā dhā dhiṅ dhiṅ dhā dhā tiṅ tiṅ tā tā dhiṅ dhiṅ dhā
x 2 0 3
sthāyī
ha ri ye – mai – kā –
sa ba su kha– dī – no – dū – dha pū – ta au ra
a na dha na la cha mī – kir pā – – yo – go –
vin da raṅ ga– dī no – –
repeat the 1st line of sthāyī
and then sing antarā:
antarā
a dha ma u dhā – ra na–
ja sa vi – stā – ra na kri pā – ka ra na du kha
ha ra– na su kha ka ra na ā – ji ja– ke – sa ba
lā– – ya ka kī – no –
repeat the 1st line of sthāyī
and start ālāp sthāyī:

STAGE 3
ālāp sthāyī
ha ri ye - mai - kā -
1.
ā - - - - - - - - ha ri ye - mai - kā -
2.
ā - - - - - - - - ha ri ye - mai - kā -
3.
sa ba su kha- dī - no - ā - - - - - - - - - -
- - - - - - - - - ha ri ye - mai - kā -
4.
ā - - - - - - - - - - - - - - - - -
- - - - - - - - - ha ri ye - mai - kā -
5.
ā - - - - - - - - - - - - - - - - -
tihāī - 1st line sthāyī
- - - - - - - - - ha ri ye - ha ri ye - ha ri ye - mai- ka-
sa ba su kha- dī - no -
repeat the 1st line of sthāyī +
the 1st line of antarā
and start ālāp antarā:
ālāp antarā
a dha ma u dhā - ra na-
1.
ā - - - - - - - - a dha ma u dhā - ra na-

2.
ā- - - - - - - - - - |a dha ma| |u dhā - ra na-|
3.
|ja sa| |vi - stā - ra na| ā - - - - - - - - -
- - - - - - - - - |a dha ma| |u dhā - ra na-|
4.
ā - - - - - - - - - - - - - - - -
tihāī - 1st line antarā
- - - - - |adha ma|u dhā-rana||adha ma|u dhā-rana||adha ma|u dhā-rana|
|ja sa| |vi - stā - ra na| |a dha ma| |u dhā - ra na-|
5.
ā- - - - - - - - - - - - - - - -
sing the whole antarā + the 1st line
of sthāyī; increase the tempo of sthāyī
and start tān sthāyī:
STAGE 4
tān sthāyī
|ha ri| |ye -| |mai - kā -|
1.
ā - - - - - - - - |ha ri| |ye -| |mai - kā -|
2.
ā - - - - - - - - |ha ri| |ye -| |mai - kā -|
3.
ā - - - - - - - - |ha ri| |ye -| |mai - kā -|

4.
sa ba su kha- dī - no - ā - - - - - - - - - -
- - - - - - - - ha ri ye - mai - kā -
5.
ā - - - - - - - - - - - - - - - - -
- - - - - - - -
repeat the 1st line of sthāyī +
the 1st line of antarā
and start tān antarā:
tān antarā
a dha ma u dhā - ra na-
1.
ā - - - - - - - - a dha ma u dhā - ra na-
2.
ā - - - - - - - - a dha ma u dhā - ra na-
3.
ā - - - - - - - - a dha ma u dhā - ra na-
4.
ja sa vi - stā - ra na ā - - - - - - - -
- - - - - - - - a dha ma u dhā - ra na-
5.
ā - - - - - - - - - - - - - - - -
tihāī - antarā + rest of antarā varied
- - - - - - - - adha maju adha maju adha maju dha-ra-na-

var.
ja sa vi - stā - ra na kri pā - ka ra na du kha
ha ra- na su kha ka ra na ā - ji ja- ke - sa ba
var.
1st line of sthāyī followed by tihāī
lā- - ya ka- kī - no - ha ri ye - mai - kā -
sa ba su kha- di - no - sa ba su kha- di - - no -
sa ba su kha- di - - - no - - -

bandiś 2
tīntāl
1 2 3 4 5 6 7 8 9 10 11 12 13 14 15 16
dhā dhiṅ dhiṅ dhā dhā dhiṅ dhiṅ dhā dhā tiṅ tiṅ tā tā dhiṅ dhiṅ dhā
x 2 0 3
sthāyī
pū - ra vī - ke - su ra
gā - ya gu nī - va ra ga re ga ma pa dha ma pa
ga re ga ma ga re sa - ni ni sa re ga - ja hāṇ
aṅ - ga ma no - ha - ra
antarā
vā - di gan dhā - ra ni -
śa - da su sa ha ca ra ma - dhya ma jo - ga di
khā - va ta sun - da ra san - dhi pra kā - śa sa
ma ya ka ha ta - ca - tu - ra

bandiś 3

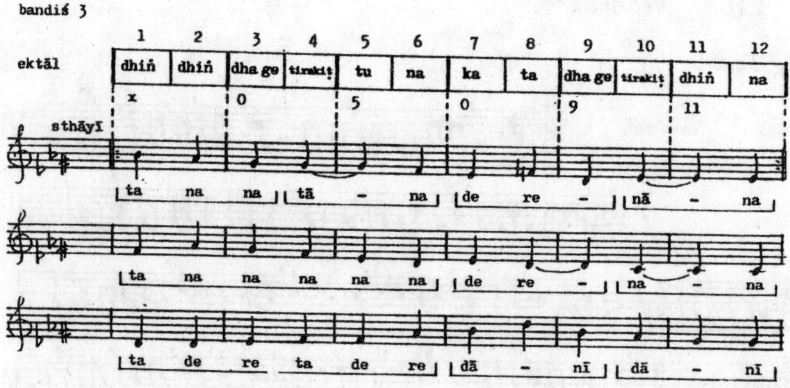
ektāl
1 2 3 4 5 6 7 8 9 10 11 12
dhiṅ dhiṅ dha ge tirakiṭ tu na ka ta dha ge tirakiṭ dhiṅ na
x 0 5 0 9 11
sthāyī
ta na na tā – na de re – nā – na
ta na na na na na de re – na – na
ta de re ta de re dā – nī dā – nī

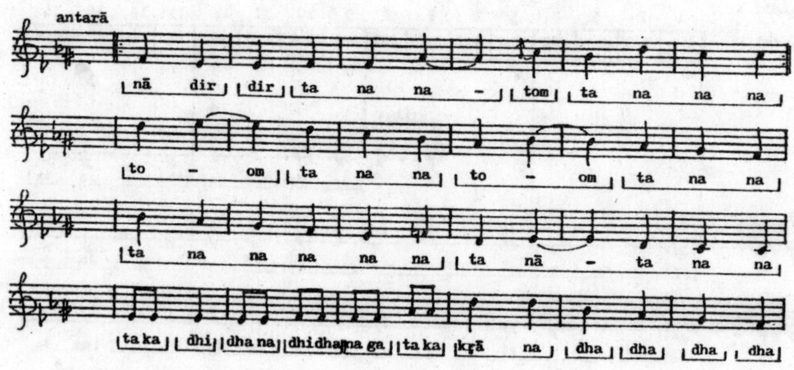
antarā
nā dir dir ta na na – tom ta na na na
to – om ta na na to – om ta na na
ta na na na na na ta nā – ta na na
ta ka dhi dha na dhidha na ga ta ka kṛā na dha dha dha dha

Rā.g To.ṛī

STAGE 1
mukt ālāp 1.
2.
3.
4.
STAGE 2
bandiś 1
tīntāl
1 2 3 4 5 6 7 8 9 10 11 12 13 14 15 16
dhā dhiṅ dhiṅ dhā dhā dhiṅ dhiṅ dhā dhā tiṅ tiṅ tā tā dhiṅ dhiṅ dhā
x 2 0 3
sthāyī
pī ya saṅ ga khe – la ta
pyā – – – rī – – – pī ya saṅ ga khe – la ta
pyā – – – rī – – – jo – va na kī – ma ta
vā – – – rī – – – pī ya saṅ ga khe – la ta
continue the 1st line of sthāyī
and then sing antarā:
antarā
mri ga ma da au – re –
ke – sa ra do – re – bhī – ja ta raṅ – ga –
sā – – – – – rī – pī ya saṅ ga
continue the 1st
line of sthāyī
and start
ālāp sthāyī:

STAGE 3
ālāp sthāyī
pī ya saṅ ga khe - la ta
1.
ā
pī ya saṅ ga khe - la ta
2.
ā
pī ya saṅ ga khe - la ta
3.
ā
pī ya saṅ ga khe - la ta
4.
pyā
ā
pī ya saṅ ga khe - la ta
5.
ā
tihāī
pīyasaṅga pīyasaṅga pīyasaṅga khe- lata
pyā - - - rī - - -
repeat the 1st line of sthāyī +
the 1st line of antarā
and start ālāp antarā:
ālāp antarā
mri ga ma da au - re -
1.
ā
mri ga ma da au - re -

2. ā - - - - - - - - - |mri ga| |ma da| |au - re -|
3. |ke - sa ra| |do - re -| ā - - - - - - - - -
- - - - - - - - - |mri ga| |ma da| |au - re -|
4. ā - - - - - - - - - - - - - - -
antarā
- - - - - - - - |mri ga| |ma da| |au - re -|
|ke - sa ra| |do - re -| |bhī - ja ta| |raṅ - ga -|
|sā - - - - - rī -| |pī ya| |saṅ ga|
continue the 1st line of sthāyī;
increase the tempo of sthāyī
and start tān sthāyī:
STAGE 4
tān sthāyī:
|pī ya| |saṅ ga| |khe - la ta|
1. ā- — — — — — — — — |pī ya| |saṅ ga| |khe - la ta|
2. ā- — — — — — — — — |pī ya| |saṅ ga| |khe - la ta|
3. |pyā - - - - - rī| - ā- — — — — — — — —
— — — — — — — — |pī ya| |saṅ ga| |khe - la ta|

4.
ā- — — — — — — — — — — — — — — —
— — — — — — — — — pī ya san ga khe - la ta
5.
ā- — — — — — — — — — — — — — — —
tihāī
— — — — pīyasaṅga khe- lāta pīyasaṅga khe-lāta pīyasaṅga khe-lāta
pyā - - - rī - — -
repeat the 1st line of sthāyī +
the 1st line of antarā
and start tān antarā:
tān antarā
mri ga ma da au - re -
1.
ā- — — — — — — — mri ga ma da au - re -
2.
ā- — — — — — — — mri ga ma da au - re -
3.
ā- — — — — — — — mri ga ma da au - re -
4.
ke - sa ra do - re - ā- — — — — — — —
antarā
— — — — — — — — mri ga ma da au - re -
ke - sa ra do - re - bhī - ja ta raṅ - ga -

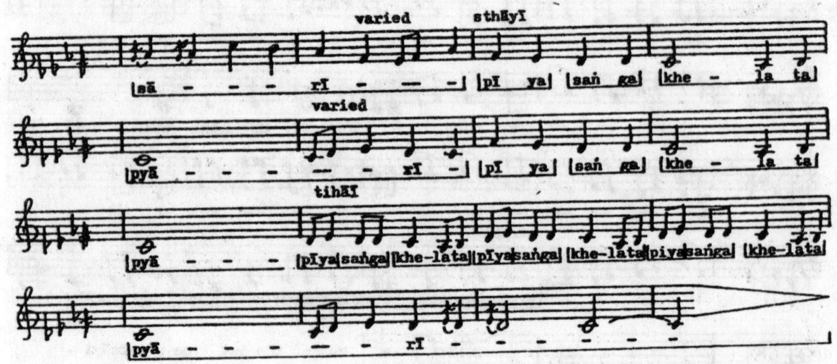
varied
sthāyī
sā - - - rī - — -
pī ya
saṅ ga
khe - la ta
varied
pyā - - - — - rī -
pī ya
saṅ ga
khe - la ta
tihāī
pyā - - - -
pīya saṅga khe-lata pīya saṅga khe-lata piya saṅga khe-lata
pyā - - - — - rī - - - - - - -

bandiś 2
1 2 3 4 5 6 7 8 9 10 11 12
ektāl
dhiṅ dhiṅ dha ge tirakiṭ tu na ka ta dha ge tirakiṭ dhiṅ na
x 0 5 0 9 11
sthāyī
vi – kri ta ja ba dha ga re ka ra ta
ma – tī – – va ra su ra saṅ – ga ta
su ga – ma sa ra la sam – pū – ra na
gu nī to – ṛī – ko – ba ra na ta

antarā
dhai – va ta ja hāṅ an – śa ra ha ta
ri ga su – ra ta hāṅ sa ha ca ra ma ta
pañ – ca ma ko u a – lpa ka ha ta
ha ra raṅ ga ko – ma ta a bhi ma ta

bandiś 3
1 2 3 4 5 6 7 8 9 10 11 12 13 14 15 16
tīntāl
dhā dhiṅ dhiṅ dhā dhā dhiṅ dhiṅ dhā dhā tiṅ tiṅ tā tā dhiṅ dhiṅ dhā
x 2 0 3
sthāyī
mo ha na gha na
śyā - ma ā - ye mo re dvā - re - ta na kī ta
pa na ga ī mo- -- -- -- rī- -- -- -- mo
antarā
śu bha di na
śu bha hai - ā - ja kī - gha rī - bhā - ga kī
- mo re - sa khī rī- -- -- -- -- -- mo ha na gha na

Bibliography

Bhatkhande, V.N., *Hindustānī Saṅgīta Paddhati Kramika Pustak Mālikā*, 6 vols. Hathras: Sangeet Karyalaya, vol. I, 1954; vol. II, 1971.

Bhatt, V.N., *Bal Sangeet Shiksha.* Hathras: Sangeet Karyalaya, 1983.

Brihaspati, K.C., *Bhārata kā Saṅgīta Siddhānta.* U.P.: Prakashan Shakha, Suchana Vibhag, 1959.

Gune, N.L., *Saṅgīta Prabhākara Darśikā*, third edn. Allahabad: Pt. Narayan Lakhaman Gune, 1987.

—, *Saṅgīta Pravīṇa*, sec. edn. Allahabad: Pt. Narayan Lakhaman Gune, 1984.

Jain, Shanti, *Chaitee.* Lucknow: Uttar Pradesh Sangeet Natak Akademi, 1980.

Jha, Ramashray, *Abhinava Gītāñjali.* Allahabad: Sangit Sadan Prakashan, 1968.

Kulshreshtha, J.S., *Sangeet Kishore.* Hathras: Sangeet Karyalaya, 1988.

McGregor, R.S., *Outline of Hindi Grammar*, Oxford University Press, 1972.

Mehta, R., *Āgarā Gharānā, Paramparā Gāyakī aur Cīzen.* Baroda: Bharatiya Sangit-Nritya-Natya Mahavidyalaya, Maharaja Sayajirav Vishvavidyalaya, 1969.

Patvardhan, V.N., *Rāga Vijñāna*, Sangit Gaurav Granthamala, seven parts, eighth edn. Jamakhandikarawara. Pune: Pt. Madhusudan Vinayak Patvardhan, 1962.

Śārṅgadeva, *Saṅgīta Ratnākara.* Madras: Adyar Library and Research Centre, 1944.

Srivastava, I., *Dhrupada*: A Study of its Origin, Historical Development, Structure, and Present State. Delhi: Motilal Banarsidass, 1980.

Subbarao, T.V. *Studies in Indian Music.* Bombay: Asia Publishing House, 1962.

Thakur, O.N., *Saṅgītāñjali*, six parts. Bombay: Pt. Onkar Nath Thakur Estate, 1977.

Index